Unlocking THE GOLDEN CAGE

An Intimate Biography of **Hilde Bruch, M.D.**

Joanne Hatch Bruch

gürze books

Unlocking the Golden Cage
*An Intimate Biography
of Hilde Bruch, M.D.*

Cover design: Abacus Graphics, Oceanside, CA

Published by:

Gürze Books
P.O. Box 2238
Carlsbad, California 92018
(619)434-7533

Library of Congress Cataloguing-in-Publication Data

Bruch, Joanne Hatch
  Unlocking the golden cage : an intimate biography of Hilde Bruch, M.D. /
Joanne Hatch Bruch.
      p. cm.
  Includes bibliographical references and photographs
  ISBN 0-936077-16-6 (hardcover)
  1. Bruch, Hilde 1904- 2. Bruch family. 3. Psychiatrists — United States—
Biography. 4. Eating disorders — United States — Case studies. 5. Holocaust,
Jewish (1939-1945) — Germany — Biography. I. Title. II. Bruch, Joanne
Hatch.
RC339.52.B78 B78   1996   96-075699
616.8'526'0092-dc20   [B]

First Edition

2 4 6 8 0 9 7 5 3 1

To Herb

CONTENTS

FOREWORD

by Stuart Yudofsky, M.D.

Psychiatrists are obsessed with boundaries. We attempt to distinguish between so-called "normal" and abnormal behavior and emotions: Where does the grief at the death of a loved one stop and depression begin? Where is the line between understandable concern and obsession? Who is to determine what is healthy self- esteem and what is narcissism? As we seek to understand our patients and their illnesses, we struggle to determine whether the key influences derive from life experience or genetically-determined biologic factors: nature versus nurture. What is mind and what is brain?

Many of the painful disorders from which our patients suffer stem from critical violations of important boundaries during their childhoods. Sexual abuse and parental over-protectiveness are but two examples. The woof and warp of the fabric of mental illness is suffused with maladaptive efforts by those afflicted to establish boundaries. The patient with numbed feelings who slashes her forearm to reaffirm to herself that she is alive; and the skeletal adolescent with anorexia nervosa who perceives her only power over her intrusive parent to be her persistent "no" when they beg her to eat are examples.

It was my great privilege to met Dr. Hilde Bruch twenty-five years ago, when I was a medical student at Baylor College of Medicine. At that time she was universally regarded as the leading psychiatric expert in diagnosing and treating people with severe eating disorders. Along with pioneer heart surgeon Michael E. DeBakey she was considered one of the "treasures" of the Texas Medical Center and of the city of Houston. Dr. Bruch was my clinical supervisor during a required medical school "rotation" in psychiatry at the Ben Taub Hospital, a charity teaching hospital. She cared intensely for each of the many patients whose care it was my responsibility to follow. No detail in understanding how their personal lives affected the evolution of the symptoms of their illnesses nor about their responses to treatment could be overlooked. I was perennially unable to answer most of her inquiries about the patients; so, in each meeting with her, I developed a long list of questions that I would later have to pursue and try to answer for Dr. Bruch the next day. Inevitably and remarkably, each of her inquiries led to knowledge and insights that were essential to the patient's recovery.

During my six-week psychiatry clerkship at the Ben Taub Hospital, I learned to appreciate how common and disabling psychiatric conditions are. I also developed an insight into how positive an impact on patients' lives could be made by a brilliant, compassionate, and energetic physician like Dr. Bruch. Although she expressed justifiable reservations about my performance and was aware of my career plans to become a surgeon, Dr. Bruch insisted that I take an additional three-month rotation in psychiatry at Columbia University's fabled New York State Psychiatric Institute, where she had previously been a faculty member. She orchestrated each facet of this experience and required that I provide her with continuous feedback about its every aspect. Although prototypic for Dr. Bruch and highly desirable for all faculty, this level of caring by a senior, esteemed professor for a medical student is unusual. Nor did the intensity of her involvement diminish after I sought specialty training in psychiatry and over the years thereafter. Dr. Bruch insisted on being a part of every key decision regarding my professional and personal lives—from whether or not I should apply for training in psychoanalysis and which academic position I should pursue upon completing my psychiatry residency to whom I should not and should marry. On the other hand, I knew absolutely nothing about Dr. Bruch's personal life. I did not know where she had been born, whether or not she had ever been married, whether she had living family members, what her avocational activities were, what were her political proclivities, etc. This, of course, was as it should be. She was the teacher, and I her pupil. With Dr. Bruch, boundaries were to be respected.

When Dr. Bruch died in 1984, I knew little more about her than the extraordinary substance of her academic productivity and pleasant distillation of the many professional interactions that it was my privilege to share with her. So powerful was her personality and enduring her propriety that even after her death I did not presume to even speculate about the sources of her brilliance, creativity and drive. Inconsistent with my usual curiosity, I did not even contemplate such obvious questions as...From what country did Dr. Bruch derive her accent? How and why did she come to the United States, train as a physician and psychiatrist, and become interested in eating disorders? What were the temperamental and experiential seeds of her distinctive personality? Upon being offered the opportunity by Dr. Bruch's niece to read this biography and write its introduction, I demurred. Had she wanted me to know about her life she would have told me. I had no right to violate this boundary. However, when Joanne Bruch told me that her aunt had come here to escape the Nazi holocaust that had extinguished the lives of most of her family, the missing piece of the puzzle of Dr. Bruch's mysterious secrecy surrounding her past and personal life was found. The pain of recounting had to be unbearable for Dr. Bruch; and repetition could callous the feelings and trivialize the hallowed memories of those who were lost. Not only does this biography illuminate the bittersweet path of a brave, great person; but it is another essential monument to other Hilde Bruchs whose lives were monstrously consumed during the Holocaust before their chances to improve and sweeten this world.

Eating disorders are highly prevalent and severely disabling. For example, anorexia nervosa, an illness in which individuals have intense fear of and preoccupation with gaining weight or becoming fat, has become increasingly more prevalent among young women in the United States over the past forty years. About ten percent of those diagnosed with the illness will die over the succeeding ten years. According to the National Center for Health Statistics, approximately one in five men and one in three women may be classified as obese. Among both groups, there are increased incidents of life-threatening medical illnesses including cardiovascular disorders and depression.

Historically, western medicine has not considered eating disorders as being within its domain for clinical consideration. During the twentieth century, however, medicine began to recognize eating disorders as significant public health problems quite worthy of its attention. Unfortunately, medical investigators fragmented the "causes" of the conditions as stemming from either psychological or physical (i.e. metabolic) sources. Consequently, little progress was made over the first half of this century by organized medicine in understanding, preventing, or treating eating disorders. The research and conceptual approaches to eating disorders by Hilde Bruch, M.D., changed this dismal record.

Pediatrician, psychoanalyst, laboratory-trained research scientist, Hilde Bruch is widely regarded as medicine's preeminent pioneer in the modern conceptualization, diagnosis and treatment of eating disorders, including obesity and anorexia nervosa. Dr. Bruch was also among the first physicians to combine biological, psychological, and social perspectives in the research and treatment of a specific group of mental disorders. Dr. Bruch was far ahead of her time in applying this powerful integrative model to psychiatric illness, a model that only recently has been "re-discovered" by medicine and patients as the most promising and productive.

Prior to the research work and writing of Hilde Bruch, obesity was considered to be almost exclusively the result of genetically-transmitted biologic diseases and syndromes that affected metabolism or digestion. The result of this flawed conceptualization was that there was little therapeutic attention devoted to assessing and changing the "afflicted" individual's eating or exercise patterns—or, more importantly, the interpersonal relationships and life experiences that may have contributed to these patterns. Dr. Bruch's revolutionary advances derived from her changing the primary focus of research attention from the illness to the person with the illness. For example, while doing metabolism-based laboratory research on obese children, Dr. Bruch noticed unusual interactions between the children and their parents. This led her to explore, carefully, relationships and unique personal qualities among families with obese children.

Among the many useful discoveries that derived from this exploration was novel insight into flawed capacities of certain mothers for perceiving critical cues from and needs of their children. Specifically, Dr. Bruch discovered that many mothers of obese children were unable to discern pivotal communications from their infant children, such as if a baby were crying because it was hungry, in pain from colic, tired, anxious or frightened, or bored, etc. Manifestly, different responses from the mother are indicated, consistent with the specific need and communication of the infant at that time. Dr. Bruch discovered that mothers who were incapable of discerning among the divergent needs of their crying infants would often respond by giving the baby a bottle. She hypothesized that the long-term results of this interaction were: a) increased frustration of the child when its "real" needs were not met; b) increased frustration and insecurity of the mother for not being able to reassure and satisfy her child; c) the inability of the child to identify accurately and respond appropriately to its own internal cues and needs; d) given that oral gratification (i.e. the bottle) was utilized generically to respond to a broad range of emotional and physical stimuli of the infant, this response pattern "is learned" and persists as the child grows older. Thus, when the child becomes bored or anxious, it is prone to confuse these feelings with "hunger," and respond by excessive (i.e. beyond the nutritional requirement) eating. It is important to emphasize that Dr. Bruch never proposed that such an experiential pattern was causally implicated in all types of obesity; nor did she claim it to be the sole maladaptive eating patterns of any obese individual. Rather, she posited that this dysfunctional maternal-infant pattern frequently was one element in a complex biopsychosocial matrix that led to the eating disorder.

Dr. Bruch believed that each causal factor of obesity should, where possible, be uncovered so that it could be specifically addressed in the therapeutic response. For example, in the case of the child whose obesity was, in part, related to his mother's uniformly responding to his disparate emotional needs with feeding behavior, Dr. Bruch would utilize both individual psychotherapy and family counseling. In individual treatment, she would help the obese child isolate and identify discrete feelings that led to eating responses. She would then help the child trace the precipitants of these feelings and develop strategies to prevent or respond effectively to the precipitants. Utilizing this strategy, Dr. Bruch demonstrated that the obese child would feel less anxious, frustrated, and impotent, and improve in multiple dimensions of his life in addition to weight control.

Dr. Bruch's approach was original and controversial in that emphasis was placed on the child's psychological insight and situational mastery, with little focus directed towards changing the eating behavior, per se. Her intense involvement of family members of the obese child in the assessment and treatment process was also unconventional. Detractors argued that this approach was harmful to the "therapeutic alliance" between the physician and the patient, and it attenuated the "safe haven" from intrusive parents that therapy provided for the obese child. Dr. Bruch countered that the child must "live in the real world" that includes the parents and siblings who are so intimately involved in the genesis, sustenance, and multifarious effects of the eating disorder. She contrasted her approach with what she regarded as "traditional therapy" wherein, all too often, the patient became endlessly immersed in the artificially-protective and isolative island of dyadic therapy.

Although anorexia nervosa, epitomized by Dr. Bruch as "the relentless pursuit of thinness," had been identified as a medical condition since the latter half of the 19th century, it was not widely considered as a discrete psychiatric syndrome until almost one hundred years later. Rather, it was conceptualized as an associated feature of certain medical illnesses such as hypopituitarism, or an epiphenomenon—a psychiatric disorder such as schizophrenia, depression, or hysteria. Dr. Bruch's extensive and effective clinical work with patients with anorexia nervosa combined with her startlingly original insights as to its defining features helped establish the condition as a discrete psychiatric disorder. She was the first to recognize that patients who suffered from this disorder had what she termed "distorted body images," an impaired perception that she stipulated as a prerequisite for the diagnosis. Even though most people with this condition ranged from normative to morbidly-low body weights, they perceived themselves to be grossly fat, and often felt embarrassed about the appearance of particular regions of their bodies—such as their thighs, midsections, or buttocks. Dr. Bruch placed intense therapeutic focus on the family dynamics of these people when they were young adults living with the parents and siblings. She discovered that the affected individual (the "identified patient") frequently felt powerless and ineffectual in the context of her family. Siblings were experienced by the patients as being hotly competitive for the attention, admiration, and love of the parents. From their perspectives, siblings experienced the patients as perfectionistic "goody-goodies" who were self- centered, closed-off from them, and who "gobbled up" both family attention and resources. Dr. Bruch examined closely the relationship of the patient with a specific parent, usually the mother, with whom they were often enmeshed. She discovered that the prototypic mother had significant problems permitting that child to develop feelings of mastery and independence within the family system, or to exhibit age-appropriate individuation from the family. Mothers tended to "violate" their child's psychological boundaries by relentlessly defining for them how they should feel about highly personal and subjective issues, who their friends should be, key life choices to make, etc. The patients were often put forth to the world as idealized manifestations of the parent's ambitions. They often performed in a superior fashion in school and sports, and eschewed teen-age rebellious behaviors, and superficially appeared to be "model children." Nonetheless, power struggles began to rage in the family over how thin the child had become, and every meal became a battle as the parent insisted that the patient eat. In general, the child would refuse by saying that she was full, or that her stomach was upset, or that the food was so rich that it would make her sick. In actuality, despite skeletal thinness, the child reported extreme anxiety that almost any bite of food would turn to disfiguring fat that would render them grotesque and unworthy. A common pattern was where the parent would "successfully" cajole the child to eat some unwanted morsels, but the child would later induce vomiting so that the food could not be digested and "turned to fat."

As with her strategies for the treatment of people with obesity, Dr. Bruch did not place therapeutic emphasis directly on the struggles and behaviors surrounding the eating; but rather, she worked with the family to permit the child to develop close relationships with peers outside the family and to develop life skills that would enable individuation from them. She dealt specifically with the parents' unconscious needs and narcissistic drives that they had groomed their child to fulfill, and encouraged and taught ways for them to gain self-fulfillment. In summary, she helped them satisfy, in their lives, emotional needs that they had relied upon the child to fill. This change cleared room for the child to risk activities that were autonomous from the family without the previous guilt and anxieties that they were betraying, through abandonment, their parent. As the patient's self-confidence in the extra-familial world built with each new initiative and success, the preoccupation with food and body size diminished.

Therapeutic focus shifted, at this point, from analyses of family dynamics to help with negotiating novel extra-familial relationships and with actualizing educational and vocational potentials.

In her own professional life, Dr. Bruch had little reluctance to challenge prevailing theories and therapeutic practices with which she did not agree. She did not back away from vigorous and heated debate with academic peers. She detested psychological jargon, whether in scholarly publications or in communications with patients and their families. She believed that if the professional's language were difficult to understand by the patient or by the student, most likely the information that the professional was endeavoring to communicate was flawed. It should not be surprising, therefore, that throughout her career, Dr. Bruch was embroiled in intense intellectual and political struggles with medical theoreticians and interest groups whose authority and power base her radical ideas and treatment approaches threatened. Ultimately, Dr. Bruch prevailed. She tirelessly presented her observations and conclusions at countless scientific symposia, and published numerous papers in rigorous, peer-reviewed scientific journals and as chapters in medical textbooks. She wrote many books specifically on eating disorders—both for the medical profession and for the lay public. As her reputation as a consummate clinician and educator grew, patients and students flocked to her from all over the world for care and tutelage. More surprising to Dr. Bruch than to those with whom she engaged was that ultimately her theories and clinical approaches became mainstream. Over the last two decades of her life, Dr. Bruch was regarded as the foremost psychiatric expert on eating disorders, and, in the decade since her death, the appreciation for her contribution has grown. Her treatment paradigm has been applied with success to other neuropsychiatric conditions such as obsessive compulsive disorder and post traumatic stress disorder. Without compromise or gratuitous ingratiation, through the power of her ideas and the impact of her accomplishment, the consummate outsider has been invited and is warmly and enduringly embraced indoors.

AUTHOR'S NOTE

When Hilde Bruch died in December of 1984, the bulk of her estate came to my husband, Herbert, whose guardianship she assumed in 1946. The voluminous, dog-eared keepsakes of this sentimental "pack rat," whose roots were locked to an earlier lifetime, revealed a fascinating story.

Part I describes early happy years and is entirely anecdotal, based on taped recollections of childhood recorded for our son, Richard Alexander, whom Hilde considered her "grandson." Parts II through X are drawn from letters to Hilde or by Hilde to other family members, or from medical papers and personal journals. Occasional reference is made to photographs.

Six interviews conducted by Jane Preston, M.D. and Hanna Decker, Ph.D. between November of 1974 and January of 1975 have been consulted throughout. Useful in providing details about Riga and Westerbork Concentration camps were *Journey into Terror: Story of the Riga Ghetto* by Gertrude Schneider and *Year of Fear: A Jewish Prisoner Waits for Auschwitz* by Philip Mechanicus. *The Guns of August* by Barbara W. Tuchman offered additional background for World War I.

I am indebted to Dr. Roland W. Tapp, Th.D. for his editing suggestions and encouragement; also to George F. Rossner for putting me in touch with Lindsey Hall and Leigh Cohn at Gürze Books. Final thanks must be given posthumously to Alice Russo whose translations from German to English made the entire project possible.

CHAPTER I

1900 - 1923

Adele

In retrospect, the years preceding World War I seem nearly idyllic. Times were simpler then and there was a natural domesticity about living. The family was supreme. It administered to life and death and all important matters in between. It was the comfortable haven where children thrived or languished, where adults bickered and made peace. Illness became the business of mothers or maiden aunts or doctors making house calls while doubling as family friends. Children played games or invented games and enjoyed being children. Mothers were buxom and sturdy and confident, while fathers headed households with dignity and pride. Days were liquid and long, and grievances minor enough to be no more than ripples on a quiet pond.

The little town of Duelken no longer exists. It has disappeared, not like Camelot into the mists of time, but by becoming incorporated into Viersen, its larger neighbor. Like the Germany it once represented, it is different altogether, yet at the turn of the century this small dot on the map of Germany was a hub of activity and minutiae of everyday living.

It was here that Hirsch Bruch met his wife, Adele, at a synagogue dance carefully arranged by parents anxious that young people should meet. Romance in these small communities where Jewish populations were sparse and chance encounters unlikely was never taken for granted, and since marriage between Jew and non-Jew was not a consideration, parents were very serious and often quite creative in arranging contacts and introductions.

Adele was bright and lively, the only daughter of the Rath family of Kempen, and as such the family pride, envied even by her own mother in her privileged position as "Father's pet." Her father enjoyed telling a special family joke to anyone who would listen but which his own family never tired of hearing.

"I have five sons and every son has a sister."

"But that's *ten* children!" they would gasp. "Such a large family. How proud you must be!" Laughter soon followed, as almost immediately people recognized their own naiveté, while Adele and her father and mother and brothers giggled right along with them.

Bathed in this warm and comfortable atmosphere, surrounded by love, Adele wished she might remain in Kempen forever, though she understood it wasn't possible. Prospects for marriage in her hometown were practically non-existent, and she and her entire family sensed the unpleasant and very real possibility of spinsterhood. Adele knew that unmarried women usually ended up in the home of a married brother or sister, acting as nanny, nurse and baby sitter, trading independence for a place to live.

Thus it was auspicious when quiet, blue-eyed Hirsch Bruch came courting. Attraction was immediate, for the young man was gentle and kind as well as handsome, and when the two exchanged vows, jubilant relatives predicted that this union begun so favorably and traditionally would settle into long and productive marriage. Seeming to confirm this, a baby boy was born nine months later, with six other children following in fairly rapid succession.

Rudolf, born in 1900, was an effective older brother. Displaying the confidence of first-born, he knew in this position only good things were coming to him. He invariably got first pick of things, toys and clothing of the best quality, since Mother believed, quite simply, that things should last forever.

Beautiful Auguste, born August 10, 1901, was dark-eyed like her mother, while possessing her father's gentle disposition. She appeared to personify all that is bright and good and promising in life.

On March 11, 1904 came the maverick, Hilde, questioning anything and everything. At first she questioned naively, like the child in her favorite fairy tale "The Emperor's New Clothes," but later with a frankness and ferocity that would drive family and teachers to distraction. That inquiring mind would later serve her well in a professional career, but at this early age when people asked, "Hilde, what will you be when you grow up?" she answered without hesitation, "Mother." Not *a* mother, but *Mother,* because for Hilde her own mother was the ideal and it would always be that way.

Artur's personality seemed "undetermined," as though being middle child were somehow pivotal, for while he resisted being counted with the "little ones," he lacked the force of his older brother and sisters. Later in childhood, he would be influenced by Ernst, his strong-willed and practical-minded younger brother.

Erna was a charmer. Loving and petite and pretty, with curly blonde hair, her family nick-named her *das katzchen,* "kitten," for those pet-like qualities. Born six years after Auguste, she shared with her sister the same birthday and many similarities in character.

Ernst was rebellious. Hating rules and authority, he once ran away, creating confusion and dismay in the normally well-organized Bruch household. He detested schooling and intellectual matters on principle, but was intelligent in a practical sense and possessed the knack for always landing on his feet. After completing the compulsory requirements, at age fourteen he quit school altogether.

Kurt, born in 1912, would not remember the easy pre-war years, but as the baby adored by all, and of whom little could be expected, he had a carefree, happy childhood. Hilde was eight years old when Kurt was born, and she, rather than her older sister, became his frequent sitter and Little Mother.

An overall harmony developed in the household despite the varied interests and personalities of the occupants, but to get this, certain procedures needed following. One rule Father and Mother established early was that the older children could eat in the dining room while the little ones were having supper in the kitchen. While this posed no particular hardship since the kitchen help was friendly and the room large and warm, it meant the difference between eating informally and going to bed at seven, or having a formal dinner with bedtime at eight. After supper, the little ones would be sent scampering to bed with a pat from

Father and a kiss and stern warning from Mother, "No talking now, and no getting out of bed."

It was a well-established routine. Father and Mother needed an hour alone in the evening, and the children after a day of strenuous play needed rest. Who could object? Only Hilde. She pouted and whined and carried on, "Why should I have to go to bed so early? I'm not little. I can read and spell and do arithmetic just like Rudolf and Auguste, and I refuse to be treated like a baby!" Probably she resented being called "little" more than she objected to the rules, but Father and Mother were firm in their resolve, resisting her bullying for weeks. Still, the pouts were wearing and the objections so persistent that eventually Hilde got her way, accomplishing the nearly impossible. For her alone rules were bent, and she was allowed to join Rudolf and Auguste in the formal dining room to eat off a beautiful table cloth and talk of important matters with Father and Mother until the bewitching hour of eight.

On Wednesdays and Saturdays, Mother went to market with at least one child in tow so that by example they could learn how to select fresh produce. Fresh fruit and vegetables were always abundant in the household even during the war years, when the garden was expanded. In addition to market and garden, farmers' wives and daughters stopped regularly at the house, pushing carriages laden with fruits and vegetables and eggs.

But their favorite day of the week was Friday, Mother's day for baking bread. So firmly was this day established in the minds of her children that Hilde, upon learning that she was born on Friday, asked in amazement, "But when did Mother have time to bake the bread?"

Black bread or pumpernickel came from the bakery, and once a week a dozen hot rolls were dropped into a small bag that hung on their door. But every Friday the sweet smell of yeast and hot bread filled the large kitchen. Mother made white bread and raisin bread and *challah* for the Sabbath, while the children stood around the long table watching and begging to help. Nothing delighted them more than when Mother had leftover pieces of dough and gave them some to make their own bread in small pans.

The oven was part of a huge coal stove, large enough to hold all the loaves, but Mother hated that stove. She hated the draft. "Inadequate," she declared. "My baking is uneven and it takes too long."

Also in the kitchen was a gas stove, but Mother's frugality prevented her from using it. Only when someone was sick or requiring special attention would she turn to it. Though Father made the point regularly that really there was no problem with money and perhaps she might ease the budget a bit, Mother would sniff that gas was too expensive. Perhaps all her complaining down the years about expenditures and work were locked into her resentment of that old coal stove. At any rate, the family understood there was no appeasing her, and her grumbling came to be an expected part of bread making, almost as necessary as yeast.

She was a splendid cook, despite her differences with the stove, and a skilled seamstress and embroiderer as well. After graduating from the Lyceum, she had been sent to a kind of finishing school for fashionable well-educated young ladies where she lived with an elegant family and learned the household arts. Had she thought about it, she might have envied her brothers their University education, but it never occurred to her to resist tradition. Like other women of her time, she expected to receive a sound education, marry, and have children. There wasn't time for introspection anyway, for soon after their marriage, Father's three orphaned brothers began arriving regularly for meals. While she wasn't exactly pleased by this development, there seemed no graceful way around it, and since she was truly fond of Leo, Otto, and Artur, she dutifully accepted the extra company at her table. Because her own family was also increasing rapidly, she hired maids to help with chores, and found herself planning meals for ten or eleven. It was a tall order, yet somehow meals were excellent.

Her frugality or economic spirit was everywhere, regulating their lives, making bargain-hunting an art. She insisted on quality, nearly always getting it, so that what she bought was excellent and durable. It had to be, since Mother expected toys and clothing to last through a whole generation of children. Only the toughest fabrics met her standards. After holding material to the light and squinting for imperfections, she would run her fingers lightly across the nap, testing for endurance by snapping the bulk of material back and forth like an accordion. Rudolf and Auguste headed the line of hand-me downs, but twice a year, at Passover in spring, and Rosh Hashana in fall, each child received a new outfit.

When they strolled to services on these high holy days, the large family clothed so fashionably attracted the attention of everyone they passed. One neighbor, anxious not to be conspicuous, peeked from behind a window curtain in his home. He saw Father in a cutaway and high silk hat, proudly displaying Mother on his arm, his slim figure tall and straight. Mother wore brown silk, trimmed in velvet with matching fur piece, all in the latest fashion, her thick dark hair swept neatly into a beautiful tortoise shell comb. The children in tandem marched behind, dignified and disciplined, but barely able to contain the joy and pride at their own handsomeness. The neighbor smiled secretly as he watched the progress of the little parade. Hirsch Bruch was the man he most admired, for with his beautiful family he was the definition of a successful man.

Rudolf got things first and was properly serious about his responsibilities. He owned a handsome set of soldiers in bright battle dress which he arranged for mock attacks when he and his best friend, Erich, played "Balkan Wars." Often they played American Indians in costumes their mothers fashioned out of sack cloth and chicken feathers, whooping and hollering and dancing in circles like the Indians illustrated in their school texts. Games and costumes were especially popular during pre-Lent Carnival, or Fasching, which began in late February or early March, when the predominantly Catholic Rheinlanders put on fancy clothes and attended masked balls. Children waited for the excitement of Fasching all year, and during the last three days before Ash Wednesday, when municipal buildings closed to honor the holiday, everyone participated, Catholic or not. They dressed festively and danced in the streets, or at the very least wore masks.

Another popular activity for older boys was *Pferdchen* or "horsey." Mother constantly worried when they played this game, warning Rudolf it was too rough. Someone could get hurt. Rudolf was unfazed. All his friends were playing after all, and no one was going to call him a sissy. Besides, he and Erich were champion players, often succeeding in deposing all other riders, so everyone respected their team.

Mounting his noble steed, he leaped on Erich's shoulders and was proceeding into battle, when he heard a crash followed by the tinkling of shattered glass. One rider had deposed another right through a neighbor's plate glass window.

The owner, a lady with a tight bun of yellow hair, came running, expression taut, voice shrill. Whose children were they, anyway, to act like this? What a lawless, undisciplined bunch of ruffians they were, a disgrace to the entire community! She intended tracking down their parents to make them pay for her expensive window. Six youthful horsemen dutifully complied by meekly supplying names and street numbers.

Father and Mother were heartsick. Of course, they paid the money and apologized to the woman. That was the very least they could do, and afterwards they sent Rudolf over to apologize. Father's concerns were grave enough to prompt serious discussion with his eldest son. How could a Jewish boy act that way? Such behavior might be all right for other children, but Rudolf ought to understand his responsibilities. His actions must be beyond reproach and never cause trouble. "Rudolf," said Father firmly, "Jewish children and Jewish families must never be conspicuous."

Friday night was special family card night when everyone stayed home and bedtime was extended until nine. After the ceremony of lighting the Sabbath candles, the blessing, the wine and *challah,* the family settled in for an evening of *Komoedschen.*

They chose this game because any number could play, while the rules were also simple enough that even baby Kurt might occasionally win with Father's not-so-subtle assistance. It was fun, too, requiring enough strategy to keep the older players alert. The ritual would begin as Mother presented a special velvet bag of pennies out of which every-one grabbed the required amount to place in the pot, or *Komoedschen.* Play began clockwise around the large oval dining room table, each player drawing cards, then trying to get rid of them by building suits. Always grandiose discussions and hypothesizings accompanied play, and the air was thick with advice on whether to throw or hold cards in order to counter another's perceived strategy. The more sophisticated players favored holding back on suits rather than exposing what they were collecting, so that in one magnificent, magician-like gesture, the winner might fan his hand on the table and triumphantly proclaim, *"Komoedschen!"*

"Oh, Rudolf. I should have known you were collecting kings when you didn't discard them. No wonder I couldn't complete my run," Mother groaned.

"I knew he had them. I was *positive*. And he tied up sevens, too," balked Hilde. "I was ready to go out next turn, but now I have this huge pile of cards in my hand."

And as so often is the case in the fortune of cards, those who gamble in order to outwit opponents are more often themselves surprised and made to pay the price for their audacity, each card costing a penny to the *Komoedschen* and the winner. But groans and laughter and secret maneuverings that weren't really surprises were all part of Friday card night and the pleasure of spending it together.

Mother had her special card day, too, when she got together with her lady friends. They took turns, six women in all, so that every six weeks or so it was Mother's chance to entertain. Her children looked forward to those days when Mother put out her finest tablecloth and crystal and silver.

"Some day all these things will belong to you children," she would softly murmur while lovingly spinning tales about each piece, a history of the heirlooms that were her dowry as the only daughter. Her children had long ago committed them to memory, and much as musicians remember beloved strains of music, the stories had become a medley of familiar tunes, the melodious fabric of Mother's gracious entertaining.

She served tea and frosted cakes, extravagantly admired by her guests and secretly admired by the children who tiptoed around hoping to be offered a nibble. Quiet they were, though elephants might have been less conspicuous amidst so much feminine activity, and while the women gently denied them it was quite plain they must wait until dessert to sample the lovely cakes. The urchins remained undaunted, indeed would have been surprised had the situation been otherwise. Her children understood this was not just another elegant tea party and card game but Mother's opportunity to catch up on all the local news and gossip. Behind kitchen doors they caught snatches of tales and laughter, and then absolute quiet as the ladies settled down to business. They took their cards very seriously.

Though card games were a welcome diversion from household duties, Mother continued to miss the companionship of family and friends in Kempen, and for her children the ten mile trip to their grandparents' became a frequent and favorite excursion. Father assembled the family nearly every weekend, hitched the horse and buggy, while they settled into a pleasant forty-minute ride through the flowered fields and open spaces that were Father's workplace. He was a cattle dealer, and on friendly terms with all the local farmers. Often they stopped at farmhouses along the way to visit, while Father discussed business. The farmers' wives were always friendly and offered berry pies, or sent the children off to the orchard to pick their own fresh fruit.

The seating arrangement in the little buggy was always the same, the older children in back, with Ernst and Erna jostling for position next to Father to assist with the horses. Mother, also seated next to Father with Kurt upon her lap, clucked constant disapproval at their rudeness. But Father chuckled quietly, giving Ernst and Erna each a turn to shake the reins. These outings with wife and children were his greatest pleasure, never failing to spark joy in his heart.

The terrain was typically flat, like Holland, which lay only twenty miles West. But there was one small rise between Duelken and Kempen, a hump which the children called "mountains," though the grade was perhaps no steeper than one foot per one hundred feet. It was known as Suechtelner Hoehen and, as they approached it, Father played a game which his children anticipated with that kind of vicarious suspense which can only be generated out of danger and fear. At the top of Suechtelner Hoehen, Father shouted, "Whoa! Whoa! The horses are out of control. They are running away and I can't hold them back. Whoa! Whoa! Help, children. What shall I do?"

As the little buggy flew down the hill, its precious cargo was torn between terror and Father's predictability. They felt the wind in their faces, the frantic thump of their hearts as the landscape blurred by. Their knuckles whitened as they clenched the sides of the buggy and glued themselves to their seats.

Then they looked at Father. Were those blue eyes twinkling? Was that a smile beneath his handsome mustache? Was he tricking them again? But then Father shouted "Whoa!" again, and with such urgency that surely this time they were in danger and the horses were running wild and all was lost.

And then they were in the little town of Suechteln and the horses were trotting tamely once more. And now when they looked at Father the smile was unmistakable.

Being a modern man, Hirsch Bruch was aware of the many changes occurring in larger towns and cities. Electricity was the latest thing: books and catalogs printing fabulous, eye-catching ads illustrating lamps and chandeliers and accompanying paraphernalia cluttered the mail. Hirsch determined that as soon as electricity came to their burg they would have it. Great excitement as the family leafed through catalogs selecting ceiling fixtures and lamp shades. Everything so new and wonderful. No more smelly kerosene, no more cleaning of blackened glass from out-dated gas lamps.

Finally the long-anticipated day arrived when electric workers busied themselves in every room, trailed by curious children. After they left, light bulbs hung everywhere, dangling from cords even in attic and basement. The sight of a naked bulb crowning her old coal stove rendered Mother ecstatic. Now at least she could *see* the beastly thing, even if she still couldn't bake in it properly. Each family member in turn felt a special pride when the very next day a notice appeared in the local newspaper that electricity had come to Duelken, where it had first been turned on in the house of Hirsch Bruch.

Another early household instrument was the telephone, which eased Mother's sense of isolation by bringing her within conversation's reach of friends and family in Kempen. Soon she lived in rapt anticipation of calls from her old town, which was probably what prompted Father's brothers, Leo and Otto, to play their prank on her.

They knew Mother was awed by her eldest brother, that merely hearing his voice over the phone could send her into a trance. On these early phones it was difficult to distinguish voices, and so when Otto assumed the attitude of the impressive and sublime Abraham, poor Mother was far too overwhelmed by the call to notice anything unusual about the voice of the caller. When she replaced the receiver on its hook, she knew without a doubt that her much-admired brother would be visiting her on Saturday. For Leo and Otto, the coup exceeded all expectation, and they hastened to inform the rest of the family. Even the children were warned to silence.

Saturday found Mother engaged in frantic housecleaning activity, with Leo and Otto lounging about in the comfortable parlor chairs supervising. "Adele, you missed some dust over there on that door frame, and those light bulbs could also stand wiping," quipped Otto.

Everywhere she looked, she saw Leo and Otto. She wished she might shoo them away like flies, and memories of those many additional meals she had prepared through the years flashed through her head. But alas, now as in the past, there seemed no diplomatic way of getting rid of them.

Leo and Otto, however, were intelligent young men with a healthy respect for Mother, who could be an intimidating presence when angered. Having had their fun, they confessed their little deception, rendering everyone a good laugh. Except Mother, who felt duped and foolish. Certainly it was not nearly so humorous as everyone seemed to think. Still, she did her best to cover up, tried to be a good sport. "Well, who would imagine? That was a good one on me," she tittered half-heartedly, while on the telephone was ever wary thereafter.

By 1912, the family saw changes in Father. He looked thinner and seemed to walk more slowly. Often he excused himself from the children's games, saying he was tired and would play some other time. Mother urged him to see Dr. Birken, their long-time family friend, and the day following Father's examination the doctor stopped by their house with sobering news. Father had diabetes, a serious illness for which there was no cure, only dietary control. But with proper diet, Dr. Birken explained, Father might expect to live many years. He advised Mother what foods to buy, how to prepare them, and what foods to avoid. Then he produced a scale and taught them to measure and weigh the amounts Father was allowed to eat, and finally he told Father how to test for sugar in his urine.

The family received the news in near silence, and Dr. Birken, who understood this peculiar calm as shock and depression, hurried to reassure them.

"We are living in wonderful times. Something new is happening every day. In science, always a new discovery, a new invention. In medicine, the same, and with such progress as we are making, who knows? A cure for diabetes could happen tomorrow."

Mother, at any rate, recovered quickly. She had no time to waste in counter-productive melancholy. All her life she had met events, good or bad, with straightforward common sense. Now it seemed only logical to combat diabetes the same way. Never had she felt more strong or confident in her aims. Her own energy provided strength and courage and hope, while hope in turn generated more energy. She declared personal war, taking the rigorous diet to battle. A shelf of small pots was added in the kitchen next to the larger shelf of beautiful black enamelware in graduated sizes, Mother's contribution to the household as part of her *Aussteur.* She continued preparing family meals in the familiar German style she was used to, and in the large black pots she creamed vegetables and made sauces. Only now she always measured Father's portion first and cooked it plainly in a little pot. Father needed to eat frequently, and the little pots were always stewing, while Mother seemed always to be in the kitchen supervising them.

Auguste's close friend at school, Frieda Fuerwentchen, was the youngest daughter in a large family of prosperous real estate and construction people. Frieda's mother was diabetic, and every spring Frau Fuerwentchen came into their home to discuss the latest medical gossip with Father. This was unusual. Perhaps it was because of their common medical problem, or perhaps she was influenced by her daughter's friendship with Auguste, or maybe she just respected Hirsch Bruch enough to enter his house, for normally Jewish and non-Jewish families, while friendly and polite with one another, did not socialize in each other's homes. Thus Frau Fuerwentchen's visit was special, something of an annual event.

Father also saw Frau Fuerwentchen at Bad Neuenahr, a spa where diabetics of means convened to socialize and take the cure. Father stayed at the Jewish hotel, but events were open to everyone for medical discussions and visiting. These conventions were an important source of medical information at a time when newspapers and journals did not print this kind of news. Visitors to the spa drank fresh spring water, walked the promenade, and attended afternoon violin concerts, which sometimes included trumpets and march music.

Often families came along to stay a few days while a loved one settled in. Friendships developed out of common bonds as spa visitors followed one another's medical progress with great interest, rejoicing in a friend's good health, trying to determine and duplicate the formula which had produced it, conversely despairing and commiserating when someone died.

The Prodigy

Hilde was different, and everyone in the family knew it. Mother worried about her daughter and secretly watched for signs of ordinary popularity, some hint of the social graces she saw in Auguste. She rejoiced when Hilde brought friends home, encouraging the relationships with milk and cookies, but when the child retired to her room for hours on end Mother would brood. She hoped school would channel some of her daughter's restless energy, that all-absorbing, driving need to achieve, for what could the future possibly hold for such a restless spirit?

Though she worried about Hilde, Mother recognized her daughter's special needs, so Hilde alone was given a private bedroom where she could pursue intellectual fancies and adolescent dreams. Beautiful books lined these walls, discards from birthdays and Bar Mitzvahs, as well as old treasures collected from used book sales or fished out of back alley trash cans. It was an odd assortment of subjects ranging from the earliest books of her childhood to the most famous classics. Some of these she could not fully understand yet, but they lined the walls anyway, ready for the day when she would fill her spirit with their wisdom. She envied her brothers their Bar Mitzvahs when they received magnificent collected works in leather-bound volumes. What did girls get anyway, except the chore of preparing food? Actually, she had to admit this was no hardship. The mixture of aromas escaping the kitchen, like an exotic bouquet, sent her spirits soaring, and the happy reunion of relatives on these occasions was more exciting than any birthday party. But she could also be perfectly content cloistered in her room, free to cut out dress patterns of her own designing or engage in the fictitious fantasies of her latest novel. In this private world, imagination knew no limits, for certainly she could go anywhere boys could go.

Her intellectual endeavors began early. By the time she was four, she had discovered the *Berliner Abendpost,* with its special children's section of stories and puzzles. One puzzle, called *Rebus,* contained intriguing hidden figures, which Hilde delighted in revealing and which she claimed as her personal possession every Saturday. She pestered her brother and sister to read her stories, promising that as soon as she could, she would read stories to everyone. Occasionally they gave in, but more often they either ignored her or displayed their indifference by wandering off, claiming they had something else to do, leaving Hilde to rely on Father's good nature—where she was more fortunate—for he hardly ever turned her down.

Patting his knee, he prepared a special seat where she clambered up to snuggle close. "Ah, Hildechen, so what are we reading this morning?" And she would show him so they could settle into that magic world where anything can happen. He read and read until at last the craving was satisfied. How truly she loved Father, and how she admired readers!

Rudolf and Auguste understood Hilde perfectly and had no intention of succumbing to her whims. They were the older ones, she the bossy little sister like a burr on their socks, a pest always there. Auguste, especially, found Hilde's tag-along company tiresome. On Saturdays when she wanted to visit her friends—*alone*—here was Hilde attempting to make friends with her friends, though she was fully three years younger. So anxious, in fact, was Hilde to be a *"Grossen,"* that frequently she bribed Auguste to intentionally forget her *Butterbrot,* so that later she might deliver the mid-morning snack. That way she would get to see Auguste's beautiful school room, and the other children would see her, and maybe they wouldn't realize that she was only someone's little sister.

Sometimes Rudolf and Auguste would be assigned a poem to learn at home, which later they would recite to their class at school. Often they would test memory and poise by practicing first in front of Mother and Father, but Hilde was always in the audience as well, her ear attuned to rhythms, her razor mind absorbing whole lines, committing them to heart with uncanny quickness. Her brother and sister balked at seeing her there acting as judge and jury, with even the *chutzpa* to correct their mistakes!

She spoke continually and importantly of school, which was to begin in April, so Mother's selection of a *tornister* for Christmas was both practical and timely. It was a handsome thing as well, and Hilde could not quite conceal her pride. She loaded it with books and strutted in front of Rudolf, a peacock displaying plumage and expecting attention. Rudolf pretended not to notice. He was so much older and a boy besides that it was impossible to be impressed by anything except her persistence. However, as always, ignoring the pest with the plump figure marching with imperious correctness in front of him proved futile, and so to be rid of her he grudgingly acknowledged the backpack, warning she better be prepared to study hard because people would be expecting a lot from someone with so large and fancy a *tornister*. Hilde was satisfied. Naturally, she would be a fine student.

When school at last began, no one was better prepared. She could recite all of Rudolf's and Auguste's poems. She could read, she could even spell a little. But her true love and greatest achievement was arithmetic. Through the years, Father had piqued his children's intellectual curiosity and sharpened their wits with puzzles and arithmetic problems. Often he awarded prizes of books or candy which he picked up on business trips. Hilde loved these contests, and her aptitude for calculations and problem solving was immediately apparent. Rudolf and Auguste, also gifted in math, perhaps lacked Hilde's competitiveness, for by the time she had been in school only a few years, Hilde was winning most of Father's prizes, and her claim to "student of the family" went unchallenged.

The joy of her first day of school was diminished only slightly by the fact that Rudolf had already left *Volkschule* to attend the *Realeschule* for boys. But Auguste was still there, in her fourth and final year, and Hilde would be sharing the one-room class with her. She packed her *tornister* with Auguste's early primers, expecting to demonstrate her reading prowess to teacher and classmates, then she carefully checked the *Butterbrot* and small sweet pastries Mother had thoughtfully baked for the teacher, and finally she lovingly stroked the bright new notebooks and pencils and replaced them in the sack. Then, with a kiss from Mother and a pat from Father, she and Auguste were on their way, joined by other children for the ten minute walk to school.

Some of these children would be attending the large Catholic elementary school which stood next to a church about two blocks up the street. The Jewish elementary school and synagogue stood opposite the small community Protestant school where Jewish students went across the street for needlework and physical education. But it was to the Catholic *Volkschule,* with its climbing bars that the children were most attracted. This jungle gym was always loaded with chattering *Kinder,* playful chimps in colorful clothing hanging from bars and chasing each other in circles round and round the perimeter.

Hilde's *Butterbrot* excursions had already made her a familiar if slightly amusing sight at school, so the teacher was expecting her, but then the teacher knew most families personally since there were only ten Jewish families in the community, and she had experienced a long association with all of them through their children. As Auguste curtseyed to introduce her sister, the teacher smiled warmly at the latest Bruch to enter her classroom. Hilde also curtseyed politely, then sighed with pleasure as she glanced around the room. At last she was part of the magical world of slate chalk boards and books!

The teacher, a large cheerful woman with silver hair and no-nonsense attitude, conducted her four-grade mixed classroom by devising individual programs out of which she had developed a phenomenal gift for understanding the complex personalities and talents put in her charge. She understood Hilde immediately, recognizing the frustrations of a quick mind. She knew the child's desire for achievement and thirst for knowledge were greater than her actual skills, and to rectify the discrepancy, placed her on such an accelerated schedule that even Hilde found no time to complain. Mother, too, was content seeing her daughter totally absorbed in learning, productive and happy. Fortunately, the teacher had recognized Hilde's genius and was able to pacify the temper without destroying the ego.

Fortuitous as the immediate situation was, it would not last long, since the precocious pupil was already plotting changes, examining the system, recognizing in it discriminations and inadequacies. German schools varied in their requirements, and students normally accepted whatever curriculum was offered in their home town. Boys and girls together attended *Volkschule* for four years or until age ten, when boys became eligible for *Realeschule,* which emphasized natural sciences and modern languages, or a *gymnasium,* which specialized in Greek, Latin, and the humanities. Because of its emphasis on classics, the *gymnasium* was slightly more prestigious, but only *Realeschule* was offered in Duelken. Since the whole educational program began with tenth grade, after four years boys entered a secondary institution in sixth grade, or *sexta.*

After *Volkschule,* girls entered a lyceum, but in Duelken, for reasons unknown, instead of going into sixth grade, the girls went into seventh. It was automatic. Four years to *Volkschule* and then to *septa.* Auguste had gone unquestioningly, and it was expected that Hilde and Erna would follow.

But educators in Duelken had not anticipated Hilde. She had calculated early that girls were being cheated, reasoning that if boys went into *sexta* after four years and girls to *septa* after the same length of time, then in order to equalize things, she must enter *septa* a year earlier. Which is precisely what she did. Nor did the sky fall in, for it was all perfectly legal. But no girl had ever before questioned the system, and now it seemed that Hilde, ever yearning to be a *"Grossen,"* was only two school years behind her sister, Auguste.

How did Hilde's family react to her unorthodox behavior? Mother called her "a real suffragette" when she assumed these independent attitudes. What a suffragette was, Hilde didn't know exactly, only that there were some "funny" women who were calling themselves this while they stirred things up in England. What she did understand was that she wasn't being flattered when Mother called her this, since it only happened when she was being obstinate and opinionated. She guessed it was reproachable behavior for a girl, something like being a "tomboy."

For the most part the family accepted their *enfant terrible,* explaining her differences good-naturedly, "Oh, that's just Hilde." Even Mother's suffragette accusations were mostly playful. Hilde was extended certain privileges, but in fact got away with plenty. To escape chores, which were evenly assigned to all the children, she would toss a pile of books on the kitchen table, moaning excessively about homework assignments.

"Mother, I have an extra report due tomorrow. I can't dry dishes. Why can't Rudolf clean the stove? My teacher wants me to present an arithmetic problem for the class, and I can't spare the time." Mostly it was simple playacting and probably recognized as such, but whether they believed her excuses or not, she was rarely challenged by other members who had already accepted her as family scholar.

Wednesday afternoons, elementary schools had half-day, honoring Frederick the Great. Mother would gather her brood, as many as she could find, to go walking through fields and woods and over the hills at Suechteln. These were the same hills they had navigated so bravely on family outings to Kempen when Father had strained to hold the horses back. The walk was a popular one because it usually ended at a garden restaurant which served sodas and ice cream. But it had a dark side as well, for it led past a tall, forbidding gray stone wall behind which lived the *Verruckten,* inmates of the county psychiatric hospital. It was a spooky place from which children kept cautious distance.

"What would happen if a madman came and attacked us?" the little ones inquired of the big ones while the big ones tried to scare them.

"Watch out! I think I saw one over there behind those trees!"

And so within these beautiful woods dwelt the fearful image of the *Verruckten,* the permanently mad, put away by relatives, hopefully to be forgotten. It was her earliest contact with psychiatry, and the image of stagnation and hopelessness was not one Hilde would soon forget.

Despite the lure of goodies and the titillating imagery of the *Verruckten,* Hilde soon lost interest in these walks. She was growing up. She had better ways to occupy herself, and it would not do to be linked with the little ones, for Rudolf and Auguste were already busy elsewhere. She settled on her favorite activity and looked for a shady spot in the garden where she could read uninterrupted her latest fiction.

In a world not much broader than the buggy ride to Kempen or a slightly longer train ride to neighboring towns where other relatives lived, the family felt unmoved to travel since their small circle of acquaintances seemed perfectly complete. Provincial contentment was modified only slightly by the input of relatives who had entered law or medicine or various businesses. Lives were simple and completely unnewsworthy, where time—measured by twenty-four hour units and begun with school or work or play—ended in card games, family discussions and bedtime. Yet outside Duelken changes were occurring, and news of these changes gradually filtered into the little town.

The *Abendpost* printed a picture of a boat sticking out of the water, and Hilde heard her parents speaking to neighbors in hushed tones about all the millionaires who had drowned on their way to America. It was the year 1912, and this was the first she had heard of a far-off place called America, which you could reach only by boat. Only very much later did she learn that of the more than 1,500 who drowned in the *Titanic* tragedy, only a small percentage were millionaires.

One day the town buzzed with excitement. Doors flew open and grownups flocked to one end of the village, while curious children wandered after them. Everyone was looking to the skies, where a huge cigar-like object was floating tranquilly by. "A Zeppelin," someone said, while a reverent murmur escaped the crowd. "Wonderful! Glorious! Such an age we live in!" And for some reason there was this inexplicable sense of pride that a giant German airship was flying over Duelken.

From another faraway place called the Balkans came news of war. Children, hearing their parents discussing it, borrowed names and battle terminology to use in war games. But mock battles were merely juvenile versions of a drama which was changing the face of Europe. Not only airships stirred German pride. There was the general feeling that German goods, German knowledge, and German industriousness were best in the world. Other countries, too, were experiencing stirrings of patriotism. "Imperialism," "Nationalism," and "Militarism" were important words great nations bandied about as they chased glory all over the globe, colonizing and founding empires.

At the forefront of the drama, his photograph displayed in the *Abendpost* and newspapers and billboards everywhere, was his Imperial Highness, Kaiser Wilhelm II, face theatrical with upturned mustaches and prominent chin, figure imposing, aggressively posed in magnificent dress uniform. He admired the British nearly as much as he envied them. Since his own mother was the daughter of Queen Victoria, he was privy to diplomatic opportunity often denied others, but seemed unable to capitalize on it. His every move stirred distrust. At a time when Britain went unchallenged as "Mistress of the Seas," Wilhelm chose to build up the German Navy, arousing suspicion and propelling the two countries into a rivalry for maritime power.

His personality also worked against him. He had a penchant for royal displays of power, which the British with their Constitutional Monarchy tended to view as faintly amusing, but more often as threatening. Of his many titles, "The All Highest," "Instrument of the Almighty," and "Supreme War Lord," the last was his personal favorite.

In 1913 there was great celebration in Germany, marking the anniversary of Wilhelm II's ascension to the throne. Marching bands assembled and fireworks exploded across the land, as this gala festival announced to the world that for twenty-five years there had been no war in Germany. People everywhere gathered to honor their Kaiser and name him *der Frieden Kaiser,* "the Peace Emperor."

But by 1914 such celebration seemed relegated to a distant past as alliances and maneuverings of the European Nations had made the outbreak of hostilities all but inevitable. As chances for peace deteriorated, Wilhelm appeared haggard and depressed. He moped and blamed everyone but himself for the failure of peace negotiations. Soon this initial period of despondency gave way to the new Wilhelm, who reappeared, cocky and optimistic, declaring himself "Supreme Commander of the Army," ready at last to shoulder his responsibilities as Supreme War Lord. However, after a few setbacks, his vacillating and panicky nature returned, and control of Germany's destiny subsequently passed directly into the hands of Field Marshal von Hindenburg and General Ludendorf.

On the whole, the German people reacted similarly to their Kaiser. Weeks of speculation had created such an atmosphere of tension and uncertainty that when the announcement of war actually came, people experienced relief. As with their Kaiser, earlier doubts were swept away by the wave of euphoria engulfing the German countryside. Optimism and goodwill prevailed as the air grew thick with patriotism.

Flags flapped smartly as townspeople prepared to honor their fine young men and send them into battle. They knew the war would not last long, for hadn't official notice been sent to Belgium promising no harm to that country in exchange for safe passage to France on the Western Front? Of course, certain warnings were also issued just in case Belgium chose not to comply, but wasn't this just army procedure, part of German good sense and organization? It sounded so reasonable that most people and even the generals were predicting the men would be home by Christmas.

On August 3, when units began arriving in Duelken, victory was already in the air. Squadrons of bicyclists came first with the important job of establishing communications, conveying German good will and warning of infractions in Belgian neutrality. Soldiers marching in precision, heady from attention, winked at girls and sang patriotic songs. In addition to canteen and bayonet, each soldier carried flowers, so that mingled with the fresh, acrid smell of new leather boots came the sweet lingering smell of perfume.

Tables covered with fresh white linen appeared in front of every house, behind which stood the *hausfrau* feverishly preparing sandwiches. Now and again when marching halted, children ran to offer bouquets or sandwiches to the soldiers. From everywhere came the sound of singing, shouting, honking and the precision beat of leather on pavement. Not since the anniversary of der Frieden Kaiser was there such celebration!

Earlier, in the palace square in Berlin, the Emperor had proclaimed he would no longer recognize parties and denominations, only "German Brothers." Hardly a family existed that hadn't sent someone, a son or brother or uncle or nephew. Still, what did it matter, now that every high stepping young man was perceived as one of their own?

Several of Mother's brothers were among the mobilized units. Rudolf and Artur biked along the parade route expecting at any moment to recognize a familiar face from among the hundreds of troops. Wouldn't it be worth any effort just to see Uncle Julius in uniform? .

Auguste and Hilde also attended the parade. As part of the flower-sandwich brigade, they stood behind a table, seriously preoccupied. Now and again some grateful soldier would grab a sandwich or catch their bouquet, wave or tousle their hair, shouting how he expected to win the war for them. The flattery induced them to work even harder, pure happiness filling their hearts.

Confronted by glorious spectacle, few celebrants recognized the irony. But alone in her room that evening, Hilde methodically reviewed the day's events. Of course it had been fun seeing so many brave soldiers on parade, nor could she deny the importance of her own contribution. Yet wasn't it strange to be celebrating a *war* only one year after celebrating the *peace?*

By dinnertime she had figured it out, and stormed into the dining room to confront the family, eyes reflecting their recent insight, narrowed shrewdly. "It was rigged," she cried. "The whole thing was a set up. Last year the great Kaiser throws a grand party celebrating peace just so that this year he can go to war. And who can object, since it is the work of der Frieden Kaiser!"

Mother and Father had gotten used to these outbursts, but were nevertheless unprepared for this one. Hilde had seemed so busy, so happy, so much a part of the day's festivities, who could have foreseen such a sudden change of mood?

But Father, ever patient, explained to Hilde that life is rarely so predictable as she might imagine, that even the Kaiser with all his power and resources could hardly have forecast the recent turn of events.

"We don't necessarily understand these decisions," said Father, "so sometimes we must learn to accept wisdom from those with greater knowledge than ourselves. Hildechen, we are not political people. What can we know of such things? But we do know we must defend our ally and sister nation, Austria, against Russia and France. And we do understand we are encircled by enemy nations and now must defend German honor. It is a matter of trust. Can you understand? Dear child, you must learn to be patient."

"They really put that one over on us," muttered the daughter.

The following day out of clear blue skies came the faintest sound of thunder. A storm brewing in the West. No. Cannon fire in Liege. The Belgians would fight after all.

The war was long and oppressive, yet even as casualties mounted families preferred giving soul and body to a losing cause rather than admit defeat. Perhaps by continuing to sacrifice they might one day extract sanity out of the insanity surrounding them.

In 1916, Uncle Julius, fighting bravely at the front, was killed in the line of duty. At least that was how the telegram read. Words spilled impersonally out of the yellow envelope as David stared at them, "SERVED HONORABLY, KILLED IN ACTION." From the day Julius enlisted, David had lived and relived this dreaded moment, which now seemed unreal. A mistake. Only not a mistake, David knew, for with tens of thousands dying, why should his young brother be the exception, have the luck to be spared?

He was not alone. The German nation suffered with him. Few families escaped the specter of death, fewer still the hardships of war. At mundane best, war meant shortages, hoarding, black marketeering, trains crowded with wounded never running on schedule, and sickness of epidemic proportion. But these superficial scars of battle were as nothing compared with the festering, unhealed wounds, the total loss of innocence that was to become the permanent legacy of war.

Because of diabetes, Hirsch had been ineligible to serve, but had experienced hardship all the same. By 1917 shortages and rationing had made it nearly impossible to procure the large amounts of carbohydrates his diet required. That particular winter was unusually harsh, and often the children stood for hours in endless lines complaining of frostbitten fingers and toes, only to learn that supply lines had been cut and food would not be coming after all. Increasing shortages brought smuggling activity. Because of its proximity to the Dutch border, Duelken became a thriving black market, sneaking contraband a way of life. For Father, food supplies were a necessity, but soon most towns-people were smuggling, while authorities turned a blind eye, and women could be seen carrying large loaves of bread, unwrapped, under their arms in broad daylight. Coffee, rice, and cocoa could also be obtained from the smuggler market.

Schools, too, encountered shortages, and were forced to close during those cold months of 1917 when fuel supplies were meager or non-existent, but the unexpected holiday did not mean children could loaf around home. Germans are conscientious, and two activities became popular substitutes for academics. Either classes went for half a day to the woods to collect fuel for burning, or else were taken by train to the next station where there was a large lake for ice skating.

Actually, Hilde preferred neither of these activities. Collecting wood was unpleasant hard work, while skating was cold and tedious. Besides, she was a terrible skater. Her ankles painfully turned in and she found herself more often on her bottom than on her feet. This particular day's outing at the ice pond found her moody and disagreeable, for here she was flopping around on skates instead of being where she really wanted to be, at home huddled under a blanket reading a book.

Her eyes narrowed as she scrutinized the large lake speckled with students from all the neighboring districts gliding or sliding across the glassy surface. The girls, she observed sourly, were wearing their usual meaningless hats of differing styles and color, while the boys wore handsome caps with silver and gold bands, indicating what school they attended. Suddenly she spotted five girls grouped together, all wearing identical red berets. Who were they, anyway, these girls, and why were they wearing those hats? Maybe they belonged to some organization, or possibly but unlikely, they went to the same school. The astringent expression faded to pleasantness as she floundered across the pond to investigate.

That evening, breathlessly, she described her successful day to Father and Mother. There were these girls with beautiful red caps who went to school in Muenchen-Gladbach where they studied Latin and other subjects not taught in Duelken. They were expecting to receive the *Abitur* and then go on to the University. Just imagine, the University! They told her that lots of kids commuted—because it wasn't far—only three stops away. They described their marvelous teachers, and they were laughing and telling tales about them and all the courses they were taking. And these wonderful girls urged *her* to come. Yes, they really wanted her to come. Oh, if only she could go there!

Father and Mother listened quietly but with great interest because an incident at the lyceum the previous spring now made Hilde's exciting discovery very relevant. It had occurred just before summer break when Hilde received her final *zeugnis*.

The *zeugnis* was more than a report card. It was a huge certificate that listed grades and contained a special section on top indexing personal characteristics such as behavior, attention, industry and regularity. Everyone at school, even "dummies," knew that any nice person could receive *"sehr gut"* in all these categories without even trying. As a matter of fact, teachers favored the categories as a euphemistic means of down-peddling poor grades they were forced to give below-average students. For a student of Hilde's caliber, whose interest in academics was nearly compulsive, *"sehr gut"* in everything should have been automatic, which is why when she opened her *zeugnis* and saw *"gut"* for deportment she exploded.

"What is this? How could I get a grade like this? I've never done anything bad. I never threw erasers around or put thumb tacks on people's seats or spilled ink. I've done nothing wrong. I'm always polite and well-behaved. It's not fair. I protest!"

It was time for dismissal and the beginning of summer vacation. The lure of warm weather and freedom should have drawn the students from the classroom like a magnet. Instead, they stood rooted at attention, mesmerized by Hilde's tantrum, fascinated by prospects of a showdown between their teacher and her number one pupil. When finally the teacher did manage to clear the classroom, only one student remained, the student with *"gut"* in deportment who refused to budge until her grade had been corrected.

This was impossible, of course, and the teacher stood her ground. So Mother was summoned to listen to the screaming, the weeping, the unbridled fury of her ill-tempered child. Where had she and Hirsch gone wrong? Perhaps they had been too permissive with Hilde, not taught her proper respect for authority. Even though she believed she already knew the answer, that she and Hirsch alone were to blame, Mother mustered courage to ask the teacher why her daughter had gotten *"gut"* instead of *"sehr gut"* for deportment.

"Frau Bruch," replied the teacher, forcing patience, "Hilde continually disrupts our classroom with explanations challenging my authority, and I can tell you that I certainly do not see her deportment as *'sehr gut.'* I will offer an example. Every day in history class we read war news from newspapers I bring to class. The students read about these various battles and locate army divisions by placing little flags on the map. This helps with geography as well as their sense of patriotism." She unrolled a large window shade-like map of Europe, pointing to a series of flags in France.

"Here you can see from Verdun how far the German armies have advanced. In this way we follow battle strategies and learn from our readings about the victories. General Ludendorf is predicting we will soon take Paris."

She turned toward Hilde, "But I don't think Hilde will agree with this."

"I don't disagree. I *never* disagreed," wailed Hilde, "I only asked why so many men are dying and why we have so many shortages. It just doesn't seem like we can be winning the war."

"There you see, Frau Bruch, what I am up against, how this undermines my teaching of the other students, not to mention what it says about newspapers and the German government."

Again she turned toward her pupil, this time speaking softly and not unkindly. "Hilde, you know how many hardships and deaths there are in war. That is why we at home must continue to make sacrifices and keep our spirits up."

But the speech was familiar and Hilde was unmoved.

"I did nothing bad. All I did was ask a few questions. In class I don't interrupt. I raise my hand first, and I always do my homework assignments on time."

"Hilde, *'gut'* is not a poor grade, but I cannot give you *'sehr gut.'* Surely you see that."

"It isn't fair. Only dumb kids and bad kids who cause trouble in class get *'gut.'*"

By now Mother was at wit's end and Father needed to be called. He pulled up with horse and buggy and, as usual, his very presence seemed to pacify, or perhaps the drama had been played out and the protagonists were tired. They parted with the teacher vaguely promising "to make amends." Though the grade was never changed, in a way Hilde's stand had accomplished its purpose, for her next *zeugnis* read *"sehr gut"* for deportment.

Father and Mother were not certain how to proceed. They did not condone willfulness, nor could they reproach Hilde for a temperament neither she nor they could change. Other family members accustomed to her differences had learned to accept the unusual behavior. Maybe they were too lenient, but they also valued and respected her uniqueness.

Though the family had resolved its own feelings, the problem itself was not easily solved. Mother's high expectation for education seemed naively misplaced as the situation at the lyceum worsened. Hilde's reputation for being difficult had gotten around, and teachers who admired her abilities were equally quick to censor alert questioning when it caused dissension or tripped them up. Far from intimidating the incorrigible pupil, the incident with the *zeugnis* had made her bolder than ever.

Soon April would be renewing her promise to Nature by sending tender green shoots pushing through barren ground, while school with its inevitable conflicts would also resume. Mother, staring from her kitchen window at the frozen remnants of last summer's bountiful garden, noted some plants on the window ledge that needed repotting. One in particular, a large straggly palm with leaves yellowed and withered in its futile search for space reminded her of Hilde. How simple if her daughter's growth could be so easily regulated.

Thus when Hilde described the *Studienanstalt* in Muenchen-Gladbach, Mother thought she saw a fertile patch. But it would require quick investigating since already it was February, with the new school term due to begin shortly.

The following day, mother and daughter took the train to Muenchen-Gladbach to talk with the Director. Yes, it was possible to enroll Hilde. Then she wrote to all the men in the army, for it was a family decision, and nothing like it had been done before. Yes, they agreed, the new school sounds like Hilde. So, while she could not real-

ize it at the time, on April 1 Hilde began commuting away from the
life she had known for thirteen years and toward the beginnings of
professional training.

The new school with its college preparatory atmosphere suited her,
at the same time the fledgling Weimar Republic was also making itself
felt, breathing liberalism into the curriculum. This freer exchange of
ideas, plus a serious and challenging academic curriculum, combined to
make Hilde's years at the *Studienanstalt* satisfying. For Mother, it was
welcome respite from the battle of academics, but for Hilde, it was an
academic feast, a potpourri of intellectual adventures such as she had
never imagined. Yet even in this rarefied climate, Hilde stood out.

In literature class, a scene from Schiller's *Joan of Arc* in which Joan
enters a room and discovers the Dauphin, knowing he is the destiny of
France, disturbed and angered her. "But how can she know that? How
does she discover him? Is he wearing a sign? She must have something
to go by. There is nothing special about a Dauphin!"

Later, after class the teacher laughed good-naturedly. "Please, Hilde,
if you keep asking questions like that I'm going to be accused of
Majestat Beleidigung." Still, nothing would inhibit the irreverent quest
for answers, where king and pauper were targeted equally. Fellow students recorded Hilde's abilities and quirks in the high school yearbook:

> She is first in Chemistry and Physics, talented in Mathematics, but
> her Latin translations are incomprehensible, causing the professor
> grief. Audacious Hilde writes about class representation rather than
> class order. Dr. Pilgram argues, hoping to trip her up. No match for
> her, so he gets angry and embarrassed.

Her years commuting to Muenchen-Gladbach, though academically
pleasing, were strenuous, since they coincided with the final months of
war and the difficult post-war period. There was also the matter of
making up a year of Latin, drudgery for Hilde because she hated languages. An English teacher in Duelken, kindly offering tutoring assistance so she could award a "B" in good conscience, received a thankless
retort from her feisty student: "Never mind, once I get out of this place
I'll never use English again." Similarly, she now complained her way
through Latin requirements, grateful she had at least kept pace with the
Studienanstalt by entering the Duelken lyceum a year early.

Auguste was not so lucky. When Hilde made plans to commute, her sister also wanted to attend the marvelous school that offered potential for University study. Unfortunately, the older girl needed to make up two years of Latin, which dropped her even further behind, making her only one year ahead of Hilde. The situation was virtually impossible, and Auguste in discouragement dropped out after only a year's commuting.

Few families placed such high value on women's education that they offered their daughters the option of advanced study. Combined with the hardships of commuting, it was therefore not surprising that only ten of twenty-eight in Hilde's class were train riders.

By April of 1917, the toll of war had reduced that number to eight, seven locals, with Hilde the lone commuter. A train ride under normal conditions taking twenty minutes sometimes never arrived at all, frequently leaving Hilde stranded in Muenchen-Gladbach. A friend offered a standing invitation for spending over nights. The harrowing schedule beginning at 6:00 A.M. and ending at 8:00 P.M. saw her living on warmed-over food with weekends reserved for resting and preparing for the strenuous week ahead. With so little time to socialize with family, the individualization that had always set her apart now became an isolation, and her own life was nearly as capricious as the train schedule.

During this postwar period, while Belgian troops occupied the Rheinland, small towns adjusted with relative ease to the occupying soldiers. For children, it is possible the soldiers' chocolate was partly responsible. There was something marvelous about these big squares, which looked like cooking chocolate and were reminiscent of far off good times before the war.

The occupation had obvious drawbacks as well. One evening after school, Hilde was delayed at the railway station because she had forgotten to bring her identity card. During evening hours, all train riders had to show I.D.s to officials. Mother was summoned by telephone, and she and Hilde required to go to Neuss to Martial Court. Officers and personnel of this Belgian court spoke only French, a fact not lost on Hilde. Always at her best under duress, she calculated her strategy while observing other offenders offering in their own defense long explanations in German. Invariably, the translator reduced each frenzied plea to two or three words, whereupon the magistrate politely asked the offender to have a seat and remain for further questioning. Mother, watching the procedure, frowned. No doubt they would be stuck here forever.

Then came Hilde's turn. With perfect composure and even more perfect French, she detailed how she was a school girl who had forgotten her I.D., contritely adding *"je regrete"* wherever possible. Explaining how hurried she had been leaving the house that morning, she concluded graciously, *"Pardonez-moi, pardonez-moi, pardonez-moi."*

The judge let Mother and Hilde go home, and they were the only ones. *"Ah, merci beaucoup, merci beaucoup, merci beaucoup!"* gushed Hilde, bowing to the magistrate. Mother, knowing only that she was free, kept saying to the Magistrate over and over, *"Danke schon, danke schon, danke schon!"*

The Politics of Change

Political winds swept Germany during the years 1910 to 1920, amounting to nothing less than upheaval. The Great War, begun as a purge from boredom, a romantic lark accompanied by church bells and flowers stuffed into soldiers' rifle barrels, ended in a bloodbath, leaving 1.8 million Germans dead, another four million wounded. His Imperial Highness Kaiser Wilhelm II, whose uniformed portrait decorated all public offices and school rooms and whose power by divine right was so undisputed he dared dismiss even Bismarck, now abdicated for asylum in Holland, where he remained whimsically detached, peacefully tending his gardens.

In Weimar, a constitution was adopted, perhaps the most advanced in political history, by people politically unsophisticated and untrained in democracy. Old institutions such as the military, the civil service, and the courts remained unchanged by the democratic reforms. Industry, managed by powerful cartels, continued in the hands of a wealthy few. The most serious defect, Article 48, allowed the President to scrap the entire Bill of Rights in emergencies, a loophole Hitler later used to suspend democracy without ever stepping outside the law.

The same *Volk* who had united heroes against a common craven enemy, now saw their dreams reduced to whimpering ignominy. Feelings of guilt lay heavy, depression hung like a stone. Some denied that Germany had lost the war at all, but had been "sold out." A popular myth sprang from the defeat, aided by unanimous resentment of the peace terms, that Germany had not lost on the battlefield, but had been "stabbed in the back" by evil forces at home. The villains were identified as the signers of the Treaty of Versailles and the founders of the Weimar Republic.

The treaty was stiff in terms of territorial loss, but even more painful to the average German was the notorious and insensitive paragraph later known as "the war guilt clause," where Germany and her allies were forced to acknowledge that they were originators and aggressors. Not one of the delegation wanted to sign, but against threat of further invasion and the need to bring peace to a starving German population, a few brave and realistic men acquiesced and accepted the shameful treaty. By doing so, they sealed their own doom and assumed a political liability they could never shake off, and a treaty that might have marked new beginnings for the German people, a chance to look forward to democratic reform and self-determination, instead stuck in their craws like a bitter pill, causing them to look backward to a happier heroic age.

It is hard to imagine the Germany that arose unsteadily and without direction out of the ashes of World War I. Trudging home in tatters like packs of mangy dogs came the despairing remnants of the Emperor's once proud army. Unemployed and disenchanted, hordes of these disbanded men drifted into *Freikorps* units, which sprang like weeds out of nowhere. These small, privately-funded armies shared a love for brawling and a hatred of liberalism.

Adolf Hitler was one of the malcontents the war let loose. Lying in a hospital bed, he could hardly believe his ears when word came of the surrender. Throughout the war, his enthusiasm had never wavered since he had never lost heart of victory, and though he lacked the leadership qualities to rise beyond rank of corporal, he had been twice decorated with the iron cross.

Loyalties were few, but he felt a sentimental attachment to *Freikorps,* although he never officially joined their ranks. They were an undisciplined, leaderless lot of lone wolves like himself, and their destructive psyche and crude nationalism struck a responsive chord in his heart. In spirit they were the direct opposite of the polished German officer class he had come to hate and distrust. Once he regained his health, he signed on for a job with a Munich army division, where it became his official duty to inform on subversive groups. On one of these errands he encountered the German Workers Party and was immediately attracted by its objective of reconciling socialism with nationalism. Like himself, it was an Austrian transplant, strongly anti-Jew, anti-Slav, and anti-Western Europe.

Hitler joined the party ranks in 1919, and rose swiftly to the top. When in 1920 the name was officially changed to National Socialist Workers Party, NAZI for short, Hitler was already the party's most important member, tirelessly organizing party rallies and establishing himself as primary speaker. True, his audience was ragtag, his speeches coarse brawling shouting matches, but for Hitler it was the beginning of a mission to lead Germany back to former greatness. He had learned from the army that an effectively organized society stems from rigid control, and like an army must take absolute command from one leader. He was ready to be that leader. He had also learned from the army tricks of propaganda, and his speeches were peppered with slogans every man could understand and identify with. He delivered these speeches to boisterous beer hall crowds who booed as often as they cheered. To squash hecklers, Hitler created a band of roughnecks known as *Sportsabteilung,* or Sports Division, which was just a disguise for the strong-arm squads known later as the SA or Stormtroopers. Eventually, out of this motley bunch of petty thugs came Hitler's personal body-guard, the all-powerful elite SS.

Thus emerged the bawling, rowdy embryo, which would in time became the massive and aggressive giant known as the Nazi Party. But few, had they recognized Hitler's name, would have taken him seriously. He and his pack of guttersnipes belonged with all the other crack-pot organizations that disrupted civilized society. They were unsavory stew pots of beer hall politics, shunned by law-abiding citizens and perceived as one more indication of the failure of government to keep order.

Though government was elected, the people's interest in their new democracy, its candidates, principles and operation was lukewarm. But putting food on the table was everyone's concern, and a hungry population resented having to hoard black market supplies for meager survival, or receiving hand-outs from Quakers, however well-meaning such organizations claimed to be. They resented flashing I.D. cards wherever they went, cursing trains forever breaking down. The feedings

and curfews inflicted by the occupying army served as constant reminders of defeat. They were the distasteful practical every day problems which would not go away. Not only were they humiliating and
depressing, but even worse to systematic, proud Germans looking to
democracy for guidance, they seemed to show that no one was in
charge.

Tradition was dying as changes everywhere created new definitions
of reality. Highly individualistic artists calling themselves
"Expressionists" searched for it, while turning out peculiar blobs of
paint, lines, and triangles they called "abstracts." Kandinsky, Nolde,
and Beckmann worked on canvas, while filmmakers discovered reality
in eerie surrealistic places and created pieces like *The Cabinet of Dr.
Caligari.* On the social scene, experiments in love were taking place,
trial marriage and "free love" the latest thing. Clothes expressed the
new freedom. Skirts were becoming shorter, waistlines dropping.
Women bobbed their hair.

It was late in the war when Hilde achieved the age of *Backfisch,* that
special day when a girl officially becomes a young woman. She was exactly fourteen years and seven weeks old, but because of shortages and
other concerns no one felt inclined to celebrate. Auguste's *Backfisch* had
occurred during the early war years when things were still plentiful, and
she had received her first long skirt especially designed for the special
day. It was somewhat like a Bar Mitzvah for girls, for there were other
family presents as well, more skirts and beautiful blouses with fancy
embroidery and draw work. Now, however, Hilde's day for celebration
passed unnoticed, and after the war styles were so changed that when
the tradition of *Backfisch* reemerged it looked as different as the new
women's fashions.

But more than postwar blues and changes in dress and hair styles
concerned the family in 1920. Father's health was failing. Chemical
changes caused by diabetes had affected his heart. He walked slowly,
and the smile which once twinkled in his eyes and hid mysteriously
under the huge mustache was no longer there. Everything that for 55
years was natural and effortless now seemed strained. Mother and the
children pretended not to notice how often Father called the boy to
hitch the horse and buggy for local business calls he used to make on
foot. They buried themselves in routine activities in order not to see his

pale face, the loss of weight and appetite. But it was there all the same, and they felt the tightness in their hearts.

It happened during the gray dawn hours of October. He had been "too tired" to take the stairs, and Rudolf and Mother shared turns through the night watching and comforting him as he slept on the sofa. Earlier, Dr. Birken had stopped by with medication, promising to return in the morning. But when morning came, the younger children awoke to whispers and sobbing. Huddling deeper into their blankets for comfort—they understood.

Never had they hurt so much. Everything ached, and they could not stop crying. Nevertheless, Mother, her own eyes red-rimmed and masked in shadows, shoved Artur, Ernst, and Erna out the door and off to school. Little ones would only be in the way. Though Rudolf, Auguste, and Hilde stayed behind to help with arrangements, the interruption was temporary. Life must continue as normally as possible.

The men of the Jewish community dressed Father's body in white cotton, the robes he wore at High Holy Day Services, for it was also the traditional burial garb. Then they placed it in a simple wood coffin. Throughout the night the men kept vigil by candlelight. They wore prayer shawls and chanted Hebrew prayers and blessings as they sat *Shiva.*

In the cold October morning, mourners gathered outside the house on Suechtelnerstrasse. They stood in small groups whispering subdued greetings and sympathies to Mother and the children, readying themselves to accompany the casket on its final ten minute journey to the cemetery. It was the same short walk the children had taken with carefree abandon to *Volkschule,* and it was along this route their neighbor had admired Hirsch Bruch and his beautiful family. Mother would not be consoled. She did not join the mourners on their somber walk, but closed her bedroom doors to all intruders and grieved alone.

CHAPTER II

1923 - 1933

Medical School

In later years when Hilde was asked why she so rarely spoke about her father, she would answer without hesitation that he died before anything happened. By this she would mean "Nazis" and "inflation." Indeed, it was the end of an era, for with Father's death came also the end of innocence and a nearly idyllic rural existence. Events were working to change their lives. Earlier that year the German Workers' Party officially became The National Socialist German Workers' Party and the abbreviated term "NAZI" entered the vocabulary, though such immediate ironies escaped the grieving family, stumbling through the myriad of routine tasks intended to make life seem normal and stable again. From relatives and friends paying condolence visits the message heard most often was, "How sad Hirsch died young with still so many children in the household, but how fortunate at least there is no financial worry." Certainly, Father had left his family well-off, Mother being the major benefactor but each child also inheriting a sizable savings account, testimony to a lifetime of frugality and parental love. But that was 1920, and by 1923, inflation had claimed the bulk of their security.

Also by 1923 Hilde was graduating from the *Studianstalt,* a young woman of promising ability with a future to consider during times when no one was thinking about anything but an eroding economy. At nineteen, she was an impressive figure, with well-defined features and a large, rangy frame. The round, steel-rimmed glasses she wore at all times contributed a studious, somewhat severe appearance, though overall the effect was not unattractive. While height and weight conveyed the impression of awkwardness, and mouth and chin were a bit too strong to satisfy feminine standards of the day, behind the intelligent eyes and vivid expression beat the heart of a woman who more than anything desired approval for her feminine self. Underneath the stern exterior hid a soul craving beauty and romance, and the girl who always wanted to be "Mother" yearned to play that role some day.

Also, like Mother, she was sensible and practical, and with savings depleted she knew it was inappropriate to daydream. Time had come to assess her future, which she did in the same analytical spirit that was her trademark in academics. Girls she judged to be of two types. There were the gracious, beautiful, desirable ones who would undoubtedly marry, and there were the untidy, clumsy, unfriendly ones who were destined to become maiden aunts. Hilde deemed herself among the latter. Usually it fell upon the oldest brother to prepare a room for the maiden sister, but Hilde knew it wouldn't happen because she would never agree to live like a second-class citizen in Rudolf's or anyone else's household. She had begun making her own decisions as a thirteen-year-old commuting to a different life, and she didn't intend changing now.

First, she considered dress designing, since it was a practical and creative career and she had always enjoyed working with patterns. Next, she thought about becoming a mathematician since she was good with numbers, but what could she really do with it? Ultimately, the situation was resolved during a family conference with Mother's brother, David the doctor, offering sensible advice. "Yes, Hilde," he said, "we all know how gifted you are in practical matters and that dressmaking offers the creativity and security you are after. But I really think it is with science and math your true strength lies, and here I believe medicine becomes the perfect marriage. After all, if you are a woman today studying math or science, especially a Jewish woman, the best you can expect is to land a teaching assignment somewhere out in the sticks."

David by implication referred to legislation dating from pre-Napoleonic times restricting generations of Jews from entering certain professions, and while most had long ago been amended "by the book," archaic attitudes had proven more difficult to dislodge. One liberal stronghold which seemed to have grown more progressive through the years was the medical profession, where admission to universities was offered strictly on merit. "Study medicine and you can do anything you want," continued Uncle David. "I'll even take you along on my rounds so you can get a taste of what it's all about."

So a practical Hilde entered medicine expecting to utilize her scientific aptitude to become a researcher, a biochemist or something similar. Every month, three uncles sent Hilde enough allowance to cover not only room, board, and tuition, but all the extras considered necessary to enrich a medical student's life.

While it seemed the wise and practical thing to do in view of her own skills and a faded economy, Hilde still wasn't convinced medicine was her calling, since first year medical students are required to study anatomy—with all that despicable memorization. She had an aversion to languages and sometimes had trouble remembering people's names, but medical terminology would be totally unfamiliar since in Germany a layman refers to body parts in the vernacular rather than the Greek. Thus, while every *hausfrau* will warn that *Lungenentzundung* is a dangerous disease, only her doctor can identify it as "pneumonia." Hilde was not sure she could ever learn to distinguish between a "larynx" and a "pharynx," and wasn't it a bad joke that in order to receive the Abitur to get admitted to medical school you needed Latin, while had she remained at the Reale Gymnasium in Duelken she would have studied Greek, which would have been so much more useful now. Just another of life's aggravating little ironies bearing no relation to logic. No doubt she would survive anatomy and similar courses, but she wasn't expecting to like it.

She began in September in Wurzburg, and over the next five years would study also in Freiburg, Munich, and Cologne, for such was the informality of German medical colleges that students were granted flexibility in sampling all disciplines before specializing. Eventually she would return to Freiburg to earn her degree.

As it turned out, not only would she tolerate the challenges of the medical curriculum but would welcome each and every day freshly enthusiastic. Partially, it was the experience of working side by side with men, conferring and sharing social and academic experiences with them. Previous schooling had been strictly segregated, the boys' school on the hill, the girls' school below, with only an occasional meeting between the two for conferences. Even though she often spoke on the train with boys whom she considered friends, and there were always brief, gruff exchanges with her brothers' acquaintances, the medical school experience was unique and strangely exhilarating.

She felt a new coed freedom and sense of belonging. A few students paired off, but mostly they gathered in groups to discuss classes or the latest gossip. Many carried Leica cameras to catch professors in action, later exchanging finished prints. Radios were the latest thing, and Hilde owned a crystal set complete with earphones, a great luxury which her uncles had considered necessary for her complete education and which now she shared with an envious circle of friends. Often at week's end, the students took off for the mountains where they hiked or skied to work off pressures, and while it was a strenuous existence, Mondays found Hilde exhausted but happy.

By November, the weighty decision to study medicine well behind her, it seemed her entire life had been no more than preparation for this encounter with microscopes and test tubes. To her great relief, medical jargon came easy, though she never took her study of anatomy for granted, and even purchased a skeleton which she conscientiously kept in Duelken so as not to lose valuable study time while visiting the family.

The rattly thing with spooky hollow eyes and bony smile was endlessly alluring to Hilde's younger brothers, who often rescued it from a lonely closet existence to place it in more friendly surroundings. Family members had gotten used to finding it grinning from parlor chairs or dangling precariously in a doorway, and even Mother was amused by the varied and fanciful poses. But these games commenced only after Hilde had returned to school, for attracted as they were by her anatomy prop, the boys were intimidated by their sister's reverent handling of the thing, knowing she would have their heads if she had even the slightest suspicion of what they were up to.

One crisp evening in early November, dead tired from a week of exams, Hilde dragged herself from the train station. Mother, Rudolf, and Auguste were waiting up and hurried to greet her, but she was in no mood and promptly excused herself. All the way home she had been picturing the warm comforts of her own bed in her own room, and thus lulled by the felicitous reverie she pulled back the puffy quilt to crawl under the soft down...with *what!*

So frozen was she, words wouldn't come. The faceless grin and bony frame had so unnerved her that even as she jumped back to avoid contact with the thing, her mind refused to register. Then gradually came short breathless gasps, as seeing Ernst and Artur leaping from the closet, her brain began to clear, triggering a stream of venom the likes of which neither she nor they had ever heard before. Like antelopes fleeing a predator, the boys sprang for safety, hurling themselves down a flight of stairs toward Mother, who intervened just in time to save them from the lion's paw. Though Mother later punished them severely, Hilde was not assuaged. A prank of this magnitude would neither be forgotten nor forgiven. However, once outside range of their sister's temper, Ernst and Artur waxed triumphant, relishing it as one of the best practical jokes they had ever played.

That same autumn, another scary incident with far broader implications than the little scene in Duelken took place, one which put Hilde's crystal set in great demand. Friends lined up to slip on earphones connecting them with news broadcasts nothing short of sensational. News reporters were calling it a *"Putsch,"* to overthrow the German Republic which was headed by Adolf Hitler and General Ludendorff.

As clearly as Hilde could tell, it had all started in the Munich Buergerbraukeller. Hitler had surrounded the place with SA troops shouting to beer drinkers inside that they were not to leave because a National Revolution had begun. Those interviewed stated that Hitler had fired a shot in the air, shouted commands and threatened force if they tried to leave, while at the same time, incredibly, former Air Commander Hermann Goering remained posted to remind them that they had no cause to grumble since they still had their beer! When General Ludendorff arrived, he promised that the army would cooperate with the revolution. Then he and Hitler and some of Hitler's "bigwig" Nazi friends led the Nazi troops, about three thousand of them, through narrow Munich streets, where finally they were stopped by a line of Munich police just before they reached the broad Odeonsplaz. It sounded to Hilde like an ambush, but broadcasters weren't sure who fired the first shot because both sides were busy denying it. No matter. A shot was fired which led to a volley of shots, and within a minute the Residenzstrasse was littered with bodies and blood. No one yet knew who had died or how many, but His Excellency Ludendorff was

unharmed and had remained on his feet dodging bullets in the best sol-
dierly tradition. The rebel leader, Adolf Hitler, had fallen to the pavement, where someone whisked him off by motor car, while certain
other Nazis, including Goering, had also gotten away. In rather anti-
climactic finish, the scoundrel, Hitler was rounded up a few days later
without incident, and although Goering escaped, it was expected that
all the culprits would soon stand trial for treason. As news wore thin,
the horror lost its fascination and students turned to the more pressing
problems of medical education.

Hilde also returned to work, feeling the incident had little to do
with her, but glad anyway the instigators had been caught and would
soon be brought to justice. That might have been the end of it had not
Uncle David arrived unexpectedly and said, "Come, Hilde, I'll take
you to Munich and you can see for yourself where it happened." It was
November 16, one week after the *Putsch*.

They stood in front of the Feldherrnhalle and stared into the gully-
like alley which opened into the spacious Odeonsplaz, they and a few
other curious spectators and a couple of Munich police keeping casual
lookout. The bloody sea of wounded and lifeless had been swept clean,
replaced by wooden barricades, but somehow the emptiness seemed
even more telling. Hilde shivered, imagining the pavement littered
with fallen bodies, sixteen Nazis and three police dead, though it
wasn't really a matter of numbers, was it? It was the whole idea of the
thing. "Did they really expect to pull it off?" That was the question she
asked Uncle David.

"We'll see. We'll see when the trial comes up. If we're lucky, they'll
all be put away for life. That's what the Constitution says is punish-
ment for treason." Then more to himself than to Hilde he murmured,
"There seems to be a lot of sympathy for Ludendorff. Someone like
this Adolf Hitler....I just don't trust it." Facing her squarely, putting
an arm on her shoulder, "Hilde, this man Hitler holds views about
Jews which are perfectly clear. He hates us all, blames us for everything
wrong in Germany. It's the Jews, the Republican government, and the
Marxists at fault, and for him it amounts to the same thing. He isn't
apologizing for last week's action, far from it. He's claiming full responsibility and calling himself a patriot. Hard to believe, but with
poor Germany in such a state, I think people are starting to listen."

In her own family they had always joked and called Uncle David the "Great Trotsky Revolutionist," but until now Hilde hadn't given it much thought. She regarded him as a man of great learning, very well read, someone who was endlessly fascinated by ideas and anxious to discuss his philosophies with anyone who would listen. But she had also seen in him the scientist, careful in research, unwilling to accept the unproven, and so practical in his approach to life that she assumed his politics in reality were much like her own, pragmatic and bonded to daily existence. She admired him greatly, and accepted him as the intellectual leader of the family. He had influenced her to enter medicine, and she respected his judgment. Obviously, he knew a lot about Adolf Hitler, which made perfect sense since Trotskyism was diametrically opposed to fascism, and she found it all strangely discomfiting.

"Well, in Wurzburg, at least among students, they think Adolf Hitler is crazy," said Hilde.

"That is good. That is good, Hildechen. What else are the students talking about? Do they talk about the Trotsky revolution? Will we see you this weekend? Your Tante Paula has been baking up a storm. I think she expects you, and I am still expecting to make a chess player out of you!"

Over the next five years while she was in medical school, she would spend many weekends in Dusseldorf with David and Paula, and though politics came under discussion only rarely, for again the climate had changed and inflation was under control, David continued his enthusiastic support of Trotskyism. When they weren't talking personal family matters, doctor and student were exchanging medical information, David being particularly interested in new techniques.

Hilde always felt comfortable in David's and Paula's home among the Expressionists Nolde and Kokoschka and other famous painters represented in the magnificent art collection. Browsing through David's vast library, she was free to read anything she liked except for this one very famous Renaissance writer which David always removed before she came. But she knew exactly which one it was, and it amused her that her Uncle, so liberal and independent in his thinking also had this small Puritan streak.

"Uncle David, I hope you've found a good hiding place this time for the Ariosto, because I intend to hunt until I find it."

"Never mind that, Hilde. Come sit by Aunt and me and tell us what the students are talking about. Do they talk about Haeckel and Darwin?"

"But Uncle David," Hilde laughed, "these things are settled. Nobody talks about evolution anymore."

Should she mention that she planned to specialize in endocrinology? No. His medical training had no place for such unscientific things, and he would probably call it medieval witchcraft. What would he say if he knew she was attending sessions in psychiatry and that some of the professors had shown a special interest in her? No doubt he would be contemptuous and call it soft-minded, ask how a grownup person could waste one's life on such unscientific things, and on this she would have to agree with him.

Altogether she had attended three psychiatry sessions: the first from curiosity, the second as a regular, the last out of personal interest. There was an oppressiveness about these classes because patients never changed. They were selected for presentation from a nearby state hospital, and Hilde remembered seeing one catatonic with semi-flexible movements successively in 1926, 1927, and 1928, whose condition showed neither improvement nor regression in those three years. So far as she knew, the patient was frozen still in this advanced state of petrification.

Alfred Hoche was one of Hilde's psychiatry professors at Freiburg. He had collaborated with the distinguished jurist, Karl Binding, to write "The Permission to Destroy Life Unworthy of Life," defending the killing of the mentally ill as compassionate and consistent with medical ethics. Ten years later the Nazis would use it to justify killing the mentally ill, but for now it merely reflected current psychiatric attitudes regarding the hopelessness of patient recovery. Hilde needed no persuasion. From her earliest contact with the "fierce *Verruckten*" occupying the county psychiatric hospital in Suechteln, she had gotten the feeling that this is the most dreadful misfortune which can befall people. So when the Assistant Medical Director came to her and said, "I have been watching you. You seem very interested. Will you come as a resident?" She had retorted, "It never occurred to me. No thanks. I don't want to spend the rest of my life with museum pieces."

Sometimes they sat at David's chess table, where Hilde tried to improve her chess play under David's patient tutelage. She knew he was anxious to find a challenging opponent, and she respected this game which only great minds could master, though she also considered it tedious and time-consuming, preferring to be studying, or gaining new insights in lively discussion, or at least working with her hands, sewing or knitting.

Paula's hands were always occupied, contributing to Hilde's sense of idleness. Her Aunt was a skilled artist, who molded pieces of such originality that she had opened a little shop where she could sell the creations. Presently occupied with silver working, she inquired nonchalantly, "Hilde, is there some nice young man in your life?"

"Nothing serious yet, Tante Paula, but I haven't given up." Though the question appeared out of nowhere, Hilde was always prepared with her pat reply since Paula asked it every time she saw her. It was one she was also hearing more and more from her own family in Duelken, and while it always brought a certain discomfort, she had learned to live with it.

"What you want is some nice handsome doctor to come along and sweep you off your feet!" Paula's standard finish was like a hackneyed refrain with a predictable rhetorical conclusion, but it meant Hilde could again relax.

When not in Dusseldorf combining medical shop talk with home cooked meals, she was high in the mountains outside Munich and Freiburg skiing and socializing with other students. Hilde was not particularly surprised to find she was no better coordinated on skis than on skates, but it didn't matter. Like other non-serious skiers she clowned in the snow snapping pictures, posing with skis crossed in the air, desperately clinging to a branch or rock, rosy-cheeked and smiling. The beauty of the mountain, the camaraderie on the slopes filled her soul with such joy, that later, inside, swapping tales of courage or exaggerated disasters over a beer or hot beverage, she belonged to this troop of skiers as much as if she had been the most talented of athletes.

Though these were the happiest of times for Hilde, following so much strenuous exercise she invariably returned from her excursions exhausted. Mondays came too soon that final year at Freiburg. Nevertheless, Hilde, always the eager beaver anxious to be noticed, had chosen a seat directly in front for her psychiatry lecture from 10:00 to 11:00. During one of these sessions, when her eyelids grew heavy and her head fell forward, she was aroused by the laughter of students and the voice of her sarcastic professor, "*Wen die Dame schlafen will dan soll sie hinten sitzen!*" If the girl here wants to sleep, let her go to the back!

A busy schedule left little time to keep in touch with family, but during February of 1928, Hilde was able to dash a "thank you" to Mother:

> I don't think your "goodies" will have to go in the knapsack, since this time the outings are not rained out, but so full of sunshine that the snow has melted except high on the Feldburg. And I had so looked forward to these four days away.
>
> In seven weeks we have our first set of exams behind us. I wish it would be over with. What I have to put in my poor head till then...brrrr. All these women's illnesses with the mess that comes after doesn't interest me.

Her letters, like her thinking, were spare, with no time to waste on superficialities. Often she condensed sentences by punctuating with dashes, the abbreviated messages reading something like the scribbled shorthand on a doctor's prescription, cryptic dispatches which only the *chemiker* can decipher. Those lucky enough to receive her rare communications were frustrated by the assignment of filling in details. Erna once complained, "You never write about personal things, what type of people you meet and what you are doing. Your handwriting is the only clue it is you who wrote the letter."

Sometimes omissions were unconscious, as though her own mind were penning in the blanks, but more often the lack of personal detail was deliberate, preferable, she believed, to outright deception. Mystery was her singular answer to Mother's incurable romanticism, the infernal matchmaking tendencies which had spread like a virus to Aunt Paula and other family members.

Vaguely she would mention a "doctor friend," perhaps a casual dinner out with an unidentified colleague, sprinkling hints of romance in the mountains so Mother might picture sweethearts tumbling in the snow. Mother must have wondered about the nameless suitors wandering mysteriously between the dashes of her daughter's letters, but so anxious was she to see her children "settled," she snatched at every phrase, hungrily responding with a thousand new questions. For Hilde it had become a complicated game of tales, her personal song of *Scheherazade*.

Orzech

By 1929 the whimsical political climate had again changed. On October 24th, Wall Street crashed sending shock waves across the world, nowhere more destructive than in Germany. Far worse than the inflation of 1923, this new economic disaster was international in scope and poignantly felt by a country dependent upon foreign loans and world trade. With millions out of work, thousands of small businesses folding and mortgages defaulting daily, prejudice was likewise burgeoning, as former owners blamed Jewish department store owners and Jewish bankers for their misery.

Not everyone was unhappy. Such times were heaven-sent for Hitler, who understood economics no better than anyone else but who was quick to salvage opportunity from the chaos. Following the *Putsch,* he had been imprisoned in the old Landesberg fortress high over the River Lech, where he occupied a room with splendid view and was treated as an honored guest. He used his time for relaxation and reappraisal and for writing *Mein Kampf,* which he dictated to his faithful secretary, Rudolf Hess. By the time he was released some nine months later, Germany seemed on the verge of an "unfortunate" economic recovery. Not wanting to trigger a fiasco similar to Munich, he marked time waiting for leaner days when he might take advantage of weaknesses in the Constitution to operate within it. The years following 1929 more than met his approval as continual suffering resulted in election after election, while each new ballot brought a further mandate for Nazism.

Hilde passed her final oral exam with the mark "excellent," entering her *Praktische Jahr* in the Hospital for Women of the Medical Academy in Dusseldorf, where she spent three months in obstetrics and three in gynecology. She might have stayed there longer were prejudice not so blatant.

Instead, she opted to complete her year of internship in the Physiological Department of the University of Kiel, where prevailing attitudes appeared more liberal. It was here she received valuable training in the practice and theory of physical chemistry, earning the respect of coworkers and administration alike. Even with the huge enrollment of German medical colleges, students with similar interests found each other, and so it was not long before she found herself surrounded by a congenial group of friends identifying themselves as "scientifically-minded."

There was also a certain "high-mindedness" about this team of doctors and would-be doctors who viewed varied ancestral heritages as propitious to scientific pursuit and who prided themselves on "impartiality." Let the rest of the world fall prey to ugly prejudice; their own friendships were bonded by more durable adhesives, the mortar of scientific process. In addition to a proclaimed admiration for science, few could deny that romance, that most unscientific of emotions, was not also in the air. Most were of an age when courting becomes serious, and unmarrieds were not unaware of the possibility of finding true love based on mutual interest and admiration.

Hilde, certainly, was alert to that potential. She had screened the field, noting with satisfaction a number of possibilities, but one young man she knew she could definitely discount. He was a scientist at the Physiolog Institut, an intern like herself, who had stepped forward the first day at the lab when introductions were being made, grinning and bowing, "So very pleased to make your acquaintance, Fraulein Doctor!" How sure he seemed of himself. Much too charming, she thought, immediately dismissing Karl Orzech as smug and superficial, someone who had probably never entertained a serious thought in his head.

As days passed, she seemed unable to shake his presence, often discovering herself sneaking glances across the long dark experiment tables through the impersonal maze of gas lines and beakers to observe him undetected. He was good looking, handsome, perhaps. Tall and slim in his long white lab coat, his hairline well-defined but not yet receded, she noted that the eyes peering through dark framed glasses to study and measure the contents of his test tubes were serious, the long skillful fingers recording findings all business. It would seem she was mistaken in her original assessment of him. Even while others took breaks, he remained glued to his experiments, and when coworkers consulted him for whatever reason, she observed how they returned to their assignments renewed with admiration for him.

Gradually she got to know her fellow post-graduates, and an assorted lot they turned out to be. Rosenblum and Weichert were Jewish, but married. Then there were Wittig, Kiese, Schwester, Lottermoler, Stehl, and Valadez. Tonio Valadez from Madrid was dark and handsome. He and petite blond Gertrud Stehl were already a couple. Richard Kiese and Margarethe Schwester were more and more often in each other's company. Orzech was friendly with everyone, but especially with Valadez and Stehl, and Hilde found herself slightly relieved that pretty Gertrud Stehl was already spoken for. Then she rebuked herself for entertaining such romantic bosh. Karl Orzech wasn't Jewish, so of course he could never be interested in her, nor she in him.

Still, she remained painfully aware of him, the homey, comfortable fragrance of his pipe smoke drifting across the lab serving as constant reminder of the serious young man who seemed satisfied to while away his hours gazing into test tubes. The obsession was infuriating. A grown woman ought to know better, ought to march straight across the lab right now, confront him about work, talk about his experiment, her experiment, something—anything—to break the enchantment. But when she watched his deft handling of laboratory vessels, his calm gentle demeanor as he evaluated his findings, she knew she couldn't do it. She was clumsy and awkward, which he was sure to notice. What if he were to judge her silly and unknowledgeable?

There was a certain comfort knowing an entire laboratory divided them, buffering her awkwardness, and she was content believing any closer relationship was pure fantasy. Unfortunately, he was an uninformed member of the real and unpredictable world. One day on his way to lunch he passed dangerously close to her station, unwittingly breaking her code and causing an immediate reaction. Her flustered sleeve had brushed a beaker, sending it crashing to the floor.

"Uh, oh, Hilde. Here, let me help you."

He knew her name! A fact so surprising and flattering she hardly dared raise her eyes when he returned with the sweeper.

"I'm so sorry," she managed, "You were on your way to lunch and I'm holding you up."

Unperturbed, methodically examining corners and crevices for splinters literally everywhere, he engaged in polite conversation. "What do you work on here? Lucky it was only glass and not your experiment that was ruined."

"Yes, I call that fortunate indeed. I am dealing with the behavior of electrolytes in semipermeable membranes. Here, let me show you the data I have collected." She was in her element, and he was smiling.

"But this is amazing! You couldn't have known, of course, but I have a special interest with electrolytes and did extensive experimental work with them before coming here. We could have been comparing notes all this time, but it's not too late. How about taking your lunch break now?"

So somehow clumsiness had been the major ingredient after all, despite her care. Once out of the fragility of the laboratory, detailing work with someone who understood and appreciated her findings, however, she felt revitalized and on solid ground. They conversed not as lovers, but with a lover's interest of science and the wonders of medicine and clinical discovery. He was surprised at what she had accomplished in such a short time, how succinctly she had learned to formulate questions, how confident she had become in evaluating data and testing their validity. She saw admiration in his eyes and knew she was impressing him with her knowledge and dedication. "We must plan our next project together," he said.

Theirs was the latest "pairing" in the lab, others expecting to see them together comparing data, though socially they seemed more comfortable discussing research and exchanging ideas with other staff members present. Nevertheless, when the group took "breaks" in the large University dining hall or the local beer hall after hours, invariably two seats were left side by side so Bruch and Orzech might sit together, and by this small act, Hilde knew they were recognized as a "couple."

Once, when she and Karl were alone, Hilde found courage to introduce University politics into their discussion. She realized the topic was "unsafe" to discuss with an outsider, but suddenly it seemed terribly important to know where he stood on anti-Semitism, which continued to be a controlling force in her life. Even though prejudice seemed not a part of this lab where she, Weichert, and Rosenblum belonged to a research team and were socially and intellectually accepted, it was obviously on the increase elsewhere, fanned by the growing popularity of the Nazi party. In Dusseldorf, where she had encountered unchecked expressions of racial hatred, she left after only six months. In Munich, the same. While she had loved the advantages of that University and the stimulus of the city, she had withdrawn after a single term.

Now, face-to-face with this young scientist whom she respected and admired more than anyone she had ever known and who professed to feel the same for her, she assembled her many grievances, confided all her fears. She trusted him to understand her most secret apprehensions, the frustrations and the anger of being mistreated and misunderstood, the uncertainty of being recognized and accredited for years of dedicated work. Her heart spilled over, while he gently pressed her hands between his own.

When at last he broke his silence, it was with the same remarkable calm that marked everything he did. Yes, he agreed, feelings in German universities did seem to be running high right now, but that was no more than "temporary lunacy." Naziism, with its tide of violence and racial prejudice, would not last since it had no place among intelligent people, and it was only a matter of time before all of Germany would recognize this by voting the rascals out.

Politically naive though she was, ripe to believe providential predictions from someone she admired, Hilde knew better. She had eyes to see, ears to hear, and what she was seeing and hearing was plenty of unchecked hatred which someone had to be supporting. Karl might be right believing that prejudice and Naziism would never find fertile ground among the "truly" educated, however small that minority had become, but by now she had encountered enough discrimination to know that there was no safe refuge for Jews even in the universities. Still, none of this seemed important when measured against Karl's understanding. He had comprehended her anxieties and in gentlest manner rebuffed her doubts. Her personal fear that he might also be harboring some secret prejudice had dissolved in a flood of glorious and grateful relief. Now, at least within the confines of the small circle of friends who counted most, she felt safe and complete. When Karl mischievously commented what a "venerable team" they made, she sensed the beginning of a new relationship, a very personal one which went beyond anything carried out in the laboratory.

Nearly at this same time, Mother decided to take more active steps in matchmaking. Always available for counsel, anxious to help love along wherever possible, one day she had taken inventory of her children's lives and felt utterly depressed by what she saw: Rudolf, 30; Auguste, 29; Hilde, 26; with nary a mate in sight. What's more, her children still refused to take her seriously, and often when the family gathered for special occasions around the large dining table they would tease her by singing about the pitfalls of the wedding knot, a woeful but humorous little ditty that ended, "and that's why I never will marry."

Auguste, at least, was cooperative, perhaps noticing as years advanced, the number of suitors declined in direct proportion. Still, the carefully arranged meetings with suitable prospects, for one reason or another had never quite "taken." Rudolf seemed plain hard to please, and Mother suspected that willful Hilde would be the greatest challenge of all. By now she was under no illusions about Hilde's vague romances. In fact, she was fully convinced that all her children, by playfully dodging her efforts, were losing valuable time and missing out on the best marital prospects. Probably they would wind up fulfilling the prophecy in that silly little song after all.

From Aunt Luise, Mother learned of a distant relative supposedly suitable for Hilde. Luise, who liked to exaggerate, burbled about the gentleman in glowing terms. "Good looking, and oh my, Adele, such a sense of humor he has! Can't you see the two of them matching wits?" She explained how Jack, like other young men previously serving time in the army, had needed to delay his medical career, that though he was four or five years older than Hilde, he was slightly behind her in training. "The perfect age for marriage, Adele, and he's as smart as Hilde, too."

That Mother doubted, but because the pairing did seem appropriate, the mechanics of bringing the "perfect couple" together were set into motion. Jack's mother, Berte Schloss, was contacted and overjoyed to cooperate. Next the marital prospects themselves were approached. Oh well, why not, thought Hilde, not often the recipient of Mother's marital designs. It certainly can't hurt.

They assembled in the Wurzburg parlor of Heinrich and Berte Schloss, two mothers and two not-so-young medics. Hilde sat between the women while Mother in a flurry of chatter admired everything from lace curtains to silver tea set. Berte seemed charming and poised. After weeks of preparation, she could afford to look modest amid the monumental assortment of confectionery and baked goods which Jack graciously offered their guests. He was obviously having fun, and Hilde thought she detected a puckish expression, some hint of irony not completely disguised by his impeccable performance as host.

"Tea or coffee, Tante Adele," he asked, "and next you must try Mother's chocolate cake because it is the best in the world."

Berte beamed pridefully. "My Jack likes to exaggerate, but we just have to accept it from him because he never lets me argue." Mother and Hilde chuckled amiably.

Inside the parlor, a shaft of late afternoon sunlight sheathed the couch, bathing the women in a warm glow, the domestic congeniality of small talk shielding them from the colder, less friendly world outside. As tea time came to a leisurely end, Jack asked Hilde to join him for a walk. She expected he would want to know more about her medical career, perhaps her doings in Kiel. Instead he teased her, "And now, my dear Cousin or Aunt or whoever you say you are, maybe you can explain just how we are related, since my mother is hopelessly muddled, and of course we both know how essential it is to get our relationship settled."

She laughed, releasing any lingering tension and because she appreciated the difficulties anyone would have penetrating the intricate web of aunts, uncles, and cousins in her extensive family tree. But Jack, as an "only child," would probably have trouble remembering even the names of her brothers and sisters. She was not quite sure herself if she correctly understood the relationship between them, but dutifully and logically she began with "Adele," proceeding slowly through the Rath chronology. Before she was half finished, however, Jack had thrown his arms up in mock despair.

"Stop," he cried. "Adele, Kempen, Gompertz, Luise, Rath. Only a wild pig can make sense of it. You will have to explain it again some day so I can get it wrong again. Promise me now that you will call me 'Uncle Jack,' and I promise to call you 'Aunt Hilde,' and then we'll always know who we are, at least."

Aunt Luise had not exaggerated her nephew's sense of humor. Hilde found it refreshing and enchanting. How clever of him to put her so at ease in this contrived situation. Wishing to continue the friendship, she suggested he visit her in Kiel, where she could introduce him to close friends whom she believed might help in forwarding his medical career. He answered that he could probably use all the help she or anyone else was offering in view of the nasty political situation.

They were laughing, excited with plans when they returned to the parlor, Berte and Adele sensing "success." Mother fairly radiated on the train ride back to Duelken, dying to know what had happened yet afraid to ask, afraid of Hilde's independent nature. Nor did she wish to

be accused of being "nosey." Instead she heaved a deep sigh, commiserating with mothers everywhere and the unjust restrictions imposed
upon them.

Hilde understood and relented. "Jack is making a trip to Kiel next
week to learn more about the Institute," she declared simply.

Schloss

His witty, light-hearted attitudes made him immediately popular with
Hilde's circle of friends, and while he was more than a full year behind
her, Jack's training had progressed enough that he felt comfortable
with medical "shop talk." Usually he remained quiet during serious scientific debate, but when discussion turned to "gossip," he snapped to
attention. Like Hilde and the others, he had attended a number of universities in as many locations. As a student of medicine he was above
average, though unremarkable, but as a student of human nature he
was acutely perceptive.

Plucking irony out of every situation, he sometimes worried that he
had fallen victim to an overactive sense of humor, as if a goiter or other
gland had gotten out of control. But seriousness evoked such personal
discomfort he courted only the ridiculous and could not help himself.
When he observed professors, whether department heads or classroom
hacks, he focused less on message than on dispatch, exaggerating their
most trivial habits: Professor Thannhauser marching back and forth
lecturing and wearing down the floor. "You must have noticed the
gully in that room yourself, Tante Hilde, and what about the way
Professor Rosenbaum wrinkles his nose and takes his glasses off when
he's having trouble solving a problem…that's always the tip-off."

Wit and mimicry appealed to Karl Orzech, whose normally sober
approach to life seemed mellowed by Schlosse's presence. Since Jack
was studying at the University of Leipzig, sometimes Hilde and Karl
would travel together to see him, or the reverse, he would visit Kiel.
Between times they corresponded, but friendship evolved between
Schloss and Karl independent of Hilde.

In the laboratory, Bruch and Orzech continued working together or
with others, and through it all developed strong feelings for one another. Their mutual liking of Schloss also contributed to ease the
strictly professional boundaries of their relationship. And when toward

the end of 1930 Karl was granted the promising position of assistant professor at the University of Berlin, Hilde was happy for him. She understood how anxious and ambitious he was for this assignment, though of course she was not in the least surprised since he was surely one of the most brilliant people she had ever met in academics.

That night when he expressed again how much he admired her, how he had come to count on her advice, she understood that this position in Berlin was a necessary training step toward his dream of heading a research clinic where the two of them would work together head to head, hand in hand, accomplishing important things. He kissed her tenderly, "I will miss you, Hildechen. Nowhere is there anyone like you, but of course you already know that. Naturally we will keep writing and seeing each other often so we won't say 'good-bye,' but here, so you won't forget me even for a moment, I am giving you my picture." It was the familiar, gentle, solemn pose she had grown to love, which flipped over read, "To Hildechen, for you to remember always my devoted admiration. Karl."

With Karl in Berlin, her own research winding down, Hilde was herself seeking changes. Through the extensive and thorough training program of the Institute at Kiel, she had become a competent scientist fully trained in the practice and theory of physical chemistry applied to biological problems. She had also collaborated with professors to publish several papers relating to experiments concerning the general physiology of the nervous system and the distribution of dyes on red blood corpuscles.

However, more and more she was becoming attracted to the human element in science. Earlier, while developing her thesis for the title of Doctor, she had been involved with children. The exercise was unique since it was 90 percent experimental, while most theses are based 90 percent on library work.

She decided to stay on in Kiel, attending the Children's Clinic for pediatric training. Her lab work concerned mineral metabolism in infants and she collaborated with professors to write a paper on brain fluid in children with acidosis, but it was the children themselves who more often claimed her interest. This appeal for working with children occurred nearly simultaneously with increased anti-Semitism at the Clinic, and once again she found herself changing direction.

For a Jewish doctor it wasn't easy. Now not only did she need a hospital for post-graduate training outstanding in the field of pediatrics, but progressive as well. Believing she had discovered such a place in Leipzig, she accepted the position of Assistant at Children's Hospital for the years 1930-1932, the last years before Hitler came into power. Because her latest move represented a flight to safety rather than a planned career change, she was forced to leave most of her experiments at the Children's Clinic in Kiel incomplete.

Letters from Karl were enthusiastic. Berlin, an exciting city, obviously suited him. Facilities at the University were modern, colleagues bright, compatible, and up-to-date in their thinking. Letters arrived punctually on an average of two per month by Hilde's calculations, perhaps not as often as she would have liked, but satisfactory considering how busy he claimed to be. Carefully, she meted return mails to match.

His letters followed a prescribed form. The first paragraph begged forgiveness for not writing sooner, listing as explanation the many activities that had kept him thus preoccupied. The next paragraph synopsized activities of the university and doings in the city. (Here it was customary for him to discuss an opera or concert he had attended.) Another paragraph directed itself entirely to her, commentaries or answers to questions she had asked in her last letter, followed by the concluding paragraph, polite commentaries and questions of his own to be answered in her next letter. "What was she doing? Did she still enjoy working with children? How difficult it must be working with little ones so sick they have little chance for recovery. How lucky to have Hildechen looking after them!" Finally he ended with a personal expression of fondness and the hope that he would see her soon.

The letters were not altogether satisfying. She would have liked something more personal to hang onto, something maybe a little less formal, but they would do. She understood the scientist in him, that part of the human soul reluctant to commit intimacies to paper. (She subscribed to the same school after all.)

Karl's letters to Jack were more relaxed. Perhaps "Onkel's" humor set him at ease. She saw Jack often now that they were both in Leipzig where Jack was beginning his year of internship. Sometimes they discussed Karl, but mostly they talked about the growing tide of Naziism and resentment of Jews, Jack wondering what kind of future a Jewish intern would have in "the new Germany." Already he had prepared for the worst, and Hilde noticed in him a nervousness and pessimism she had not seen before. She understood. Jack's position in medicine was less established than her own, and while supposedly the Nazis weren't a majority, they were easily the most visible party, with their uniformed SA, swastika arm bands, and rowdy, flag-waving rallies. Their dramatic show of strength in the 1930 elections had brought increasingly frenzied shows of nationalism and undisguised opposition to Jews. While nobody openly admitted to buying *der Stuermer,* the perverted and viciously anti-Semitic tabloid continued to gain in sales.

Still, Hilde clung to the hope reason would prevail, feeling relatively secure at Children's Hospital where, with other Jewish staff members, she continued performing duties without incident. Letters from Orzech to Bruch and Schloss also continued at an acceptable rate.

During the spring of 1931 all three attended a medical conference in Dusseldorf. Since they were practically in her neighborhood, Hilde phoned Mother to prepare for visitors. With Mother, of course, food and hospitality were never in short supply, and as the trio chattered and joked in her cordial parlor, it was easy to believe "old times" had returned. Each fairly burst with conversation, tales from the workplace accumulated over the year, fond remembrances of the past, breathless excitement over new activities, delivered in the comfortable and familiar company of close friends. Here was a warmth and glow which Hilde had not experienced since Kiel. The others must have felt it too, since Karl later sent a postcard to Mother thanking her on behalf of Jack and himself "for a delightful afternoon," a message which Mother delightedly relayed to her daughter. To Hilde, it was confirmation that things had not changed, that among close friends they never would change no matter what happened in Germany. But that was 1931, and the very next summer something happened to change her mind.

For Europeans, July and August are favorite vacation months, which is why 50 percent of the hospital staff are assigned to take their leave at that time. As it happened, during the springtime months, Hilde developed a peculiar sore throat which behaved suspiciously like scarlet fever, and to prevent possible contagion and allow a full recovery, her usual six week vacation time was changed to May. Consequently, when summer rolled around, she was the sole Jewish member left on the skeleton staff. Elections were held the final Sunday of July, a day otherwise undistinguished until Hilde strolled into the dining room to join colleagues for the usual medical banter, and suddenly all conversation ceased. The eerily stony silence was as telling as it was frightening, since she knew immediately they had been discussing politics and that every last one had voted Nazi. If so-called liberal-minded "good friends" behaved this way, what room was there for her on staff of this or any other hospital? Immediately she resigned, figuring that once she left the employ of hospitals which were mostly government controlled, she could no longer be subjected to arbitrary dismissal based on racial discrimination.

Alternatives were evaporating, the only option now to go into practice herself. While the decision was purely political, she couldn't help feeling a little excited at the prospect of being a children's specialist, bound no longer by bureaucratic directives, dependent only upon her own sound knowledge of medicine.

After examining various sites, she chose for her office a rented apartment near Dusseldorf, a two-room suite on the busy Marktplatz of Ratingen. To the designated "waiting room" she added the homey touches of pictures, colorful drapes and rugs, as well as wee tables and chairs where her young clientele could sit and play. Her office was similarly warm, furnished with a roll-top desk, couch and several chairs in addition to the necessary examining table. To one side, a cabinet covered with sterile white cloth held small instruments and dressings along with an electric sterilizer. Another table held the ultraviolet lamps, special lamps for examination, and a baby scale. Equipment representing her many years of interest in laboratory science also found space. High on shelves where little hands could not find them were extensive chemicals and special burners for heating, a centrifuge, and her beloved microscope.

She was fortunate that her family as usual was behind her. Rudolf had lent her the substantial sum of 5,000 D.M. to pay for office equipment, but his money combined with an equal amount from her own depleted savings were barely enough to meet expenses. Still, it had all been worth it when on October 15th, less than four months after the election and the scene in the hospital dining room, she hung out her shingle to begin practice.

Was it not a gamble? A young, female, Jewish pediatrician, trained primarily for laboratory work, no references, no clientele, equipped only with the desire and determination to earn a living in the worst of economic and political times for her own race? Perhaps. But it was not in evidence when she opened her shutters. After seeing only four new patients the final weeks of October, she saw their numbers increase rapidly until in January she had logged thirty-one new patients plus "repeats" and long-term treatments. She was gratified, declaring the new private practice a success. But if so, it was the briefest of successes. Adolf Hitler's popular showing at the voting polls had resulted in the offering of the Chancellorship to him, and following his swearing in on January 30, 1933, Hilde observed a gradual but steady decline of new patients.

She had written both Karl and Jack of her decision to go into private practice, but the letters differed considerably in content. To Karl she spared details, stating only that she felt the move "a necessary change at this juncture of my medical career," adding how she expected to enjoy the independence of "going it alone." He responded that indeed it sounded like a fine idea, that he felt certain it was a positive step for her.

With Jack, of course, she shared the Culture of Rejection, Disappointment, and Discouragement. Written explanation seemed extraneous, yet for the sake of morale they traded disillusionments, receiving encouragement for minor triumphs, sympathy for further setbacks. Jack was still struggling to complete his internship in Leipzig where the climate for Jewish personnel had deteriorated rapidly. The harmless humor which so amused Hilde and her friends in Kiel had turned bitterly invective. In letters satirizing Nazi propaganda, snide sarcasms told a tale of resentment and frustration. He empathized with Hilde's situation, of course, fully aware of events at Children's Hospital which had compelled her to open private practice.

She suspected Jack knew of her feelings for Karl, though they had never discussed them. How could she when she was fearful even to reveal them to herself? Hitler had come to power, her medical practice was dwindling, both adequate reasons for alarm, yet now an even greater fear enveloped her, one that somewhere deep inside she had anticipated and dreaded all along. Hadn't she always known it was unnatural to expect loyalty from an Aryan? She flipped Karl's brief New Year Greetings over to read again, yet there was nothing here to indicate these polite wishes might be his last.

Should she consult Jack and ask if his letters, too, had stopped? She rejected the idea immediately. No need to air feelings yet. Perhaps Karl was simply busy. It was only March, after all, and there was no law saying he had to write twice a month. If a letter should arrive tomorrow, she would have revealed her feelings for nothing, and then how silly she would look!

She threw herself into her work, or tried to, wondering if things could get any worse for the Jewish citizens of Germany. It was impossible to forget even for a minute who controlled the country. Companies of brown-shirted storm troopers of the SA and uppity black-coated guards of the SS were everywhere, constantly parading the streets, jackboots echoing. Anti-Jewish propaganda, now officially sanctioned and supported by every resource of government, blared ugly messages across air waves or plastered obscene headlines in newspapers and magazines.

Finally it all crescendoed in a boycott. Hilde saw nothing legal about it, only expert organization. On the morning of April 1, when she arrived to open her shutters to begin the day's activities, two uniformed, well-armed storm troopers were stomping back and forth in front of her office. They asked if she "had business" on the premises.

"Of course. I am the doctor."

"You are a Jew," they sneered, "and we have orders to warn people against entering establishments like yours."

Still, they grudgingly allowed her entrance, at the same time positioning themselves as sentries on either side of the door, fearing perhaps that her right to enter might be regarded as a weakness, an example for others to come piling through. They needn't have worried. Not many people were out this early, and the scattered few walking dogs or taking morning strolls stared curiously with no intention of breaking rules.

Inside, Hilde bolted the door and leaned against it, bracing herself against trembling nerves, whether from fear or rage she couldn't tell. Then, mechanically, she phoned the day's appointments telling them not to come. She didn't say "why," and when some wanted to know when they could reschedule their appointment, she didn't know this either and simply told them that if it were urgent they would do better to consult another doctor. Then, without another word, she locked her office door and left.

Outside on the Marktplaz as further evidence of boycotting, Jewish shops and offices were being picketed and one large department store "watched" by a platoon of storm troopers. Placards with a yellow spot on a black background were affixed to shop doors identifying Jewish enterprises "lest anyone should mistakenly overlook the bullies standing guard," thought Hilde dryly. A passing truck was covered with large handwritten posters, "Boycott all Jewish shops and department stores! Don't consult Jewish lawyers! Avoid Jewish physicians!" Inside the cab were two SA, one with a bull horn shouting, "All good citizens of the New Germany, please observe the Boycott! Jews are our misfortune!"

On the train back to Duelken she witnessed similar scenes in other towns, new outrages. Still she registered little emotion, and no one on the train spoke or volunteered a hint that this day was unlike any other. Once home alone with Mother, however, Hilde howled her pain and anger, until she saw in that dear woman's face such despair and grief that she found herself trying to soften the impact of this latest catastrophe which she knew with absolute certainty would prove fatal to her fledgling practice. "Never mind, Mother. It's over now. Perhaps tomorrow will be better."

But tomorrow was not better. Although the boycott was officially called off, her office, located on the main street of a small town, remained under constant observation, and a Nazi big shot living right next door seemed always ready to oblige with "unofficial" calls. His proximity and visibility were more than enough to intimidate patients, but then came a cruel editorial in the local newspaper:

> To the Wohlfahrtsamt of Ratingen: There is a children's doctor in Ratingen who is Jewish. The Bureau does not approve her for reimbursement but continues to send patients to her office who then are considered private. Because of National Socialism they become fewer each day. Now we request this Bureau take away her right to treat patients and hope such short notice is sufficient.
>
> This is what we have to say to that Jewish doctor: For the few Jews living in Ratingen there is no need for a Jewish pediatrician, and a Jewish doctor should not treat German children. Ratingen already has enough competent doctors to treat its people and the percentage of Jewish residents is too small to warrant her services. We hope in

the near future our German thinking townspeople will oblige us by
behaving in the true spirit of National Socialism.

Whatever the boycott left unfinished, this scathing message completed. With only five new patients appearing at her office the entire
month of April, this Jewish pediatrician of six months' standing closed
her office doors for good, moving herself and newly acquired office
equipment back to Duelken, where Mother and town doctors assured
her she was safe, and where Mother urged her to set up practice in their
home.

"Plenty of room for an office right here, and what could possibly
happen to you in your own hometown? These are neighbors and
friends who have known you for years, people who liked and admired
your Father and respected his business honesty. Hilde, you know how
everyone loved Hirsch! They trusted him in everything, and of course
they were right. He always selected only the best cattle for them, such a
fair man he was! Why, he treated all his customers just like family. He
hardly knew the difference. They will remember that! And don't forget
that the families you went to school with will remember you as an excellent student and will have to know what a fine doctor you have become. Believe me, these are good people. Our friends and neighbors
are just as offended as we by these terrible acts. Only last week Frieda
Fuerwenchen stopped by to ask after Auguste, and I told her what had
happened to you in Ratingen. She was horrified, but agreed with me
that nothing like that could ever happen here. You will see, Hildechen,
your practice can still be a success with support from all these people
who know and admire you."

The breathless monologue left little space for interruption, but in
fact Hilde loved the familiar ramblings that meandered through happier times before lighting upon what Mother surely believed was true,
that there was still a future for her loved ones in Germany. All-in-all
Hilde thought the argument a good one, and with her entire future
now hopelessly grounded it would have been comforting to embrace
Mother's philosophy as well as her offer. Still, she remembered the chill
of a hospital dining room on a warm summer election day when professional and personal friendships proved worthless, and so she answered softly, "I may not be so wise as you, Mother, but I've had a
number of experiences that make me believe the Nazis mean exactly

what they say. You have not seen as I did how Munich looked a week after the *Putsch,* and you have not read articles by a psychiatrist who believes there is life not worth living, and you were not blocked by two brutish bastards from entering your own property."

There was another reason, too, more painful, more shameful than all past insults combined. It was her private agony, an untreated puncture wound of the heart continually festering. When Mother wondered why her daughter continued making frequent excursions back to Ratingen, that terrible place where she was ill-treated, Hilde fibbed that she was expecting unsettled payments. While infuriated by this lack of self-restraint, she felt driven by an uncontrollable urge to sift through the Ratingen mails for a familiar envelope containing some handwritten message explaining all. "So sorry I haven't written—but—I have been busy with teaching and research—I broke an arm skiing—I was sent to Greenland to treat Eskimos."

What a fool she was! Instead of raiding mails, she ought to be shredding his picture along with its inflated pledge of undying admiration, expunging evidence of her relic past by tearing up all snapshots of him and the "group" with their silly smiles and ridiculous frozen poses. If only she could let go, shed those reminders as easily as he seemed to have shed his promises.

She still had not said anything to Jack, nor had "Onkel" thought to mention Karl recently, probably because he had so many troubles of his own. With internship finally complete, his next logical move should have been to specialize at some hospital or clinic the way Hilde had done, but now even the most undesirable assignments were impossible to come by, and of course, Jewish medical personnel were always prime for dismissal. He was reduced to opening a private practice, but without a source of capital, his only hope was to find medical people in similar circumstances and pool resources. In addition, Jack had recently received the depressing news that his father was seriously ill, that he would now probably have the burden of supporting not only himself, but needy parents as well. Then on April 22 came another crippling blow: a Decree Regarding Physician's Services with National Health Insurance was declared which appeared to bury any lingering hopes for Jewish doctors still expecting to eke out a living in Germany. It was crucial for doctors and dentists to serve on a Health Insurance Panel since services paid out of Local or Guild Sick Funds yielded nearly nine-tenths of the medical practitioner's income. The Decree of April 22 barred "non-Aryans" from panel practice, except for certain "privileged non-Aryans" described as those who had fought at the front, served in a military isolation hospital, or lost a father or son or husband in the World War.

Fortunately, Schloss, a veteran, qualified, as did Hilde's other friends, Weichert and Rosenblum. Now in the mad scramble following this latest catastrophe, they found each other, and hoped, among the three, to find enough money and equipment to open a private practice. But the continuous search for money coupled with the uncertainty of succeeding tended to magnify even minor disagreements, and since theirs was an unnatural alliance born of stress, each never stopped searching for more palatable alternatives. Admittance to the *Kassenarztliche Vereinigung,* the "Kassen," was far from automatic even for those qualifying under the Decree, as Jack made plain in his anxious letters to Hilde:

Leipzig, February 21, 1933

Dear Bruchhilde!

How nice you didn't forget me. Your gift of the appointment book was a two-fold delight. First, because you are a very nice person, and second, because I now have proof in black and white that I belong to the race of people with good taste.

I'm still alive, but that is the only positive thing I can say. My future is up in the air. To try and settle in Leipzig? Terrible! I hope you, at least, have a war-connected brother or father. Do you have any advice for me? I can go anywhere from the North Pole to Honolulu, but I have to be ready to support my near-death father. Hope you are all right.

Schlosschen

Leipzig, May 17, 1933

Poor, poor Hildechen,

I am so sorry to hear about your practice. How I would like to offer sage advice, but I am like a priest in a vise. Everything goes wrong. I asked for admission to the panel in Leipzig, and now am waiting to find out what they say after they recuperate from the shock.

I still can't be a friend to Rosenblum. He gave Weichert his equipment and apartment, but for Weichert to go it himself is too expensive. It would be nice if you would let me know what equipment we might have from you. Weichert is getting pushy. I don't like to put you on the spot, because I know that you don't know yourself what you might need.

I don't think your residence in Duelken is a good idea, but Hildechen, it is better than nothing. What makes you think I am angry with you? I yell at more substantial subjects than little medicine girls and am only grateful.

Your Onkel Doktor

Leipzig, July 3, 1933

Dear Hildechen,

Long ago when I was still a doctor, I wrote reports to former colleagues. This is such a report. My plans for foreign employment fell through, so I will remain here if the blankety-blank Insurance office agrees. I've decided to accept your suggestion and take the plunge with Weichert. Rosenblum is going to Palestine and would lend us his furniture. With your instruments we could manage without too much money, though I hope the time is near when you will be able to use your own equipment. If all goes well, I'm hoping to open in August. Would you come and help? But as we all know, the best chances in this world are flawed, all others are doomed. Now we know why we are the "chosen."

For now, "*Sieg Heil,* Hildechen!"

Onkel Doktor

At least it appeared that Jack had come to some kind of resolution, and she hoped it would work out with Weichert. Realistically, everyone had to discover his own solution, the least abrasive and disruptive way out of the disaster they were all in. She hoped that as a veteran Jack would soon be admitted to the all-important Kassen practice. She remembered how in Ratingen she, too, had applied for Kassen, feeling assured of early admittance since she was the only pediatrician in town. But of course that was before the Boycott, before the heinous editorial and restrictive April Decree, and before her own realization that in Germany there could be no safe place for anyone on the black list. Her homeland had treated her as a second class citizen, denying her even the right to earn a decent living, and she would not stand for it.

Her reaction to being deserted by so-called friends was even stronger. Karl still had not written, lacking even the grace to phase out their relationship with polite untruthful explanations. She didn't dare write him either, knowing she would blurt out all the wrong things, insults provoked by months of anger and rejection, which he would surely interpret as pain and humiliation. If that were to happen she would be stripped of the only thing remaining, her dignity.

She resolved to leave Germany, the sooner the better, the only question being "where." Countries still claiming to be in a depression were not exactly spreading the red carpet for refugees who might claim jobs needed by citizens. France was definitely out because the French government zealously guarded visas and made emigrations temporary. America, land of the free, seemed distant and drastic, but as a matter of fact her torch of freedom was not exactly glowing for impoverished physicians without job prospects either. The best bet seemed England, where she might circumvent strict employment regulations by listing herself as a student in midwifery.

Having decided where to go, she also needed an "excuse" for seeking entry, which she found with an International Pediatric Congress scheduled for July in London. Finally something positive, and if all worked out she would be out of Germany in a matter of weeks, hopefully making contact with the Jewish Refugee Committee in England. Mother and other family members were disappointed, of course, but on the whole they had gotten used to her bouts of independence. "If Hilde wants to go to England, let her go to England," they declared, feeling little more than that their present troubles would soon blow over, that governments come and go, and that the small communities were safe in any case.

She scheduled one last social call in Wurzburg where Jack had moved to be with his Mother to help with his ailing Father. Hilde was anxious to bring him up to date on her plans. Already she had received a visa for England and was scheduled to attend the Congress in mid-July. Jack proclaimed the midwife strategy "excellent," and though less enthused about his own prospects, once more inquired whether he might have her medical instruments now that her plans for England were finalized. She declined. "Who knows? I might still need them, but

I'll leave them in Duelken to be sent either to England or to Wurzburg."

Catharsis

Unexpectedly, the visit with Jack also became her "release" from Orzech, when her frustrated relative, trying to put his own life in order, admitted consulting Karl about admission to the Kassen. "Can you believe my so-called 'good friend' would have nothing to do with me? Claimed I had nothing to worry about since I am a veteran, and then discarded me as easily as yesterday's ticket stubs!"

Hilde, saying nothing, raced home to cast her thoughts in writing. "Onkel" would have been amazed by her zeal in his defense. She described him as a patriot who had served nobly at the front, his performance as admirable as theirs now was shameful. Arguments supposed to be logical and dispassionate in order to woo the scientist in Karl, after a paragraph or two unleashed seven month's frustration in curse words and accusations. Even while penning it, she realized that beyond defending Jack there was little of substance in what she said, that an angry tide had washed rationality and logic away. No matter. Her future with Karl was over, as the tickets in her purse representing a sea of fresh beginnings proved. She reread the letter only once. It was impassioned, non-scientific, but completely truthful, and she hurried to post it before she changed her mind, awaiting almost certain reply. She was in England when it arrived. Mother forwarded it.

Berlin, August 15, 1933

Fraulein Doctor,

It pains me to address you this way, but I can't understand what has happened between us. I've done nothing to be reproached for and I must believe there is a lot of misunderstanding between us. As you know, such situations have occurred before with Schloss. You can't imagine how helpless I feel before your strong words.

I know we haven't written each other for a long time, but that, too, has happened before and we always took it for laziness which in our profession comes easy. In the meantime, the only thing I remember is this letter from Schloss, which I answered the best I could. I didn't think he had anything to worry about since he was a veteran.

I think you should know that I did look around for ways to help him, but with no success.

I feel your accusations are personally and shamefully unjust. I can't imagine having done anything wrong or cowardly, though I know I am no hero. But to make such a judgment takes a person who knows me better than you do. I'm sorry you don't simply state what you accuse me of. I have spent all this time at the Institute of Berlin working hard and haven't had a chance to earn all the curse words you sling at me.

If you ever thought me a friend, which I doubt, you ought not pass judgment before talking to me. That's my definition of friendship. It was for this same reason I was mad at Schloss the time we visited the Berlin Zoo. The fact you can judge so easily, shows you irresponsible. I take it from your letter you would like to find me at fault. This I will not accept. Since I have a different definition of friendship, I'll try again to clear up this terrible misunderstanding. I hate to think your letter will be the only memory we have of each other. But I must leave it to you to search your memory again. Today you might think my letter is begging. I have to take that, too. But I will honor my version of friendship.

Karl Orzech

His naive expression of astonishment at her "rudeness" in calling things by their real names incensed her. Could he really see nothing shocking in what was happening in Germany? Was he so blind he did not notice former Jewish "friends" begging favors, *groveling* to remain in the medical profession, a field where Jews had proudly served and contributed to Germany's fame? As for his detached discussions of "friendship" and "honor" typed impersonally so as to further disguise any personal involvement and his implied assurance that he was sure her temper would quiet when she came to her senses, she would certainly need to set *that* straight. Removing from her folder the Ratingen Kinderarztin stationery, she penned,

Dear Doctor,

I knew beforehand you didn't understand me, but that you would go so far as to read shameful injuries, insults, and accusations into my writing never occurred to me. Or are "painful disappointment" and "sadness" terms which are no longer understood in the new German language? I do have a copy of my letter. You don't have to help with my memory. I would again use the same words even if I had waited another two weeks with my letter. My decision was not rattlebrained or frivolous. You had seven months to right matters. Now you claim it's all in my head, but I assure you it is not, and my verdict is the same. To give "reasons"—one, two, three—I cannot—and it would be useless to try with such lack of understanding.

I don't know if somewhere in your busy and unworldly work you can remember a person who comes from a different culture in Germany, and just maybe can't be understood by the new German. I think of Parsifal whose crime I never understood before. His lack of questioning about the suffering of others, understanding, or feeling for them, was the result of his own insecurities and official duty. But of course you can't use that excuse for yourself. You are a clear thinking man who knows exactly what he does or doesn't do. For you, it was a well-thought-out decision when we didn't write each other out of "laziness." May I offer an explanation? (Though I can't imagine that in Germany, especially in Berlin with its own Ministry for Enlightenment, it should be necessary.) May I tell you that between yesterday and today there is such a gap that my world outlook got lost in it. The bridge that crumbled between Aryans and Jews should have been your job to repair. I, the scorned, homeless, "subperson" could not expect to influence you, but a word of understanding from a friend would have been a good deed. I did not expect heroism.

These are my thoughts concerning you, and now I believe you can no longer claim "shameful injustice." At first I didn't want to answer, but the thought of our old friendship, (which is buried with a lot of other things), made me explain again. You will now read in my first letter, not insults, but an explanation of a difficult sad existence. It is a parting from the past and old friends who proved to be no friends.

Hilde Bruch, M.D.

CHAPTER III

1933 - 1935

Romance in Germany

By leaving for England, relegating to memory the happy carefree experiences of childhood, vaguely unfulfilled dreams trapped and buried forever in the soils of Germany, Hilde set a course she would never reverse. It had not been her intention to leave that soil forever, and she might have done so less willingly had she fully understood the permanence of the separation. Like her loved ones in Duelken, she believed current politics in the homeland temporary, an unlikely but inexplicable malady whose toxic symptoms, like the mysterious and outdated Black Plague of yore, could not help but wear out with time. Once outside that atmosphere of intolerance, however, she would discover relative contentment, knowing only a narrow ribbon of water separated her from those she loved, that for visits she could always return.

In Germany, her brothers and sisters found different replies for these dark days, and Mother in the past often despairing that her children would never find love or settle down as young people are expected to do, now saw love blooming in every corner. So abundant were cupid's darts, it was as if the gentle god were making reparation for previous neglect, and at a time when life might have been otherwise bleak, infectious bursts of happiness seeded barren earth, sending forth tiny exquisite blossoms.

Auguste, already thirty, was first to marry. What had this promising and beautiful young woman been doing while sister Hilde industriously completed medical school and residency? Realizing she could never sufficiently cover the Latin requirement at the *Studienanstalt,* Auguste had returned to complete her secondary schooling at the lyceum in Duelken. Untrained for anything specific, the next ten years were lusterless and indecisive, while she waited for a husband, teetering that fine line between youth and aging, marital eligibility and spinsterhood.

When the time came, it took her rather far afield, Mother having exhausted the supply of young bachelors in the immediate area. Leo Goldschmidt was from Cologne. Similar to Auguste in temperament, he also had been passed over by numerous matchmakers and was well into his thirties when this latest chance for marriage arrived. Like Auguste, he possessed the self-assurance which comes only of maturity and experience, of discovering love at a time when such pleasures might easily have passed him by.

Courtship was brief, expedited by their ages and the growing political unrest. It was decided until more permanent arrangements could be made, the young couple would share living quarters with the parents in Cologne, Leo continuing to work the family business, which as an only child was his to inherit. Difficulties soon arose. Business was poor and not improving, and though his new wife was not one to complain, she was visibly uncomfortable in the household of her in-laws.

Auguste's brother Rudolf had long ago wearied of contrived romancing, but Auguste thought she knew him well. Little more than a year separated the two eldest and together they had developed a certain sobriety toward life, possibly because each had been given so much responsibility. Auguste saw few shortcomings in her brother. He was smart, amiable, and the person everyone turned to when things went wrong, not simply because he was oldest and in charge of family business matters, but because he possessed untutored wisdom, the kind that is solid and reliable. Like others discovering love, Auguste wanted the whole world to share her good fortune, but plans regarding her wily, headstrong brother needed to be shrewd and specific.

In the village of Kempen, Mother's hometown, lived a young woman with alluring dark eyes whom Auguste had known since childhood when they had met by chance during one of many family visits. Though closer in age to Hilde, the little girl in fact had more in common with the older sister, and soon the two children were regularly looking forward to Mother's family reunions, that special time when they could retreat into a private world of girlish gossip. Time had never really changed the relationship, since the two grown women still enjoyed exchanging confidences on planned but infrequent visits.

Perhaps because she had known her since childhood, always regarding the young woman as Auguste's friend, Mother had overlooked the obvious, not realizing Selma Goldschmidt was the perfect spouse for Rudolf. So Auguste believed and also thought it unlikely Rudolf would remember her friend. The coincidence of sharing the Goldschmidt name (although their two families were unrelated), Auguste considered a good omen, believing with a little luck they would soon have another name in common.

Bringing the principals together was not exactly story book stuff. Caught off-guard and slightly suspicious, Rudolf seemed disconcerted finding a newcomer sharing the family parlor with his sister. His manner was embarrassingly brusque. Selma, too, showed signs of discomfort, as if suddenly realizing she was the center of something important. Adding to the confusion, Mother belatedly recognized a match-in-the-making and appeared from the kitchen with the traditional courtship bonbons in hand. What saved the situation was that, once introduced, Rudolf did indeed remember Selma, Auguste's playmate from Kempen, and immediately lapsed into soft, nostalgic memories about times when life was wondrous with possibilities for a boy.

So Auguste had her way, and the two couples, one married, the other betrothed but making plans, were often in each other's company. Already Auguste was expecting a child, and Leo discussed with Rudolf the possibility of leaving Germany altogether. "We would start fresh. New country, new opportunity. And we wouldn't have to go far, only across the border to Holland where they are sure to appreciate good German sausage. Business here, Rudolf, it just doesn't come because people are afraid to buy from Jews."

When asked his opinion, Rudolf was lukewarm. For months he had stared at similarly discouraging figures in his own accounts, recognizing in them more than a temporary business slump, but also knowing he would never leave the country merely for the sake of opportunity. Germany was his home, his rock, the place where he had experienced ups and downs but mostly contentment for nearly thirty-two years, surrounded by loved ones in the heart of the Rheinland. Happy memories overwhelmed him as he also remembered in less impassioned terms his sense of responsibility. He was the steady one the family always counted on. Of course he must stay, do what was expected and right. There was no other answer. Things were bound to turn around, anyway, for historically Jews had stood firm against tormentors and harassment, and today was today but certainly not tomorrow for Germany, a modern, educated country. Most important of all, he must consider Selma, the wonderful woman who had promised to follow him through life forever.

He had already confided his intentions to in-laws, Johanna and Albert Goldschmidt, also his fears of not being able to provide adequate financial support. Albert had pooh-poohed the concern. Goldschmidts were well-off, and while Albert's own business wasn't presently booming, it had shown consistent profits through the years. Thus when his future father-in-law invited Rudolf to join him, Rudolf saw a solution for himself and Selma and also for the family in Duelken. By vacating his position as professional head of the family, he would be promoting Artur or Ernst to a situation of responsibility while offering them a livelihood, and by residing in nearby Kempen, he would still be close enough to offer advice whenever his brothers asked it.

No such magic ring surrounded Leo in Cologne, a tiny city where already the atmosphere seemed charged with prejudice. Without much choice in any case, Leo and Auguste chose to emigrate to Holland, a country where language and custom were unfamiliar, but where the newlyweds with a baby on the way could strike out on their own.

Though she no longer lived in Duelken, Erna, too, was very much a part of family activity. Now grown, nearly twenty-four, she was still the "kitten," pretty and lively. Six years to the day separated Erna and Auguste, and they were as close as sisters can be considering the difference their in ages. But because the younger sister had developed from girl to woman during threatening times when for a Jewish woman not to have means of support was foolhardy, Erna's ambitions were different from Auguste's. Then, too, she had been strongly influenced by Hilde whose career in medicine had proven the possibilities for a woman.

For interests Erna did not look far, for she had inherited from Mother a natural love and gift for gardening. When she decided to attend horticultural school near Dusseldorf, she renewed ties with Tante Paula and Onkel David Rath just as Aunt and Uncle were losing touch with Hilde.

By the time the Nazis had ascended to power, Erna had taken a job in Neuendorf, a vacation resort on the East Sea, (now the Baltic), where life was carefree. Fresh salt tickled her nostrils whenever she bent to tend her plants in this breezy, expansive climate where air itself seemed easier to breathe. Yet even here during those warm summer months of 1933, routine had been altered. In former seasons, guests to the pension, mainly from Berlin, arrived late in summer after school vacations had begun, staying maybe a week or two before returning to work refreshed and ready to renew the cycle. This year, instead, they came early in order to recover from the shock of losing jobs. They were the elite of German Jewish society, doctors, lawyers, teachers, musicians, actors, and civil servants, ranging from postal carriers to high government officials who had been fired directly or were forced to resign through pressure from their employers. Some few had chosen to leave on their own rather than suffer humiliation and almost certain dismissal later, as in the case of one guest, a professor at the Academy of Fine Arts in Berlin, who had vacated his position because his wife was Jewish.

Erna drew both vegetables and flowers from the extensive gardens surrounding guest house and cottages, carefully selecting only ripest fruits for the kitchen, arranging daily fresh bouquets for the linen covered tables in the dining room. It was a friendly informal place where guests often stooped to assist in pulling weeds while admiring gardens or commenting on weather. No doubt the owners were responsible. The husband, a retired newspaper man, thoroughly enjoyed his guests, never failing in his easy manner to engage them in small talk. He and his wife lived in a big house on the hill overlooking guest house and cottages. Religion was what they found in their hearts, liberal and freethinkers, both, though he was Jewish and she was not. The pension was under surveillance.

Early one morning staff and guests finishing breakfast heard the droning of boots on gravel followed by a heavy pounding at the door. An important-looking official accompanied by six subordinates burst through the entrance hall. Terrified guests were warned of house arrest and not to leave while the search remained in progress.

The leader snarled, "What newspapers do you read, what books?" A single sweeping of his arm cleared the neatly lined shelves of the pension library. Only the lady of the house, having known this petty tyrant from boyhood, remained immune to intimidation.

"What do you think goes on in a respectable place like this? And what gives you the right to disturb our guests while they are vacationing?" Sarcastically, "Are you sure you've been entirely thorough in your search? Personally, I think you've missed something in that attic up there!" She pointed to the ceiling, chirping rapidly as though trying to distract raiders from the nest, hoping by her own fearlessness to relax the innocents in her care. A ladder and tiny trap door led to a loft.

At another time the sight of six burly men with hefty commander squeezing through such a narrow space might have seemed comical. Now no one snickered. And finding nothing but a few dust-covered broken chairs, the innkeeper's boyhood acquaintance was anything but charitable.

While this was happening, Erna suddenly remembered potentially incriminating letters she had left on top of the table in her cabin. Some few contained harsh statements about National Socialism, but mostly they were the baffled complaints and naive commentaries of family and friends who did not yet fully understand the hateful new regime or the penalties for criticizing it.

Earlier in the interrogation, she had stood frozen at attention like the others, eyes riveted to the floor. Now while everyone was preoccupied with the attic, she gradually began inching her way toward the door. Dressed in gardening attire, slim and perky, she looked anything but suspicious. Still, her heart was pounding as she raced to the scene of her crime where, shredding the evidence, she flushed it down the toilet.

Apparently no one noticed her absence except for the pension secretary who nodded discreetly when she sneaked back. If nothing else, it was a valuable lesson in secrecy. Now she knew she must let go her former gentile friendships if only to protect them from suspicion or interrogation for associating with a Jew. Yet even as she was instructing Mother to withhold her address from these good friends, her open, warm nature rebelled at being forced to seal her past like the petals on a flower.

She was not the only youthful castaway in Neuendorf, and soon she met Viktor Ries, a former student who had been preparing to graduate from the Academy of Fine Arts in Berlin when he was involuntarily relieved of the necessity of taking final exams. During his final semester as a candidate for a Master's Degree in silversmithing and metal sculpturing, an administrator had realized it was not in the school's best interest to graduate a Jew, so Viktor was roughly ordered to pack his tools and get out.

Thus, instead of being master in silver working, he assisted Erna in the gardens, thankful to hold a job. Though drawn to Neuendorf because the owners of the pension were old family friends who promised to find work for him, as a Zionist he firmly believed only in Palestine would life truly begin. While Viktor shared this dream working the warm soil of the garden beds with Erna, the two fell in love and soon were plotting that future together.

There were complications. To be admitted to Palestine one needed to demonstrate Jewish connections by passing an examination in Hebrew, and now Erna began studying Hebrew in earnest, assisted by old Hebrew texts rescued from Mother's attic. Evenings she and Viktor attended classes in Berlin where a realistic pioneer from Palestine warned of unemployment there.

Summertime brought an end to two salaries, and a wedding date was set for September 1. Preparation was minimal since the young people were anxious to be on their way. Mother, though happy for Erna and her husband and the opportunities awaiting both, harbored even without realizing it, a growing sense of depression. Erna was the third and last daughter she was relinquishing to a new land because of unfit conditions in Germany. Unlike the others, this arrangement appeared permanent. Hilde had entered England as a "student," so Mother expected her to return as soon as conditions improved, while Auguste's emigration seemed even less significant because of the short distance between Duelken and the Dutch border. With proper identification, Mother could easily cross into Holland, though normally she planned staying a week or more when she visited.

At the train station in Berlin, Mother wept even while encouraging Erna and Viktor on their journey, the daughter offering reassurance that it wasn't "forever," promising to look into every possibility to have her to join them in Palestine. Mother forced a smile at this loving but naive gesture: What could Viktor and Erna know about the complexity of ownership? What did bride and bridegroom possess beside the clothing on their backs, a few suitcases of wearing apparel, Viktor's jewelry-making equipment, Erna's gardening tools, and maybe a few pots and pans for housekeeping? In their pockets, also, each carried ten D.M., the full amount of currency the German government allowed to leave the country. At that, the young people were probably lucky owning nothing since it meant they had nothing to lose.

England

On July 14, 1933, Hilde disembarked at Harwich, several days before the scheduled pediatric conference, having "talked her way" into England by listing herself as a student of midwifery. Her passport granting leave to land "on condition that the holder does not enter any employment paid or unpaid while in the United Kingdom" would seem to preclude any possibility of receiving a medical post, particularly a paying one. Nevertheless, by the time the Congress was over, Hilde had discovered the Jewish Refugees Committee with its remarkable philanthropist chairman, Miss Alice Model, whose assistance in the next weeks would prove invaluable.

A single letter written to the Undersecretary at Whitehall extended Hilde's leave, eliciting the prompt reply, "permission granted till the end of August next for the purpose of continuing your studies in midwifery." Meantime, Miss Model lined up jobs in several locations around London, and soon Hilde was working as clinical assistant at Jewish Maternity Hospital and in the Outpatient Clinics at London Jewish and Elizabeth Garrett Andersen Hospitals. Later, she would become an observer of child behavior using anthropometric measurements to research the relationship between physique and mental disorder in Emanuel Miller's Child Guidance Clinic in the West End of London.

Pay was poor, the work not nearly challenging enough to suit her well-trained scientific mind, but the people she met were extraordinarily sensitive and generous. She was befriended by the president of the Pediatric Congress and his wife, who introduced her to physicians all over London. Miss Sylvester Samuel, sister of Sir Herbert Samuel took special pleasure inviting her to lectures at the Royal Society. By simple virtue of being a "refugee" she gained access to places ordinary persons could not enter, and relationships originally fashioned of necessity blossomed into friendships destined to endure a lifetime. Out of such humble beginnings originated the vast network of contacts which would later be extended like a lifeline to other family members.

"To be honest," Hilde declared, "there is nothing as exciting as being on your own in a new country living one day to the next." The smallest details fascinated her, and after accepting a dinner invitation her first week in England, she was both surprised and entertained by the way Britishers handle a fork. "All my table manners and Uncle Otto's training are down the drain," she wrote Mother, "just watching an Englishman eat peas on the back of a fork. Now that is a balancing act! Strange that something assigned so much value can vary so much."

Given her student-midwife status she knew not to expect much; there would be no great opportunities in clinic or lab, no responsibilities proportionate to the independence of practice she had known in Germany. Her greatest disappointment, one which she could not rationalize, was what she perceived as the overall British approach to medicine. She called it "old-fashioned," and knew positively she would not be among those German refugee doctors who traveled to Scotland to take medical exams in order to practice medicine and remain permanently in England.

As she angled for alternatives, a steady flow of letters out of Germany brought her up-to-date on the mess she had left behind. Mail from Wurzburg reminded her of her last visit at Schlosses, the misery of her relationship with Karl peaking at a time when Jack was nursing his own anger and grievously tending a dying parent. Though Heinrich Schloss survived barely another two weeks, her powerful love and admiration for Orzech suffered a slower death, lingering in one form or another, and eventually emerging as a kind of clawing resentment. Now to exorcise even these feelings she composed one final note:

> I didn't intend to write, because of course you won't understand, but I can't keep silent about your conduct. After all that has happened to me the past year, the worst was personal disappointment in a person I truly considered my friend. Now that I've been long enough and far enough away from the homeland to think about it without bitterness, the only feeling I have for you is contempt, (sympathy or excuse

being impossible). I needed to express these feelings in order to make fresh new beginnings.

Signing it "H.B.," dating it "London, December 10, 1933," she in fact never sent it. Satisfaction came through scanning the terse message and absorbing its finality. Truly her heart was in the last line. How comforting to wipe clean the slate, release all painful reminders of Karl. Were it only so easy to sever ties with a special corner of the Rheinland where childhood dreams are born and nurtured and nearly every day the mind is flooded with memories of a hometown and a family who still lives there.

How were they really? English newspapers brimming with news of Hitler and his Nazis revealed nothing about Mother or her four brothers. To uncover these mysteries she needed to play detective, read and re-read mail from Duelken searching for clues, but information regarding personal hardships created by Nazi politics was hard to come by since Mother tended to linger on the comfortable and familiar, avoiding unpleasantries which might upset her daughter.

Family trivia and local gossip cluttered the pages of her letters: "Ernst and Kurt are at the Sport Club and send their love. The fruit harvest was good. We filled all the glasses and sold some, since our main eaters are not here anymore. Uncle Leo is moving to a villa by a windmill, so now Tante Berthe can lord it over her sister." Only very occasionally did a careless line sneak through revealing by implication the ugly atmosphere surrounding them. "Rudolf and Selma got a new radio. Mine has seen better days, but I won't fix it, because I don't like to listen to it anymore. In the evenings instead I read and do needlepoint."

One thing her letters did excel in was news of the grandchildren, supreme joy of her life. She now had two, Margot and Herbert, with Selma expecting another. When Auguste two years earlier had given birth to Margot, the first grandchild, this experienced mother of seven was on hand in Winterswiyk to lend expertise. But confidence soon faded after the baby came. Greatly embarrassed, she later confessed to Hilde, "I was never more scared—handling something like that so small and fragile." Hilde, herself so well-trained in the handling of newborns, had laughed. Understandably, Mother was intimidated by this tiny wiggly mass of humanity because her own babies had spent their first six weeks in the care of a midwife, who not only assisted the doctor with delivery but remained as nurse and helpmate afterward.

She switched her attention to letters from Jack, which, while more informative than Mother's, were infinitely more pessimistic. No doubt they reflected the true Germany, but filtered through Onkel's jaundiced eyes they certainly were defeating. Jack's gloom was justifiable, of course, obliged as he was to support his mother while the medical firm of Manfred Weichert and Jacob Schloss struggled for patients, funds, and medical supplies. But the constant pressure had undermined any pretense of trust:

> Your brother sent your instruments and I took inventory so I can keep an eye on "light-fingered" Manfred. I left your microscope in Duelken because Schatzky gave me his. So far I've heard nothing more about his promise to send for Mother and me when he is settled.

Six months later "light fingers" were no longer an issue since Manfred Weichert had quit to emigrate to the U.S.A. Weichert's good news was Jack's catastrophe, leaving him without choice but to emigrate himself. "There is a University in Boston who thinks it can use me—as professor of blood sugar in a cold room—or something like that. I expect for language I will have to use both hands and facial expressions."

Hilde was amused and relieved to recognize in his writing something of her old friend. "Now we must talk business. Us talk business? Ha! What shall I do with your instruments? They aren't worth much. No point selling them. Some I could take with me. Or should I send them to your mother in Duelken? More importantly, couldn't we say 'good-bye' or 'hello' somewhere? Maybe Southampton or Liverpool, someplace close to you. I'm leaving early May, most likely on the Cunard Line. It would be wonderful, Hildechen! And now, write soon."

In the end they would choose to meet neither in Southampton nor Liverpool, but in Hamburg, Germany, where both would board the *SS President Roosevelt*, Hilde debarking in London, Jack continuing on to Boston. University Hospital had barely given Jack enough notice to close his office doors and settle business affairs. Nevertheless, he had managed to scratch a note to Hilde, "I leave all arrangements to you since I know your aptitude for detail, which I have no time for myself. Mr. *President Roosevelt* intends to leave Hamburg May 16, and since I'm a peace-loving man, I have no objection."

During her week's return to Germany, Hilde expected to play "doting Aunt-Pediatrician" and lose some of the homesickness which plagued her even after these many months away. While visits with family promised to be wonderful, time with Jack would also be well spent. The return voyage to England was sure to provide enough visiting time aboard ship to experience first hand his excitement, learn the details of his appointment. Who could predict where life would lead either of them? The sailing might even prove romantic now that her feelings for Karl were buried forever, for wasn't it conceivable she and Jack might someday struggle with the hazards of practicing medicine in the new country together?

All in good time. Her first business must be to obtain a visa to the United States. She would need a money deposit with affidavit of support from someone in the States, or else some proof of employment. Right now she had neither, but Jack might possibly help with the latter. Probably he could advise her about applying for medical positions in the States, or at least she would learn how he had gotten his.

She was ready for change, dissatisfied with her present work. At the same time she did not consider the time in England wasted. This year of casting about while scrutinizing life in her Nazi homeland was a temporizing measure which had worked to her advantage; for while she continued speaking English with a heavy German accent, her verbal and written command of the language was much improved. As a matter of fact, Hilde was decidedly comfortable with both the English people and their language, having made remarkable friendships and many useful contacts among physicians and refugee committees. Even so, she could not help but feel a tinge of envy for Jack with his "whatever it is post" in Boston, knowing the time had come when she, too, must move on. Her visa without extension was due to expire in the next months, and she knew she could never return to Germany where conditions for physicians were ever worsening.

She met him in Hamburg at boarding time, and seeing him after so many months stirred her heart. Drinking in the familiar features, she felt briefly at peace comparing a year's worth of experiences. She had anticipated finding him in high spirits, and indeed he was "glad to be

out of Hitler's shit house," as he put it, but if that could be characterized "optimistic," his mood only spiraled downward from there. When
asked the story of his success, he replied tersely, "You're asking what
button I pushed to get this job? Well, your guess is as good as mine.
Dumb luck, shooting craps. My turn on the dice, maybe. And what
good is it anyhow when I can't scrape enough together to get Mother
out of the hell hole, too."

Hilde understood Jack's concern for his mother. The refugee's
plight of leaving major responsibilities behind was commonplace.
Quite often, the emigrant managed to earn enough in his adopted
country to support himself, yet not nearly enough to provide ship fare
or affidavit for relatives. Entire families were sometimes forced to endure separations lasting years.

While she sympathized with Jack, especially since the death of his
father had left Berthe quite alone, during the span of her friendship
with him Hilde had gotten to know his mother. The two women had
exchanged confidences concerning Jack's mood swings and Berthe had
written letters seeking advice and reassurance. Hilde had no trouble
providing either, but neither did she worry unduly about Jack, believing that once securely settled, his humors would stabilize. Most certainly she did not worry about Berthe, who possessed an inner tough-
ness her son perhaps lacked and whose life where he was concerned
amounted to one unselfish act after another. For Berthe there was only
one consideration, opportunity for Jack in America, and so to prepare
for that day when he would send for her, she cheerfully enrolled in
English classes.

Thus, Hilde found Jack's outburst outrageously overdrawn and self-
pitying. "As usual you pull a long face when everyone else would beg or
steal to go to a free country where there's every opportunity for success.
Who wouldn't trade places with you? More to the point, how on earth
can you judge a new job, its salary and conditions of employment, or
for that matter, anything else about America when you haven't even
been there!"

Realizing she could not count on Jack, already her mind was drifting toward more realistic solutions. "You are much too impatient," she
retorted. "You want everything at once, but as a matter of fact, it all
takes time, though eventually everyone I know has done well in
America. I have an uncle who went to the United States in 1903, and

without knowing a word of English moved to Nebraska to work in a store. Then three years later he started his own 5 and 10, and at that time there were only two other stores like it in the whole state."

Her mind was racing now. Of course, how could she have forgotten Onkel David Kaufmann, Mother's cousin in America! His was a success story the whole family bragged about. Most likely he would send her an affidavit of support because he was generous and had already helped her cousin Bruno with an emigration.

"My Onkel David three years ago became president of a bank in Grand Island, and by now is probably running the whole community." Voice and spirits soared as one by one she remembered new rungs of accomplishment, though it appeared nothing would budge Jack's outlook. Still, she would concede nothing, and by the time she sighted familiar shapes of London outlined on the horizon from atop ship deck of the *SS President Roosevelt*, the plans percolating in her mind were nearly formulated.

"Wiedersehen, wiedersehen," they shouted to each other at dockside, embracing fondly, promising to write. "You'd better," she cried, "Just as soon as you land, because I expect nothing less than a complete record of daily life in Boston."

As she watched the ship pull away, Jack making crazy faces and waving spiritedly from the ship's deck, she thought, "He'll be okay. It's just his nature to ambush disappointment by painting the gloomiest picture imaginable. When he gets to America all that will change." Even now, as the ship blasted warnings or farewells or whatever it was ships did, steaming slowly up the Thames and out to sea, she could still make out a tiny image jerking about on deck, Jack dancing like a marionette so she would not lose sight of him.

After receiving good news that Onkel David would sign her affidavit, she returned once more to Germany, excitedly hugging nieces, nephews, brothers, sisters, aunts, uncles, cousins, neighbors, friends of neighbors, anyone who ventured near, clicking her camera repeatedly, since who knew when she would pass this way again? She wanted to meet Ilse, Rudolf's infant daughter, born in her absence, and to look in on Berthe Schloss. Berthe continually worried about her son's black moods, and Hilde promised to keep her informed.

Once back in England when Hilde wrote Jack of the visit, an enthusiastic piece regarding procedures in the new world, ironic naive inquiries of a fellow novice traveler, she expected he would find it clever and amusing. Instead, his reply was briskly sobering:

> I can't decide whether you are right or wrong in your decision to come here because I feel prospects in this country are small for all of us. At least for now I have enough to eat and a thieves' den for a room. That's it for plus, everything else is minus. I tried my best to meet your request for contacts, but since I'm low on the totem pole, I didn't get very far, and I'm afraid even the best connection in Boston would be of little use to you, anyway, since there is not even the will to help.
>
> Be sure to do everything possible to get a job before you get here, even if it isn't much, because sooner or later you will need to eat. So far as meeting you, I would suggest you contact Weichert (if you can't get anybody else). I'm sorry I can't meet your ship in New York, mainly because it's too expensive, but you ought to have someone with you the first few days. Thank God, you speak English. That helps a lot. In a day or so, Americans will understand your King's English. Unfortunately I can't say the same for myself. As to your mental outlook: Don't be overly optimistic, but be confident that in this land of opportunity you will somehow succeed.
>
> Hopefully your vacation in the old homeland was a good one, and that you saw only beautiful things to store in memory, because over here, you'll see misery for a long time. Thank you, by the way, for your nice letter with all the news of Wurzburg. Mother wrote how much she enjoyed your visit. You are right, she is the best person I have in this world.
>
> *Schloss*

Her heart sank. Was she about to make the worst mistake of her life? Was Jack's letter the only reason for the heaviness inside, or were latent insecurity and homesickness finally catching up to undermine months of competent planning? Uncle David believed she would be successful in the new country and had verified it by signing an affidavit. The whole Jewish Refugee Committee of London was behind her, friends envied her, and clearly everyone admired her initiative. In any case, she had better pull herself together since there was no turning back now that she had blabbed ideas everywhere and to everyone bared her soul by committing thoughts, words, and dreams to America.

America

Miss Model, along with several other Committee members, had come to see her off at the train station as part of a planned gala farewell which included champagne, so she was feeling confident and more cheerful than usual. At dockside, however, she began questioning the madness that had brought her here, specifically her zeal for bargain hunting. Had she been insane booking a "freighter" on an American export line, instead of a sensible ocean liner? True, she had saved considerably on fare, but next to the *SS President Roosevelt* this thing was a dinghy. She questioned whether it was seaworthy enough to break harbor, let alone get her to America.

To counter the quirky sensations rising from her stomach, she paused to observe other passengers now arriving in a steady stream. They bustled on deck, hauling steamer trunks, furniture, and hand luggage, which they placed on dollies to roll up the gangplank, seemingly oblivious to peril. Suddenly she knew they couldn't all be crazy, that behaving like a frightened rabbit would only mark her as the neophyte traveler.

Inside, the ship looked even smaller—if that were possible. Judging from the size of the beds, the cabins were meant for midgets. Three narrowly spaced appendages jutted from the right wall connecting at the far end with a ladder. An attractive woman appearing to be in her mid-forties was removing clothes from a suitcase on the lowest berth and glanced up long enough to introduce herself as "Miss Radcliffe." Hilde was sorry she hadn't come aboard sooner since now she was left with the dubious choice of top bunk or middle. Still, her humor remained intact and both laughed when she jokingly opted to be the "filling in the sandwich." It was purely a "good sport" pose, however, since the ladder worried Hilde considerably, while a recently injured leg contributed to her awkwardness and uncertainty. As she practiced going up and down the flimsy rungs she wondered how much worse things might get when they hit open seas.

Miss Radcliffe offered to set Hilde's luggage next to her own for purposes of unpacking, and while the two transferred clothing to a pull-out closet, examining the tiny metal wash basin that pulled out next to it, they exchanged bits and pieces of information about themselves. "First impression—mutual liking," wrote Hilde later in her diary, though mingled with it was something resembling relief that they would be able to get along in these cramped quarters for the next ten days. Frequently both women cast eyes heavenward offering silent thanks that the third bunk was still empty; but at the last minute, breathless and flustered, Mrs. Harold arrived and flew into action.

It was too much for Hilde. She excused herself as civility would allow, remarking that housekeeping chores would "keep," as indeed they would in this postage stamp-sized roomette where definitely three was a crowd. Breathing deep the harbor air, feeling the spaciousness on deck, she slowly began to revive. But upon closer examination, her surroundings left her stunned and gasping, for suddenly she was seeing everything reversed as surely as if she were peering into a mirror. Starboard, port, aft, stern, all those nautical terms she had memorized to prove herself the thoroughly knowledgeable sailor were worthless if a mere fifteen minutes in her cabin could disorient her even before the ship pulled anchor.

The one reassuring sight was a young couple whom she recognized from an earlier stroll. They were still leaning against the same place on the deck railing, chatting placidly, apparently unmindful that their view of London had changed completely. Hilde's frantic pacing as she checked the view first on one side, then the other initially distracted and puzzled them. Finally a great smile of recognition broadened the man's face and he called out, "No, dear lady, you are not seeing things. You are entirely correct that St. Paul's is now on the other side of the ship because, you see, we have turned in dock since you went below."

"Thank heaven you have rescued me from certain madness!" she exclaimed.

"But you must allow me to complete my diagnosis: A mild case of cabin fever understandable in these pinched quarters. And my sure fire treatment for it? Several hours a day on deck in fresh air and sunshine."

She laughed, "You sound like a doctor."

"Uh, oh. Found out again. Guess you never quite get away from it," he chuckled, drawing enthusiastic agreement from his wife, who replied, "We are the Kendalls, heading back to New York from a medical conference in London. Forrest is a biochemist, but on this trip I'm happy to say we were both vacationers. What a marvelous city London is!"

Kendall extended mitt-like paws, and she felt her spirits soaring. That another doctor could be on board had caught her by surprise, although how could she have known when the passenger ledger omitted titles, listing her own name as "Miss Hilde Bruch?"

"Oh, I'm so happy to meet you," bowing graciously in mock formality, "Hilde Bruch, refugee doctor, currently unemployed, presently bound for America hoping to change luck and status." Everyone laughed.

"So what are your plans now, Hilde Bruch? Where will you stay?"

"The answer to both questions is, 'I don't know, I don't know,' but I confess I have an even more urgent worry. My worst nightmare is that no one will show up in New York to meet me because I'm told in America women can't go ashore alone, that instead they send you to somewhere called Ellis Island where you have to wait until someone comes to release you. I don't have anyone."

She blurted it out having only heard rumors of emigration procedures in the United States and visualizing customs as miles of holding pens filled to overflowing with people begging for release. She had done all she could to avoid this quagmire by writing Uncle David (who was sorry he was unable to make the trip from Nebraska), Jack who had declined because of expense, and Weichert who couldn't get off work, but had succeeded in solving neither the problem nor her fear of the proceeding.

"Well, we can't have you wasting away on Ellis," said Kendall affably, "so our first priority when we land in New York will be to summon a posse to your rescue."

"After that, we must examine your job prospects," added his wife.

Were they genuinely concerned? The light-hearted responses made it hard to tell. After all, she had floundered into their lives looking more like some drunken sailor trying to reestablish bearings in an unfamiliar port than a doctor expecting to practice serious medicine. Regardless, she liked them, sensed they also liked her, and was grateful for the friendship however it came packaged.

Nine o'clock: three loud blasts signaled they were on their way. For awhile she watched familiar shapes on the Thames, lights blinking in buildings silhouetted against a dimming sky. Then excitement and energy also fading from what seemed nearly the longest day on record, she headed toward her cabin and pallet to sleep surprisingly well, lulled awake only occasionally by the muffled roar of engines and the comforting action of waves moving lightly beneath the ship.

Sunshine filtering through the cabin window the following morning seemed to enlarge the cabin, while the ship, now in full light, also looked more imposing and important. Refreshed from sleep, Hilde wandered familiar narrow hallways in search of coffee, breakfast, and a bright new day's experiences.

By afternoon, a lighthouse off the coast of England marked the final landmark of the old world, and as the ship roared out of the Channel and into open seas, crew members took orders for free cocktails to inaugurate a "welcome aboard party." Games were in order, too, but looked so childish that Hilde spurned them in favor of less organized socializing. Moving purposively between knots of people, introducing herself and trying to remember names, later in her cabin she reinforced the memory by scratching on a note pad those she could recall: "Winklers, Semples, Mrs. Pfeiffer, Casas with two children."

The following day was much less pleasant, as winds created choppy seas and erratic motion which affected nearly everyone. Pale subdued passengers headed for the ship's dispensary to receive Dramamine and comforting reassurances of better weather ahead. Nevertheless, throughout the night the storm continued gathering strength, so by morning forward progress was all but halted. Informed passengers spoke of a "hurricane" gone to sea after hugging the coast of America. True or not, the captain avoided mentioning it, stating only that they were in no present danger, that radio weather bulletins indicated the worst was over, and that in the meantime the ship's staff would be doing everything to keep them comfortable.

Still the little craft continued pitching, the deck under siege of salt spray declared off limits, chairs and tarps secured. Cabins, close and stuffy, which seemed to intensify symptoms of vertigo, became unfriendly refuges. Hours hung heavy. Many found their way to the interior lounge where, because reading was impossible, they dozed in chaises or visited quietly with neighbors.

The next days saw gradual calming. On their eighth day at sea, came definite sight of land: Cape Race, Newfoundland, four miles away, and on Monday, October 1, 6:00 P.M., the first lighthouse off Massachusetts, simple and majestic in the glowing sunset. "Night:

nearing Boston—lights twinkling with increasing density—searchlights, the ship guided into harbor and ordered to quarantine."

Hilde rose at 5:00 A.M. to watch dawn spread across the many small islands and forts in Boston Harbor. At 8:00, with ship finally docked and landing cards issued, passengers were allowed to debark, citizens first. When it was their turn, she and Miss Radcliffe scurried down the runway hailing a cab to take them to the Statler Hotel, Miss Radcliffe's favorite lodging in Boston, where Hilde took the opportunity to telephone Schloss. Later, the two ladies strolled around town eating ice cream cones, peering through shop windows, and returning to the ship by subway, which Hilde found disagreeably dirty.

It was nearly noon when Jack arrived ship-side, depressed and dissatisfied. Clearly his condition had deteriorated since their visit in England when he still held hope, however thinly, that things might go favorably in America. While she had known through letters things weren't going well, she was unprepared for this exhausting display of anger and self-pity. Despising the dispensary where he worked, he hated colleagues even more, branding them unfair. They were slave drivers, he the overworked, underpaid refugee/serf doing menial and degrading jobs in an understaffed, poorly equipped lab. Nobody but a poor choiceless slob like himself would have agreed to their terms.

It was an earful she didn't need just now, burdened as she was by her own doubts. Of course, it had been weak and foolish to phone Jack. She knew perfectly well the contagious nature of depression, that by exposing herself to its destructive forces all those carefree feelings that had earlier buoyed her with a sense of adventure would likely evaporate. Yet, even knowing this, the need to see him had far outweighed the risk. She longed for the sight of a familiar face.

She spoke brightly about locating something suitable for him while searching job markets for herself in New York. Perhaps the Refugee Committee would make suggestions. She praised Berthe and counseled Jack to be strong for his mother's sake. "Her courage alone is not enough. She needs you, and is counting on you to get her out of Germany."

He nodded, spirit temporarily assuaged. "If only I could save something from the pitiable salary I earn. You see, at this rate it will be years before I can send for her. Would you help by looking for something in New York? But I'm afraid I'm hoping for something that isn't there."

Hilde promised she would look into prospects for refugee doctors in New York City. "We will get together when I am settled," she remarked lightly, while he facetiously promised "to write seldom."

As the ship pulled out of harbor, she watched him moving slowly in the distance until finally he was swallowed into the crowd of visitors lining the pier. Her last night on board was quiet, occupied by writing a regretfully untruthful letter to Berthe Schloss.

"I Love New York"

October 3, 11:30 A.M., the first houses of Long Island appear haphazardly, then in steady rows along the coast. A gong rings for passengers to attend lunch in the dining room. At 12:30, Chief Engineer Schlitz himself appears on deck to identify points of interest in the city. Starboard, a Swedish ship bound for South America sends greeting with three high toots while we answer back with three low ones. Moments later it is only a green stripe. We are surrounded by skyscrapers, awesomely high in the fading light, crisp lines beautiful against a blue sky.

Hilde, with a tourist's knowledge of the city skyline, recognized the more important landmarks even before Schlitz confirmed them. Finally, the Statue of Liberty—nothing had quite prepared her for this sight. Her skin quivered, and she felt a melting weakness in her knees. Eyes, too, were filling, and momentarily she was afraid she might make a spectacle of herself by weeping openly in front of everyone, because of this solemn symbol's magnificent promise of freedom.

Soon sentiment gave way to anxiety, when people began organizing belongings, hugging and waving "good-bye" to shipboard acquaintances. For most, America was already home. Skeptically she regarded the many sentimental people promising to stay in touch.... "Blessed be the tie that binds," she thought watching them race to the arms of waiting loved ones without a second look backward.

The Kendalls, too, were cheerily on their way, after first reassuring Hilde that they would send a "rescue squad" soon. She felt uncomfortable watching them go. Their shipboard friendship had meant a lot, likewise the medical exchanges with Kendall. He had been anxious to impress her with medical progress in America, promising a tour of the hospital at Columbia Presbyterian Medical Center where he worked. They had even set a date so she could talk with Dr. Rustin McIntosh, head of Babies Hospital, conceivably to land a place for her on staff.

That was almost too wonderful to contemplate, and now watching the young pair waving to her from the pier, flushed with the excitement of being reunited with their family, it was easy to believe they might forget her in the confusion of reestablishing routine after so many weeks' absence. Feeling slightly morose, anyway, after cheering 99 percent of her fellow passengers on their way, she headed down the narrow stairwell to her cabin luggage, which had been packed since yesterday tea time. Expecting lengthy detainment, she felt confused to hear immediate rapping on her door. The Kendalls, even with a bag of miracles, could not have freed her so soon.

What a surprise to be greeted by Mrs. Gertrude Borg, who had been informed by Miss Alice Model and the Refugee Committee in London of her arrival, also Mrs. Finkelstein and Miss Kaufmann from the National Council of Jewish Women. Uncle David had thoughtfully sent a business representative, and the Kendalls had already located someone to send over from Immigration. *Five* people when she was expecting none!

It was decided that she would stay at Gertrude Borg's luxury apartment on Riverside Drive, high above the Hudson. In later weeks, she would learn more about the philanthropic activities of her hostess, the committees and health organizations she headed, but what would always impress her most was Gertrude's capacity to minister to homeless and bewildered individuals like herself, uprooted newcomers who arrived without means or pedigree.

The next day was a treadmill as she sought permanent residence. The Women's Organization sent her to Immigration who sent her somewhere else, who returned her to Immigration; but somewhere, she was fortunate enough to stumble upon Congress House, where she agreed to share rent on a furnished apartment.

That night in her room, she jotted to Mother first impressions of New York:

> The town seems big and important and so easy to get lost in I always count buildings and windows. Fifth avenue is the most marvelous street of all, very wide, and lined with glamourous shops. Still, every-

thing isn't quite what you want to believe, because just off Fifth Avenue you can turn a corner and see slums, the houses of the very poor....

Altogether I am exhausted because there is so much to see and do. Already I am invited to attend a baseball game next week, and expect an even busier weekend coming up with a tour of The Columbia Presbyterian Medical Center, and a visit to the Metropolitan Museum of Art.

Columbia Presbyterian Medical Center, Saturday, October 6, Kendall greeted her at the front desk, friendly as ever, slightly apologetic he could not spare more time. She replied that the demands of research keep their own time table. An hour later, she had seen most of the vast hospital complex, which struck her as surprisingly well-furnished and organized. She noted diet room and kitchen, special wing for heart patients located near the operating rooms, and finally the pulse which keeps the body running, rows and rows of research labs. What impressed her most was the large professional staff relative to the number of patients, indicating well-informed personnel and excellent patient care.

Kendall had kept his promise about making an appointment with McIntosh, and in a few days she would be seeing the head of Babies Hospital while participating in a staff conference, Grand Rounds, at the same time. When he excused himself to return to matters in the lab, she thanked him deeply, and then with her own tour and business complete, headed toward the city's beckoning skyline. As the day was overcast, the buildings appeared even larger in the fading light.

A clear schedule was her incentive to investigate New York's mysterious underground and make a trial run to Brooklyn Hospital, where the following day she was scheduled for an early interview. In doing so, she perhaps demonstrated more spunk than wit. Four times she found herself on a wrong line, each time widening the breach from familiar territory.

Soon she was indifferent to the location of Brooklyn. All she wanted was to find her way out of this maze of tunnels with flashing blue lights and filthy yellow tiled stations, where spastic doors spat out apathetic riders. Finally surfacing for help and by now visibly limping, she located a policeman. Her accent, thickened by stress, had become a garbled mixture of German and English, the "interview-perfect" dark dress a mass of wrinkles, her carefully rolled hair undone and resembling a sloppily constructed birds nest. Although she pictured herself straight out of the old country and for the briefest moment inborn pride burned out of habit, truly she was beyond caring.

When he explained how close she was to home, she gasped, rotating her arms, "But that means I've been riding for hours round and round in circles." Only now she, too, was laughing and had regained enough composure to ask directions for tomorrow's interview in Brooklyn. This time he insisted she take the subway, and scribbling her route mumbled, "You can do it, I know you can, so much easier than buses—the local gets you right there."

By now she was feeling positive kinship for him. Certainly some explanation of her ignorant behavior was in order, and so she told him how she was a newcomer, a doctor fleeing Germany, leaving family behind.

"And you're letting a little thing like a subway get you down? Dear doctor, whatever you do, don't go back there. My grandmother is Jewish, so I know all about that madman, Hitler, and his goose-stepping henchmen. Get your family out, too—fast—because anyone left standing in this guy's way is going to get it, and Jews are first in line. Poof!" He slapped his hands together. His chilling words, "never go back because they will kill you," followed her home. Nighttime brought nightmares: A frustrating scene in which Mother, clasping grandchildren to her skirts, beckoned from the opposite bank of a river, wanting to swim across but fearful of the children drowning, refused to try. There were no boats around, or if there were, no one thought to look for them. Dilemma unresolved, she wrestled herself to consciousness, waking hours leaving no time to brood over matters in Germany.

Finally, October 19, the all-important session with Rustin McIntosh: She was surprised that the head of Babies Hospital, neatly dressed in a dark vested suit, was not much older than she.

He greeted her warmly, "Dr. Bruch, I've looked forward to our meeting. You have a great fan in Dr. Kendall." After some introductory small talk, McIntosh asked about her work. "Dr. Kendall has told me something about your training, mentioning work in physical chemistry with specific studies on the behavior of electrolytes. Did he say you got your degree at Freiburg?"

"Yes," she answered, listing other training sites, detailing only the most important.

When she mentioned Leipzig University Children's Hospital and her two years' assistantship there, he interrupted, "Oh, Leipzig, the hospital I visited there impressed me as excellent. I also met Professor Rosenblum there and liked him, though I can't agree with all his ideas. Still they are interesting, and I've often wondered if they should be investigated further."

Delighted by this unexpected connection, she responded, "Did you also know that Dr. Rosenblum has emigrated to Palestine?"

"Yes, I'm afraid I did hear that. Unfortunate for him, yet how much more tragic for German medicine. Every day highly qualified displaced physicians like Rosenblum or yourself confront me. I only wish I had openings to give all of them jobs."

At this first mention of the competition, Hilde felt worried. She had never expected it to be easy, but believed that with perseverance and hard work, success would ultimately come. Now she wondered whether she would even be offered the chance to prove herself.

"Right now I am interviewing at all the area hospitals, seeing what is available. I want to learn how they do things in America. I believe I can contribute from my own pediatric training, but first I need to learn something about the way they practice pediatrics in America."

"That's what we most like to hear—that you want to learn something. Maybe we can help you with that. Dr. McCune is doing studies on newborns, and with your knowledge of electrolytes I think you could really fit in. Interested?" No time to answer. "I'm going to send you down to the Poli Lab where you can talk to him yourself."

In the lab she introduced herself to Donovan J. McCune, M.D., arranging to meet for further discussion later in the week. Returning to her room at Congress House she discovered a letter from Dr. Plant requesting a second interview for a position in chemistry opening up at Beth Israel Hospital. Things were looking up. That night she wrote Mother:

> In some ways it is a city of opposites. I visited the Empire State Building and St. Patrick's Cathedral, which are every bit as majestic as you are led to believe. But there are some unspectacular and very inexpensive things about the city, too, namely food. (You know me

on this subject.) Fruit vendors everywhere—it's hard to get away from them, and non-farming apartment dwellers like myself can enjoy luscious fruit very cheaply. Orange juice is sold in white tiled buildings all over the city—that's because oranges can be shipped cheaply from Florida or California. Also I get lunch at a fascinating cafeteria where you put coins in and a door opens to give you a sandwich or drink or cake—whatever you want. I can't explain here, because you've never seen anything quite like it, but I think you'd be intrigued by the idea, and the food is good. Still my greatest weakness is ice cream sodas.

I'm doing fine and will soon be interviewing again at Babies Hospital, with Dr. McCune who might be able to use me in the lab. Also several other hospitals are interested. The Refugee Committee and other people I meet are very helpful, and I wish you were here to share my excitement. Please write. I worry not hearing from you, also Erna in Palestine, because she doesn't write either. But what I really want to know is how are my little nieces and nephew? You know I can't brag unless you tell me!

McCune's Lab

She had mentally prepared herself for her meeting with Dr. McCune, expecting to appear cool and knowledgeable. But in the end, she supposed it hadn't mattered since he was too preoccupied to notice her or her commentary. In his enthusiasm for his projects, he tended to describe and show everything at once so that she was swept into a whirlwind, unable to take it all in. When finally the lab tour was over and he looked up, as if seeing her for the first time, she was totally surprised by his comment, "With your training, I think we should work excellently together, and the sooner we can get started the better."

Delighted, she nodded agreement. It would be wonderful working with him, knowing what she could contribute, and though both knew she still needed official notice of the position, they headed confidently to the cafeteria. When after lunch Dr. McIntosh called her to his office and proposed placing her on staff as Instructor of Medicine, allowing co-participation in laboratory projects with Dr. McCune, her heart pounded with excitement. Then, by her own account, she did something "dumb" by inquiring about salary.

"But I thought you knew your salary wouldn't come from Columbia University. All we can do is offer the official appointment and temporarily waive medical papers needed by the State of New York. I'm sorry we can't offer money, but budget proposals for the year have already been accepted."

Crestfallen. "Of course your budget is settled for the year…. What a silly mistake! Where do I apply for a stipend? I don't want to sound naive, but I'm not familiar with procedures here."

"I suggest you see Dr. Farmer Loeb at the Emergency Committee in Aid of Displaced Foreign Physicians. But I assumed you had already done so and informed him of our discussions. I hope it won't cause a problem now, but I'll be happy to explain to Dr. Loeb what we've proposed here."

She was angered by her own stupidity. Somehow it was always bureaucratic details that tripped her up. As usual she had bull-headedly plowed ahead, never bothering to inquire whether there were rules which needed following, and "independence" once again had been her undoing. Though she excused herself for not knowing hospitals expected you to arrive with your own bundle of money, it wasn't as easy forgiving herself for appearing foolish in front of McIntosh.

By the time she saw Dr. Farmer Loeb the following morning she was feeling more conciliatory toward herself. Clearly he was impressed, and she, relieved not to be reprimanded for breach of procedure, deduced that at least for Loeb she had saved one step in the process of handling too many refugee doctors. But when he advised her about procedures for getting medical license and papers in order, she again pronounced bureaucracy preposterous.

"You will need references verifying activity as well as performance from the earliest years in medical school to present. If I were you, I would examine my papers tonight, find out what's missing and write department heads, first in Germany because things are so chaotic there, then follow with your year in England. Once that's complete come see me again and we'll proceed with forms for Albany. You'll need an examination in the English language. In the meantime, I'll inform Dr. McIntosh of our meeting and let you know what happens."

Tonight she would write Hober and other professors, hoping for quick response, but who knew how they would react? No doubt she would take high marks from Rosenblum, especially after she relayed compliments from her interview with McIntosh.

In the end, the muddle in Germany probably worked to her advantage, since both McIntosh and the State of New York understood the difficulties in presenting a complete medical portfolio on demand. As in England, she enjoyed unconventional latitudes, and two days later, without papers or verification, Dr. Hilde Bruch began working with Dr. Donovan J. McCune in the laboratories of Columbia Presbyterian Medical Center.

Anxious though she was to prove herself, she soon discovered the old confidence was no longer there to command. Instead, confusion reigned on turf where ground rules were different. In the lab, the first sodium analysis had gone slowly, her movements lethargic as motions in a dream, but McCune was patient. Then later, during a review of old cases, she redeemed herself with a diagnosis which in his words "demonstrated marvelous clinical training."

She wore a bright "American smile" to work, pressing herself not merely to demonstrate her capabilities, but to exceed all expectation. With mountains of new material to assimilate, discipline and organization were essential. Appointments, professional and social, crammed her calendar. To save time on transportation, she left Congress House, and with her eighty dollars per month stipend leased an apartment at Bard Hall on the University campus, where she received Uncle David and Aunt Celia Kaufmann, newly arrived from Nebraska, as her first "housewarming" guests.

Finally the first letter from Germany arrived. Mother described business as so poor she and Ernst were considering giving up. "Also, I haven't been myself lately. Can't say why, just that my usual energy isn't there." Her concerns extended to Kurt, whose apprenticeship at a department store had abruptly ended. Would Hilde see if she could find something for him in America? Nearly anything would do, since he was strong, willing, and so conscientious about his English studies that language would not be a hindrance. She had requested the same of Erna, but everyone knew that those emigrating to Palestine were having a hard time. Though Kurt was studying Hebrew and had entered a Zionist agricultural training program, she wondered how he would manage there. She believed things were a lot different than Erna's semi-optimistic letters indicated.

At first, Hilde considered sending a telegram, because if Mother were ill she had to know. Then, rather than cause alarm unnecessarily, she decided in favor of a newsy letter describing happy outings with Celia and David. A show at Radio City Music Hall and a lecture, "Russia as I Saw It," had enchanted all three, which later they had discussed in great detail while strolling through Central Park. "A memorable sight, Central Park South with the rocks lit up from inside out," wrote Hilde. On another occasion they had motored through the Holland Tunnel to New Jersey visiting a brewery there and sampling free cold beer before returning to New York via the George Washington Bridge. "Magnificent structure, and one of these days when my feet are up to it, I will *walk* across it."

She promised to scour the city looking for job opportunities for Kurt and to ply Uncle David for suggestions. "Please write and let me know how the business goes, also your health—it is hard to be so far away."

Hilde's cheery news combined with improving conditions in Duelken apparently did the trick. Mother immediately answered that she had found a buyer for one of their pastures and that Kurt was temporarily working in Duisburg readying himself for possible emigration to Palestine. Regarding Hilde's job coup, she expressed amazement. "It is hard to believe you found work so soon and your career has taken off like that. I hope it reaches the skies. I know you will need to work hard, but you want to show them how much you learned."

So, thought Hilde, things are slightly improved, but what does that signify? You needed distance to gage the barometer accurately, to understand that sporadic bursts of fair weather were not unlike the temporary remissions of a serious disease, deceptive variations in a prognosis which overall didn't change. Still, she too welcomed the brief glow of Indian Summer blunting November's chilly promise of winter.

Not that the frantic pace of her own life allowed time to dwell on Germany. Days flashed by on an agenda anything but routine. Only her faithful log notations kept activities unscrambled: "Morning, newborn ward; afternoon, animal lab with lunch on roof garden (must have met a half dozen people—wish I felt more secure with names and faces), dinner in the Intern's dining room."

Though still not allowed to participate, she had come a long way toward understanding clinical discussions. Her analyses were also improving, if impeded somewhat by a natural clumsiness. The one thing continuing to hold her back—since it was at the very heart of everything she performed, yet not a part of her training—was statistics. The fact was she had never even heard of this subject until confronted by it in McCune's lab. To complicate matters, McCune, tolerant of most things, was finicky to the point of obsession about the compilation and tabulation of numbers.

In order to formulate her findings, she requested private working space and was granted desk privileges in the corner of a rarely used classroom on another floor. Here in this funny office she passed many hours trying to make sense of figures, and where her conscientiousness did not go undetected by pathologist Dorothy Andersen, also located on the same floor. Soon the woman renowned for work on cystic fibrosis was offering assistance, eventually becoming Hilde's "sounding board" for interpreting the statistics of her basal metabolism studies.

Despite the guidance of friends and colleagues like Andersen, pressures on Hilde increased, and in the excitement of assembling data it was easy to ignore twinges of homesickness and self-doubt. Her antidote to all problems was work, work, and more work, weekends not excepted. Social events, though pleasurable, were geared to learning more about the new country, and with great satisfaction she noted some of these extra-curricular activities:

> Thursday: Dinner at Waldorf Astoria, 850 guests in the big ballroom. At our table, Mr. and Mrs. Borg, her cousin and husband, Dick. Cocktails, long speeches, good music. Got a little tipsy, hope no one noticed. Home with Borgs at 1:30.
> Friday: Evening at Dr. Andersen's for a real American dinner, broiled steak, hubbard squash, popcorn. Elegant apartment, wonderful humor—Happy as on board ship. Left after midnight."
> Saturday: Dinner with Kendalls at Bard Hall—Lounge not private enough for conversation—made date next week to see a movie.
> Sunday: Called Carmel Finkelstein to walk across George Washington Bridge. Evening concert at the Beethoven Society: Friedrich Schorr, Wolf and Brahms—trio of flute, alto and harp. Beautiful.

In rare scattered moments salvaged from the rigid schedule, she indulged herself with reading, fiction or non-fiction, English or German, while into the wee hours of morning she answered mail, condensing her busy life into a few sentences, punctuating them, "I'm fi-i-ine...." November brought special news which she immediately conveyed to Mother, believing it sounded even more impressive in translation. "Today in the university mail I received the official document appointing me Instructor in Diseases of Children in Columbia University, by authority of the Trustees.

Later this week will be my first Thanksgiving here, which I will spend with the Borg family. This holiday makes me feel humble. I have every reason to be thankful to America."

Just days after debarking the *SS American Trader* in New York, Hilde had written Jack a full report of initial activities and impressions of the city. While she was unable to pinpoint specifics regarding job opportunities for him, she felt chances would be improved by personal interviews and a first-hand check of area hospitals. After all, what worse could happen than that they would have a nice visit together?

But as always, obligations to Mother Schloss and salary came first, and Jack's reply left little doubt as to mood. "We will have to wait awhile with our rendezvous, if not for the 'miracle,' at least until I'm better off. You wouldn't want to see me now, anyway. In this state I'm no good to anyone. Even if I could steal enough money for the trip, I couldn't spare the time. Here, I'm always in jail, suffocated by routine work."

Hating the tone while admitting its logic, she would not blame Jack for not risking hard-earned dollars on train fare for a trip which would likely prove a wild goose chase. She had been premature in her suggestions and expectations and now had only herself to blame for hurt feelings.

Once her own appointment at Babies was established, however, she felt optimism more justified and wrote that the same stroke of good fortune might just as easily hit him. Although his answer was immediate, it was as negative as hers was positive.

"I'm returning your good wishes, glad everything has worked out so well for you. Thank you for your concern, but in thinking it over, I come to only one conclusion, that I am far too miserable right now to let anyone see me. Again we must put our meeting on the back burner. Be content with your wonderful new position and try to forget my gloom. I think you were right with your first impressions of America, though for me it was different, and you mustn't imagine the mood I was in during your visit to Boston is rare. It is constant, and comes from the dark side of my nature."

He signed off, "Let me hear from you," while she wondered what earthly reason she could find to do so. Wouldn't it be better to end it now? Didn't she owe herself a fresh start, and wasn't it just possible that descriptions of her own successes only exaggerated Jack's failures, contributing to his depression? Even now it was difficult to determine where truth lay, whether Jack was victim to the exploitation he claimed, or whether such demons were of his own making. Regardless, if there was one thing Hilde had learned from her early weeks in America, it was the importance of appearing "fi-i-ine," and she knew Jack was doomed no matter how well he performed in the workplace should he persist in revealing only the "dark side of his nature." Americans had no time for it. Still, she could not or would not abandon him.

A letter from Erna sending March 11 birthday greetings took her by surprise. Of course, that was the day she would turn thirty-one, which also meant on the 23rd Mother had a birthday. She must remember to send a letter. Where had the years flown, or for that matter, where had so many days of winter gone? Glancing at her calendar log for hints of last month's activity she was unsettled to discover blank pages instead of entries, although according to her disposition, "a lot" had happened. Trying to reconstruct these now indistinguishable lost days proved frustratingly impossible. Only a single incident in the lab stood out, even now painful to recall.

Invariably one or another of her fingers wore Band-Aids, and for a while these white strips were the subject of wise-cracking, her "badges of courage." Then, when it became obvious she was merely clumsy, the joshing stopped while eyes tactfully turned away. However, on one particular occasion, she had ripped a glass stick across her left index finger creating a catastrophe impossible to ignore. A worried McCune rushed her to Dr. Schillinger in surgery, though not before blood had spurted everywhere. McCune was compassionate, calling her "a good sport" while Schillinger administered local anesthesia, skillfully repairing the damage with seven sutures.

Thoroughly frightened herself, Hilde had made light of the incident by relating a Grimm's fairy tale where a tailor boasting 'Seven at one blow!' because he had swatted and killed seven flies at once was mistakenly credited with actions of bravery. Everything had worked to the braggadocio tailor's advantage, his "gallantry" in the end being rewarded with the hand of a princess and half a kingdom. Jovially, Hilde warned her colleagues, "This was just the first blow, the second soon will follow."

At the time her colleagues seemed amused by her spunk and wit, but in the weeks following, Hilde thought she noticed a definite "coolness" in McCune. When she could no longer stand the estrangement, she confronted him the only way she knew how: point blank. She said she had noticed tension between them which she calculated to be 99 percent the result of her accidents or miscalculations in the lab.

Caught off guard, McCune had little to say except that yes, he too was under the impression she was clumsy and that it might be interfering with research. That was all, but considering the words had been mostly her own and the confrontation had taken only minutes, it was surprising how even now his reply stung.

By the time McCune had stopped by her office later to apologize, she had already made certain resolutions. Vowing to be less accident-prone in the lab, she intended to prove her dedication by expanding personal working hours. As a bonus, maybe the additional time and numbers would help end once and for all the question of sodium content in blood plasma of newborns, which was looking more and more negative all the time.

Simply put, she would get along with McCune because she *had* to, though truthfully it wasn't easy for her collaborating with him or anyone else. She had never been any good at it, preferring always to work alone and at her own pace. Left without that choice, she supposed she ought to be grateful for McCune's discipline and careful instruction. Instead, his passion for statistics was driving her mad, and secretly she accused him of losing sight of essentials.

As responsibility with its corresponding figures stockpiled, she found she could no longer contain them in the laboratory. The numbers followed her home, dancing in her head far into the night. She discontinued logging days, and turned to sedatives at night in order to sleep more soundly and conserve precious energy for the Center.

Always she worked hard at the calculations, placing them in columns, commanding them to order, and while she was quite certain she had accomplished a great deal this past month—McCune seemed pleased—it was peculiar she was having trouble remembering things.

A letter from the ever-despondent Jack this time sounded different, his usual doom and gloom seemingly pre-empted by more urgent needs:

> Stop, there *is* something which could bring me to New York. I have learned they give an English language exam there. You are the expert in this field and have to know some of the details. Where should I apply? Is it Albany? How much money would I need for a trip to New York? I'd like to get as much accomplished as possible while I'm there—anything you might suggest as well as anything I can think of. Among other things, I want to see L. Farmer Loeb, who was formerly Assistant in the First Medical Clinic, Berlin. I hear he is now some big wheel in a committee for displaced doctors. Have you heard of him? In any case, I think you will have no trouble locating him with your connections, and I would be grateful.
>
> Bearing in mind your eternal refrain that it's easy to answer letters "if you just sit down and do it," I will be expecting to hear from you shortly. Also, if you could answer some of these questions I would be pleased.

Not a personal word anywhere, yet after months of urging, it now appeared he would be coming after all. Oddly, it made no difference. Out of loyalty alone she pulled her writing paper from the drawer, supplying the information he requested and extending the expected welcome.

That night her sedative-free sleep was disturbed by images so kindred to some barely recognizable truth that her subconscious was reluctant to let go. Once awake, her practical and scientific self took over and she reached for pencil and paper to record the vivid dream, intending to consult a psychiatrist about it later.

> I have just received an announcement that Schloss is engaged to a very young girl. Confirmation comes in writing which is rose and light blue on cream. I don't remember the text, but am curious and wonder if I know the girl.

I feel very sad and angry, and once again I am on the ship. I know I should answer the announcement. But suddenly I rip it into small pieces and put it into an empty chocolate box. Then I am upset because I can't find a steward. I want to hurt Jack by not acknowledging the announcement.

I stand on deck waiting for a deep perfect wave, and then toss the box in. I watch it being carried further and further to sea. I understand it must disintegrate, but now I would like to have it back.

Later I am somewhere at a party where lots of tables are set up. I have arrived too late and stand at the top of the stairs looking down as Jack dances with the girl. I do not recognize her, but she is wearing a black velvet dress, and now I feel sad only for him, although I, too, am very sad as I awaken.

Drowning

"March 25, 1935: Hilde Bruch, M.D. was admitted to Presbyterian Hospital in a state of deep coma following a self-administered dose of barbiturates." Mute to cause, the clinical statement furnished no clue about seductive forces compelling this desperate action, and energies that spring from the murky depths of the psyche are always open to speculation. Friends and colleagues questioned why no one had recognized signs of depression, wondering if anyone had ever really known Hilde Bruch. Their image of a courageous woman insatiable in her drive for achievement yet bursting with enthusiasm now lay naked and vulnerable to revision. That a person so skilled at forging destiny should juxtapose fortune by willing herself to die seemed nearly impossible.

Only in retrospect did associates reproach themselves for equating achievement with contentment or failing to realize that Hilde's feverish urges for work probably masked other needs. Maybe they should have noticed tension residing beneath the confident pose where depression and terror also fought for control. But if such vague impressions now were present, they were sadly after the fact, and the patient, once recovered from her poisoning, was not offering any explanations.

She revived to confusion, intense pain, and immediate horror that the dreams of a lifetime were lying in shreds. The greatest terror of all was in not understanding why she had done it. A dark, invasive spirit had prevailed at the very time she was achieving her greatest success, and during that brush with mortality she had also discovered the outer limits of her own being. Now, bitterly resentful of these mental restrictions whose existence she had not known before, she rebelled. Drowning in a whirlpool of conflicting signals, she reacted the only way she knew how, by denying the significance of the self-destructive forces even as she wallowed in the wake of their despair.

To describe her as uncooperative is an understatement. Never in her life humbled, she now was confused, frightened, disappointed in herself, and aching with depression. Like a cornered panther, she lashed out at everyone and everything constrictive: the hospital with its endless regulations, the grilled slits purporting to be windows on walls which pressed inward, hindering breathing, censorious doctors disguising judgments beneath blandly smiling masks. It took no imagination to believe she was back in Germany reliving the persecution.

Except this was Presbyterian Hospital, not Germany, and here she would take a stand, passionately fight for her rights, demand to see Dr. McIntosh or Dr. McCune to learn why she was being holed up and not allowed use the bathroom. She insisted on getting the names of all doctors responsible for treating her like a baby so she could order them off her case.

While doctors contended with frequent temper tantrums and unreasonable requests, it was nurses, irritating by their very availability, who bore the brunt of her anger. In or out of her room, whispering in hallways, they were ever-ready targets whose attentions she viewed as either fawning or presumptuous. The need for privacy so intrinsic to Hilde's nature had been seriously violated by the ward's rule of keeping patients' doors open at all times. So humiliated and enraged was she by the constant exhibition of herself to anyone walking down the hallway, she forced her doctors to waive the regulation. This only served to exacerbate frustration when nurses invariably out of habit forgot to close her door, while she, in her extreme displeasure, bellowed sharp accusatory words after them.

Indeed, she did confer with the Doctors McIntosh and McCune, who assured her that her position at Babies was not at risk, but what she surely needed now was rest from the work and treatment for exhaustion. She disagreed, protesting vehemently that she was in the middle of something too important to disrupt. After all, she was "fine."

But this time the arguments fell on deaf ears, as resumption of her position at Columbia was made conditional on "a leave of absence for the restoration of health."

Following one week at Presbyterian she was transferred for long-term recuperation to the Bloomingdale Hospital, a psychiatric institution in White Plains. Given no choice about confinement in any case, underneath the bravado was a person still shaky and uncertain enough to recognize the necessity of additional treatment, even gruffly accede to it, though the action was one she dreaded.

Perhaps some of that fear had to do with recurring impressions from the past, oppressive images like the *Verruckten* of Suechteln waiting out hopeless lives. Like those poor souls, she, too, was isolated and wondering who would come to rescue her from behind gray stone walls.

She had made it perfectly clear that any communication with family overseas would constitute an infraction of ethics she would not tolerate. Only one person, Uncle David Kaufmann, was notified of the illness, and that only because legal regulations required it.

When informed, the Grand Islanders were more stunned even than the New Yorkers had been. David and Celia, fresh from memories of their Eastern vacation, remembered Hilde's bubbling enthusiasm. Cousin Bruno, her longtime childhood friend from Kempen, recalled a self-assured girl who had developed into an ambitious woman, rather headstrong, but certainly not given to "moodiness." None could offer the faintest explanation for why things had changed so dramatically, or whether the patient once recovered would ever again resemble the Hilde everyone knew.

Though David was at first struck dumb by descriptions of a poisoning so grossly out of character, he gradually began to recognize a familiar strain when physicians over the telephone complained that their patient's ornery behavior was interfering with treatment. Greatly relieved, he assured doctors he would get Hilde's cooperation, then passed the good news on to Bruno and Celia, who laughingly agreed that Hilde could not have changed very much if she was still calling the shots.

David, unable to come to New York to handle financial matters or sign admission documents, proposed sending a business representative as proxy. But Hilde was righteously horrified about placing her life in the hands of a stranger, and scribbled a note, which received immediate reply two days later when Uncle's spokesman, himself, hand-delivered it:

> Just received your letter from April 6th, and I gather by my reading that doctors get sick just like other people. I do not doubt that your physicians have only your own welfare in mind when they prescribe quiet and relaxation, a furlough from work. All reports confirm that you are well-liked at Presbyterian Hospital, and that everyone is working diligently toward your recovery. Remember, you are the patient, and a patient does what the doctor tells her.
>
> I trust Mr. Rentlinger completely. He has been my partner many years, and has 26 years experience in the business. Any arrangements he makes are okay with me. Try to be an "A" patient as you were an "A" pupil.

At Bloomingdale, Hilde perceived Time the constant enemy. Bad enough to be missing out on ordinary activity and conversation, but what really made life unbearable was that a loathsome hospital hierarchy now controlled her life. By mid-May, she had had enough, and penciled her displeasure to Dr. McCune:

> I had so hoped you would come up on Sunday just to demonstrate your new car—and to have a look at what kind of a half wit I am being taken for. But you are not the only person who did *not* turn out: as a matter of fact, nobody came to see me at all. And so I feel utterly lonely. But that is not the only reason I feel unhappy here. I really think six weeks of being kept like an idiot is more than an average person can stand. And I have not been outdoors now for nearly seven weeks. I think the trees I can see from my window are beautiful. But that is not enough to satisfy my longing for exercise and fresh air. So I have decided to leave on Saturday next (5/18).
>
> Now I would like to ask you a great favor. I am a bit afraid to leave quite by myself. Wouldn't you like to come and take me to N.Y. in your swell new car? I think it would be lots of fun, at least for me. And would you kindly ask Goetsh to drop in at Bard Hall to get my room ready for Saturday? It was rather in a mess when I saw it.
>
> I am not quite sure whether I shall be able to work straight away; but I'll be alright in a week or two.

Hoping things are getting on well with all of you, and with best regards to Mrs. McCune and Goetsch and the 6th floor.

I remain,

*Your Hilde, das alde schaf
(the old sheep)*

Some old sheep. Of course, she wasn't pulling the wool over anyone's eyes, and she was not in charge to make it happen, so she remained at Bloomingdale yet another four months. It was not time wasted. Though temporarily waylaid by depression, her scientific mind relentlessly searched answers, and this time it was neither to the fearful *Verruckten* nor the hopeless catatonics of her medical school days she turned, but to herself.

Wishing to know more about the mystery within herself which had generated so much pain it had nearly claimed her life, she no longer dismissed mental illness as someone else's problem or half-sightedly viewed the hulk of a victim without seeing the person, whole and suffering. She had undergone a metamorphosis, yet having shed the old skin, she still awaited its replacement.

Neither was psychiatry the study in futility she once supposed. Having witnessed them herself, she could verify powerful mind forces pulsing in a dimension not subject to physical law. Nevertheless, she believed these dynamic forces, with study and comprehension, ought to be predictable and controllable.

To pursue such truths, her interests shifted from what had been purely physical to the mental and abstract, but the refocusing was gradual, one in which the strengths of clinician and scientist were never far away. At least for now, the only thing she really wanted was to return to a job in the laboratory where she might again deal with the tangibles in life.

CHAPTER IV

1935 - 1938

New Directions

Autumn leaves were falling when Hilde returned to a brand new work assignment, one which captured imagination and personal involvement as nothing before it ever had. She was asked to develop an endocrine clinic for children, 90 percent of whom were "fat." Here was not the intellectual exercise lab work with electrolytes had been, but a chance to study and treat real patients with disturbingly chronic conditions of overweight. Included in the study, also, was the rare condition, hypothyroidism, (relatively easy to diagnose because of retarded development, sluggish behavior, and often cretinoid features), though it was not to such an obvious problem as this, but to obese children without recognizable deformity she was drawn.

Perhaps she empathized with problems of overweight because they were her own as long as she could remember. Dieting was unfashionable in her youth, though Mother in subtle ways had tried to curb Hilde's enthusiastic approach to food even while her brothers brazenly pronounced such tactics futile by nicknaming her, *"die dicke,"* (the fat one). Now, years later, this young career woman of thirty-one believed she had been more or less successful in controlling the scales, though it had required constant vigilance along with the common sense acknowledgment she never would be "thin."

Hilde had no difficulty understanding the source of unwanted pounds. They came from eating too much, from food, plenty of it, of all variety, and in her own case, a special craving for chocolate. Naturally she would not be slim as long as she loved eating so much. Oh, but here at the clinic she was hearing something different: fat children saying they ate little or nothing with parents corroborating the claim. Since this was an "endocrine clinic" and there seemed no reason to doubt the referrals to it, Hilde obediently proceeded, as with the more obvious glandular cases, methodically measuring children's weight, height, and maturation rate.

Gloom accompanied these examinations, since parents, child, and medical staff alike believed puberty would be delayed, growth and development retarded because of endocrine deficiency. How shocking then to learn that tests, instead of supporting current theories of endocrine dysfunction, more often contradicted them. These overweight children, far from being mentally or physically slow, were often ahead of their peers, while maturation rate was more in harmony with children who might expect an early puberty. The great mystery then, was why, without evidence, the medical world accepted them as examples of hypothyroidism or hypopituitarism.

Hilde's scientific training brought confidence to her own findings, so now it was simply a question of discovering where and how errors had occurred and why the medical community continued to perpetuate them. More relevant and personal, of course, were the children themselves—how to develop a program to treat them effectively. If she were correct, the solution might be ridiculously simple: a restricted but common sense diet coupled with increased activity.

While Hilde revitalized her own energies seeking answers to medical questions as these, she remained under constant pressure for funding. Already her fellowship from the Refugee Committee had expired, and in order to remain on staff at Columbia continuing attractive assignments, she needed to look elsewhere for pay. Fortunately, the Josiah Macy Foundation offered a grant which was renewable annually, and for the duration of the obesity studies she would oblige them with regular reports.

That was the professional side. Personal life was dominated by increasing concern for family. With the 1936 Olympic Games scheduled to soon begin in Berlin, it was proving impossible to convince loved ones that past dangers still existed. Pogroms had been temporarily halted, signs banning Jews taken down, while Germany, gracious

Hostess to the World, put on her most attractive face in an all-out effort to seduce guest nations. Hilde was skeptical of the pretty pose and the longer she remained outside her native country, the more wary she became, wondering how to persuade her more trusting dear ones who saw the Olympics only as an important sporting event, while gratefully appreciating that once again life seemed peaceful and nearly normal.

Frustration manifested itself in chronic exhaustion and apathy. Following confinement at Bloomingdale and as part of the recovery program, she had begun seeing Dr. Gotthard Booth, under whose therapeutic care she would stormily remain for five years. Privy to her darkest thoughts, Booth became a lifeline of rationality when moods were blackest. Still, fatigue remained and progress in treatment was not easily demonstrable. Work proved the more effective palliative, since here she could see tangible results, and increasingly she immersed herself in this self-administered therapy, burying her past with remarkable ease the same way she had her breakdown, leaving behind barely a ripple.

As a matter of fact, inquiries concerning her confinement were surprisingly few, possibly because her formidable personality discouraged questioning by the merely curious, while the medical community, once over its initial shock, honored her privacy by interring the incident deep in its archives. To innocents inquiring why on earth they hadn't heard from her in so long, she offered innocuous or ironic reply. Earlier, she might have leveled with Jack, but now when he wrote, "What happened? First I get a disturbing letter from Dr. Schoenheimer and now this mystery letter from you while neither tells what really happened," she retorted paradoxically, "Twins leave a lot of possibilities open!" Interesting that the illness that had nearly claimed her life now provided the insight to clear her vision. Except in her own yearnings the romantic relationship with Jack never existed because he had never been free enough of his own obsessions to care deeply about her or anyone, except perhaps his mother, who was part of the obsession. For better or worse, like it or not, she was on her own, entirely alone.

Family members proved more difficult to foil. Sometimes she hedged, as with Erna to whom she sent a snapshot of herself, scribbling nonchalantly, "I have been sick," only to learn that the explanation wasn't nearly adequate to satisfy her curious sister. Replied Erna, "It must have been a very long illness if you needed that much time to recuperate. We assume you were careless in your lab with poisons, or was it something else? Why such a big secret about your illness? Your picture is funny. In it you look like an easygoing governess, and you have lost a lot of weight. Still you look like a very young girl, and we are happy to have a look at you."

Even with an ocean between, Hilde could sense Mother's anxiety. "The mail has got to be terrible these days. You must know how worried I am because it has been since the end of March that I have had news from you." When the daughter, from her hospital room in Bloomingdale, replied vaguely that she was temporarily "under the weather" but better now, busy with this and that, Mother replied suspiciously, "It is very strange that you write with a pencil and don't say anything about your work."

In the end, Hilde could bear to be nothing less than truthful with the person who knew and loved her best, and to Mother alone she scribbled the word, "depression." Any further description of the illness was brief, down-peddled to include reassurances of waiting job and speedy recovery. But Mother got the message anyway. "I feel terrible that you are in such a deep depression. It is hard for a mother not to be able to help her child. You must have tried to do too much."

Later rereading that last line, Hilde laughed at Mother's "everymother" diagnosis, marveling at the strange, naive wisdom it contained. Certainly it was on target where she was concerned, though it was advice she would not heed.

The Tightening Noose

To understand how things were in Germany, Hilde needed only to measure the mails, and throughout 1936 letters were few. It brought peace of mind at a time when her fevered brain most needed it, allowing her to slip into ordinary working routines. Unfortunately, that interlude was short, and Mother's letters soon began arriving regularly, this time with a difference.

Political triumphs at home and abroad had bolstered confidence and inspired Nazi officialdom to enforce the "Jewish Policy" with impunity. The plan: to wipe Jews out economically, send them packing for good. In rural Duelken, where Jews were respected contributing members of German trade and culture, it was possible as late as 1937

BRUCH FAMILY TREE

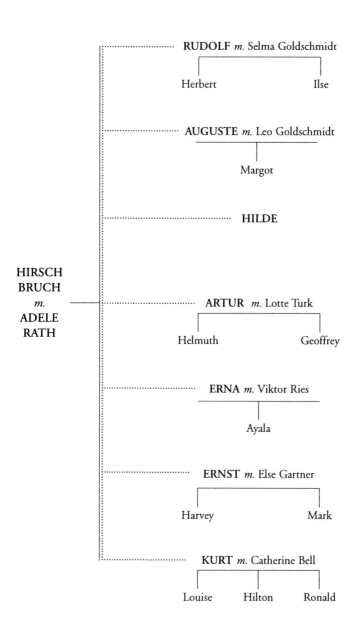

RUDOLF *m.* Selma Goldschmidt

Herbert   Ilse

AUGUSTE *m.* Leo Goldschmidt

Margot

HILDE

HIRSCH BRUCH *m.* **ADELE RATH**

ARTUR *m.* Lotte Turk

Helmuth   Geoffrey

ERNA *m.* Viktor Ries

Ayala

ERNST *m.* Else Gartner

Harvey   Mark

KURT *m.* Catherine Bell

Louise   Hilton   Ronald

Engagement photos of Hilde's parents,
Adele Rath and Hirsch Bruch in 1899

Adele Rath Bruch in 1938

The Bruch children in 1910:
(from left) Ernst, Erna, Artur, Hilde, Auguste, and Rudolf

The Bruch Family in 1914:
(from left) Artur, Hirsch (seated), Auguste, Ernst,
Rudolf, Adele, Kurt, Erna (seated), and Hilde (with doll)

Hilde in 1917, age 13

Classmates at the *Studienanstalt* in Muenchen-Gladbach in 1921.
Hilde is standing on the far right.

1924

1937

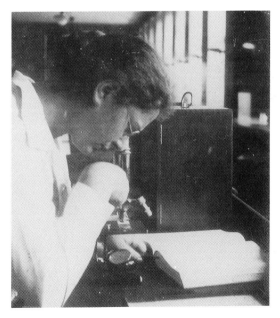

Medical school in Germany, 1926

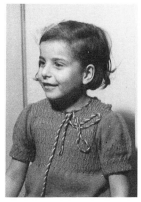

Selma and Rudolf in 1940 (above)
Ilse, age 3 (right)
(Herbert's parents and sister)

Helmuth, Lotte, Geoffrey, Herbert, and Artur (home on army leave)
in England, 1945

(clockwise from above) Ernst and Else's engagement photo, 1938; Kurt in New York, 1938; Erna (later known as Ester), 1936; and, Hilde and Kurt, 1940

Draft of letter to Karl Orzech (1933):

I didn't intend to write, because of course you won't understand, but I can't keep silent about your conduct. After all that has happened to me the past year, the worst was personal disappointment in a person I truly considered my friend. Now that I've been long enough and far enough away from the homeland to think about it without bitterness, the only feeling I have for you is contempt, (sympathy or excuse being impossible). I needed to express these feelings in order to make fresh new beginnings.

for Mother and remaining family members to believe with careful management they could wait out these terrible times in Germany.

Now with financial ruin threatening everywhere, emigration became the only hope. Priority went to young people. The older generation still reluctant to be uprooted, often compromised by visiting sons and daughters in kinder lands. Mother's letters to Hilde reflecting these changes concentrated on the resettlement of her children. Three sons remained on German soil, while the fourth and youngest, Kurt, worked as a waiter in France.

Artur and Lotte Turke had married in June of 1934, and by December the following year, were parents to a son, Helmuth. When Artur's first job, an apprenticeship with the large department store, Cohen & Epstein, Duisburg, folded, he was taken into business by Father's younger brother, Uncle Artur, until Uncle's business was also forced to close. Now, the young Artur Bruchs of Rheinhausen were anxiously looking outside Germany for assistance, and foremost in their thoughts were Uncle David Kaufmann and Hilde in the United States of America.

The financial situation was no better for Rudolf, who still clung to a dying cattle business in Kempen, having settled into the first floor of his in-laws' home to save where he could. Nevertheless, the oldest, most secure and settled of the sons wrote a different-sounding birthday letter to his sister:

> Late, but from the heart, congratulations for your birthday. We read all your letters at Mother's. What have you to say to our loves? They make life worthwhile. We are sending a picture of them peddling their bicycles across our yard—the product of the sale of our pet rabbits. This weekend will be Oma's birthday, and already we are learning songs for the party.

Though the perimeters of their lives shrank daily, out of habit or stubbornness Rudolf and his family adjusted, so it was not until August of 1938 that Rudolf, writing to Hilde from Holland, acknowledged defeat:

> I'm taking the opportunity to answer your letter from a free country. From Mother's letters, you already know how it is for us, but no one can truly understand unless they are involved. For a year we've had

no income, so our little money dwindles day-by-day. They canceled our license to sell livestock and even though we were able to get a year's extension, in practice it has already ended because farmers get fined if they buy from a Jew.

We have no choice but to emigrate. For us, North America would be best, and during the past months we have been taking English lessons. Now we are hoping for an easing of entry regulations, or that you can find us a sponsor. We are told that if you don't have enough money yourself, you can get a co-sponsor. Hopefully they will let us keep our passports, good until October, 1939.

In Duelken, still hoping to resuscitate Mother's business, Ernst stared at pasture lands formerly filled with grazing cattle, now standing empty as sad reminders of earlier, prosperous days when Father had purchased heifers in lots of twenty to fifty head in order to keep local farmers well supplied. Since cattle dealing was one of the few occupations open to German Jews before Napoleonic law changed things around 1865, Hirsch and other Jewish cattle men possessing the hand-me-down wisdoms of generations had honed their skills into art. A farmer disappointed with milk production from one or several of his cows, perhaps needing more butterfat to supply his area, would call upon Hirsch to make up the difference. Sometimes money was exchanged, sometimes a trade negotiated should Hirsch decide the farmer's non-productive dairy cattle could be held and fattened in his own pastures and later sold to a meat supplier for slaughter. Whatever deal was struck, the farmer trusted the cattleman's judgment, and a handshake was more than a promise, it was a guarantee.

How different now with Mother gradually selling lot after lot in order to raise money to buy ship tickets, which under the circumstances seemed only sensible. Painful though it was letting go the past, common sense reminded them that with Ernst having trouble getting rid of even a single animal, pasture space was wasteful expense. Yet despite this depressing business situation, Ernst managed to salvage some pleasure from life.

When a friend from Cologne asked him to be his guest at a holiday ball because he knew this lovely young woman Ernst might also enjoy knowing, Ernst, always gallant, anxious to meet the ladies, promptly accepted the invitation. The girl was Else Gartner, companion to his friend's mother-in-law, who had been hired by the family to occupy endless hours when time hangs heavy and depression becomes too hard to bear. The woman Else watched over had grown so despondent witnessing her children emigrate she had tried to end her own life. Else, possessing a maturity and wisdom well beyond her nineteen years, seemed a perfect choice, for with the woman she was as compassionate and loving as any daughter.

On this particular night, she was given permission to attend the ball in a chauffeur-driven limousine along with other members of the family. Through narrow corridors which were the streets of Cologne the elegant vehicle proceeded slowly so that its occupants could stop to greet friends along the way.

Ernst, traveling on foot and recognizing the family automobile, boldly set his entire six foot three inch frame in front of it, signaling frantically as if life itself depended on getting a lift. But when the door opened and he beheld Else, lovely in a frock of her own designing, flushed and pretty with excitement, he could think of nothing better to do than continue clowning. With low cavalier bows appealing to Else but pointing at himself he whispered breathlessly, "Fraulein, he's still available!" Then just as quickly was off, stepping jauntily, while inside the limousine everyone laughed.

In fact, Ernst was bewitched on sight. At the ball, Else already had a beau waiting, so tradition forced him to sit out the first dance. But after that the evening was his to woo and charm her, to whirl her about on the dance floor until even the most casual observer could see the relationship was serious. As indeed it was, for on March 13, 1938, the day when Else's grandmother turned ninety, her parents in Mayen held open house, making it a dual celebration by announcing their daughter's engagement to Ernst Bruch of Duelken.

Even before they set the wedding date, the couple started investigating possibilities for emigration; their best bet, the U.S.A. Else's relatives living in New York had income to sponsor and space enough to provide temporary housing while Ernst and Else looked for employment in the States. However, when they asked an American processing official how long he believed it would take to reach their quota numbers 15,026, 15,027 he replied, "Put it this way, I wouldn't hold my breath."

Meanwhile, Mother was also becoming restless, torn between the need to wait for her boys and their families to settle and a fear she alone would be left in Germany. When she learned from Auguste that Erna was expecting a child in early March, the happy news confused her. Tentatively she had planned to visit Erna that fall, but now it seemed preferable to wait until after the baby came, when she could be a more useful grandmother. Still the decision was not simple, since who knew how long Ernst would continue overseeing things in Duelken making the visit possible? In the meantime, she responded the way she always did to these events, by knitting and crocheting love into baby clothes, so that in a few short weeks she had assembled enough wee articles to make any baby feel cherished. Even this brought complications:

> This week I sent a package of baby clothes which only cost twenty D.M., but still I worry Erna and Viktor won't have money to claim it. I know how many kind friends you have who can help, so I'm begging you, Hilde, send some money to Erna so she can get the box.

A Medical "Break"

Hilde sent the funds to Erna by return mail, "to baby Ries with all my love, Aunt Hilde." Thrifty enough that small sums posed no problem, for larger amounts she still needed to call upon Uncle David Kaufmann. She had imposed on him often, most recently for a personal loan to establish private practice.

Forever ingrained in memory was the censorious manner in which her promising practice in Germany had been dissolved, although curiously she also remembered those few months of working independently as probably the most personally satisfying of her life. Again she was proposing to spread her wings of independence, only this time she could claim the advantages of being affiliated with the great research and teaching facilities of Columbia Medical Center, a combination of hospital and private practice not possible in German medicine even had she not been stigmatized.

David did not disappoint her, confirming that she could count on $500 to $1,000 to help with office expenses whenever she was ready. Besides needing a larger apartment, she would need additional medical equipment, and so she wrote Schloss to send any instruments of hers he was holding. While they had not been in touch recently, she knew

Berthe had finally gotten to America and that Jack must be happy, relieved of his greatest worry; but by the tone of his answer, neither mood nor instruments were subject to recovery.

> Last weekend, I went through the whole place looking for your things, but only found the few items listed below. You'll have to buy the rest and send me the bill, and tomorrow Mother will pack and send what we have.
>
> Good luck on opening a practice. You are fortunate to get this far. If I had the money, I, too, would settle down, but I'm afraid it will not be possible for me ever to do serious research again. ·
>
> Thank God, Mother is so well-adjusted. Her little love for America makes everything worthwhile. That is the one small plus I have gotten from three years' labor.

Letting his letter fall to the table, she contemplated the refugee's unending sorrow: Either it was a question of job, as in Jack's case, working beneath one's capabilities, or worry for family stranded abroad, as in her own, but everything boiled down to one common denominator, MONEY. She envied Jack for Berthe, he envied her a career, but neither was free of frustration or depression.

Office visits to Gotthard Booth were now as frequent as letters from Europe. She balked at her inability to spare loved ones the unspeakable indignities she was reading about, and Booth, like some false calm in the eye of a hurricane, came to symbolize her impotence in shielding them from the ravages of the killer storm. By January, 1938, Hilde felt herself sliding slowly into a familiar abyss, and in order to personally track her temperaments and prevent another breakdown, she bought herself a diary to record moods, "also past moods, as much as I can recall...."

Three short years of coping with these swings in temperament had at least given her a certain confidence in her ability to outlast them, and she vowed she would never again allow the fantasy of suicide to relieve her of responsibility to herself or family. Work was a powerful and effective antidote, and so amid multiple entries of "very blue," "depressed," "discontented and fatigued," "very lonely," "bad session with Booth," were also small bright spots relating to her studies.

May 4 brought a tremendous boost to her morale. The incident abbreviated in her annals, "presented paper *The Growth Factor in Obesity in Childhood*—drank too much—slept poorly," was in fact an occasion of major importance, when months of painstaking research bore fruit and culminated in recognition.

It had not begun that way. When she and her colleagues climbed out of their car in Great Barrington, Massachusetts, Hilde hadn't known whether she would even be given the chance to present her ideas to the Pediatric Research Society. As a young unknown with low priority, her name and topic were marked at the bottom of the program with an asterisk, "time permitting"—a nasty situation, but she had prepared carefully just in case.

Then suddenly she was up on the podium saying fat children cannot be hypothyroid if they are taller than average and bone age is ahead of schedule, and she had the slides, six in all, portraying children standing next to graphs of their growth rates to prove she knew what she was talking about. By the time the presentation was over and offered for discussion, the room was buzzing, hands everywhere waving. "Of course you are right," everyone proclaimed, "exactly what we've been thinking all along." For evidence they cited personal experiences, one after another, and an hour after everyone had adjourned for cocktails, testimonials were still going strong.

Long after she had retired, the evening's stimulation continued to wear into her sleep. She supposed that in her excitement she had been heavy-handed with liquor, so much seemed to be pulsing in her poor head. Story after story after story flickered and faded like birds flocking to roost, but where would they find rest, these hapless wild things without perches? Another image flashed by: she was a judge witnessing piles of unrecorded information, truth unpursued. Nothing made sense in these semi-conscious states, until suddenly a picture flipped into focus as clear as on the day it happened.

She was sixteen, a pupil at the *Studienanstalt,* where the literature teacher had assigned class members the exercise of selecting a favorite saying from a list of aphorisms. "Choose the one that suits you best," she had instructed her protégés. One student, Hilde Bruch, had immediately flung her hand up, crying out, not waiting to be acknowledged. "I see mine, and it is perfect! *'Schadliche Wahrheit, ich Ziehe sie vor dem nutzlichen Irrtum. Wahrheit heilet den Schmerz, den sie vielleicht uns erregt.'*"

The teacher was smiling broadly. "'Damaging truth, I prefer it to advantageous error,' yes, Hilde, that certainly is you, and I would have been most disappointed if you hadn't picked the Goethe quotation. You see, I too have been playing a little game trying to guess which quote each of my pupils might choose, but yours was the only one I could be absolutely positive about."

The dream awakened her and for awhile she lay musing in the early rays of morning, pleasurably remembering those early school years. From the moment she first saw that quotation, she had understood its special power and significance. Then and there she had adopted it as her *leitmotif,* which even today was providing answers.

Her disposition had not changed through the years. She was still questioning authority when it ran counter to reason, refusing to compromise truth for the sake of orthodoxy. That stubbornness, the cause of so much grief and unpopularity in her past, had yesterday gratifyingly paid off. She alone had taken a stand on issues her colleagues, with much the same opportunity and convictions, had been unwilling to risk.

While the gathering of research pediatricians in Great Barrington was small and informal, likewise its scope of influence, it provided the verification and impetus she needed to stay with her investigations. Already she was preparing papers on medical misconceptions about obesity. One related to Froehlich Syndrome, with the hypothesis that lack of familiarity with Froehlich's original report had resulted in misapplication of the basal metabolism test. The other had to do with the basal metabolism test itself and a misunderstanding about what the test measures. Errors like these needed exposing to explain what had gone wrong in the current treatments of fat children, and hopefully the airing of negative evidence about endocrine dysfunction would lead to new and positive approaches.

Unfortunately, when it came to actual treatment, things proved more complicated. Dieting and exercise, her ludicrously simple but rational formula for losing weight, met immediate opposition. Mothers balked or acted threatened when asked to follow treatment plans, while children stood by looking apathetic and helpless. The basic weight-loss program seemed doomed, but to Hilde this poor mother-child cooperation was itself significant, since it suggested something important was happening between the two principals that food should have such an abnormal emotional hold. She suspected that the failure of these children to lose weight was deeply rooted in complex psychological problems within the family.

Casual observation demonstrated that her obese referrals were unique. Incidents not dramatic of themselves occurred with such regularity it was impossible to deny their significance. In pediatric examining rooms so small there is room only for one chair, it would seem natural for mother to sit, leaving child to stand or lean against the table waiting to be examined. But with mothers and fat children seating arrangements got reversed. When Hilde suggested 'maybe mother would like to sit,' more often than not mother herself defended the arrangement, "It's okay. Let him sit."

These same over-protective mothers often dressed and undressed children ten years old and older, while son or daughter obediently accepted the service. Medical histories taken directly from obese patients were often interrupted by mothers prompting or correcting them. In fact, without testing, it was difficult to believe these children were smart or physically advanced since they appeared the opposite, socially immature, dependent on mothers who apparently encouraged the behavior.

That isn't glands, thought Hilde, looking for psychiatric explanations but finding in everything she picked up a presupposed glandular disturbance. If, for example, she wanted to know why both mother and child insisted the child had grown fat on practically no food, she could read in some journal "the absence of a large appetite is characteristic of glandular obesity," although to Hilde it seemed far more likely the mother was misinformed and unrealistic about her child's needs, or that either or both were simply lying—for whatever reason. Inactivity or similar behavioral disturbances associated with obesity were rarely mentioned in medical journals, but when they were, these too were attributed to malfunctioning glands.

There were other problems: Almost all psychiatric literature of the thirties, like psychoanalysis itself, was exclusively geared to the individual. Family members were important only if the relationship was part of a sequence of events traumatizing the patient; but, to Hilde, interaction of family was vital to understanding the whole problem of overweight, and so she proposed a program of studies which included not only mother and child, but brothers, sisters and father as well.

By studying family as a unit, Hilde and other optimistic staff members hoped to discover certain uniformities, trends from which to develop programs for prevention and treatment. Soon it was obvious their approach was simplistic, that many different forms of obesity existed even in childhood. However disappointing these results, the focus of the study itself was significant.

At long last the child was being viewed as a person, a dynamic being with potential for self-expression rather than a wooden laboratory puppet. In some distorted way, the development of obesity was part of an active process involving child, family and total environment. Hilde sensed it, but felt increasingly handicapped by her lack of formal psychiatric and psychoanalytic training. Frustrated by dead ends where answers appeared to lie outside her scope of knowledge, she decided to leave the intelligent pursuit of them to an indefinite future.

Instead, she readied herself for private practice by moving into larger quarters, at the same time diversifying her extra-curricular activities by taking driving lessons. In an automobile, she showed the same manual dexterity she had in the laboratory handling glass test tubes.

"So what?" she shrugged, stripping gears while her instructor tightened and winced, "by now he has to be used to people doing dumb things like that." Later she recorded, "a little stupid at driving today."

September came to an unexpectedly bright finish with good news from Kurt. As expected, when the Paris Exhibition closed, all foreign workers were ordered out of the country. Fortunately, the manager of the large Paris hotel which had hired Kurt was favorably impressed and recommended him for a job on the Holland/America line, where he was immediately offered a cabin class stewardship on the *Niew Amsterdam*. The luxury ship docked regularly in New York. Always close to the brother she had "mothered" as a baby, Hilde wept tears of joy when he surprised her with a visit.

She had moved to a new location, 35 Hamilton Place, to begin private practice while maintaining her staff positions as Instructor of Pediatrics at Columbia Medical Center and Assistant Attending Pediatrician at Babies Hospital and Vanderbilt Clinic. Regular visits with Dr. Booth continued. Life seemed benignly uncomplicated November 10 when radios everywhere blared news which she interpreted simply but fatefully for her diary, "terrible news from Germany."

A few days later a wire arrived: SOFORT FUER RUDOLF FAMILIE BUERGSCHAFT VERSCHAFFEN = MUTTER. She obeyed the message immediately, telephoning Uncle David for the sponsorship. It was the first of many yellow envelopes she would open precipitously, only to act upon with limbs of stone, because unfortunately the time when it was easy to get people out of Germany had passed them by.

Kristallnacht

November 9-10, the historical *Kristallnacht,* or "night of broken glass," was Nazi officialdom's answer to the assassination of Secretary vom Rath in Paris by a Polish Jewish student. For the perpetrators it meant "spontaneous" demonstrations and arrests of Jews throughout the Reich, an order efficiently and mercilessly executed by the SA. For the persecuted, it meant hours of unrivaled terror, a prelude to even more anxious days and nights to come. Exposed to danger beyond their wildest imaginings, the attack literally changed victims' thinking overnight. Young, old, rich, poor, healthy, infirm, every Jew who still drew breath now desperately sought a way out of Germany.

Even so, depending on where one happened to be at the time, intensity of pogroms varied. "In Duelken," wrote Mother hoping to reassure Hilde, "we have been lucky. Nothing happened here, though it cannot be said of other places. I have seen it." It was true her house and goods were untouched, but were she totally honest, she would have mentioned Ernst's arrest.

"What's this all about?" Ernst had demanded as the thugs grabbed him, only to receive the terse reply, "Jews have no rights. Jews get no answers."

Ugliness in Kempen went unchecked. Rudolf and Selma, her parents and brother, Leo, were huddled around the radio in Rudolf's small first floor apartment, when gangs with clubs crashed through the parlor window and beat down the heavy front door. Shouting obscenities, uniformed hoodlums grabbed the three men and held them, while others scattered toward the bedrooms, Selma frantically rushing after them.

"Please, our children are asleep in there. They're only just babies, please, please don't hurt them."

"What makes you think we're interested in your Jew-brats? Just get them out of here," one of them sneered as she gathered the trembling limbs and fled, leaving behind her the sounds of splintered glass, the thud and crashing of things being thrown.

Outside she recognized the children's table and chair set already in pieces, toy chest with toys smashed and scattered among the shards. Presently being flung from the gaping aperture once an upstairs window was grandmother's wardrobe, lamps, books, and feather bedding, all torn. Terrified and silent, the children clung to the skirts of mother and grandmother, watching first their own tiny room, then the larger world of their parents and grandparents systematically destroyed. Father wasn't here to protect them the way he always did, maybe because he and Uncle Leo and Grandfather had already been taken away.

Indeed, Rudolf had not said "good-bye" to wife or children before being rudely shoved with other Jewish householders into an arresting van. Now he feared for them, and somewhere in the distance believed he heard their voices over the crunching of glass. Within him stirred vague long-ago memories of a day when he was a boy not much older than Herbert: Father had warned him Jews should never be conspicuous, advice the son had prudently heeded all these years.

Rudolf and neighbors were taken to holding prison in a nearby town, but since the designers of that little jail never anticipated so many law breakers, cells were crowded and uncomfortable. Local guards were indifferent, but fortunately lacked the SA's propensity for cruelty. In describing the situation to Hilde, Mother was brief and direct:

> What shall I say? We are in good health, yet very depressed. We can only hope that our sons, brothers and husbands come back to us in good health.
>
> On Saturday we went to Anrath just so the men could see and speak with us. Tomorrow we go again—regulations won't permit us to stay long. Selma is nearly at wit's end, the apartment almost destroyed, and little Ilse again not well, but even that doesn't compare with the future of the men. We can't do a thing now but hope. Somewhere there must be help for us.

Auguste echoing from Holland:

You can't imagine what stories we heard these past days at the border. The worst cannot describe such brutalizing. We ought to be glad they didn't make cripples of our brothers. What can we do to help these poor people? Hopefully they will find freedom with a visa to another country, but they can't get a permit here because we have no work. Do you have connections in the United States? I hope that in your free America someone will be able to help. If they come, it will be with nothing, because those gangsters have stolen their last penny. Please write as soon as possible.

In New York, Hilde frantically looked for ways to speed emigration. Remembering a woman on staff at Babies whose father was a former congressman, she wondered whether he would vouch for her to expedite matters in Stuttgart. Indeed, The Honorable Schuyler Merritt of Stamford, Connecticut, did what he could by writing the Immigration Department and Secretary of State on behalf of Adele, Rudolf, and Ernst. The result came several weeks later in the form of a pamphlet containing information about United States immigration laws which Hilde already knew by heart, also a copy of Merritt's letter along with the State Department's response:

> There is no way whereby quota applicants may be allotted numbers out of their turns, since to do so would be according them a special preference for which the law does not provide, and moreover would be unfair to other applicants who are awaiting their turns in the regular order and who are likewise anxious to effect their early entry into this country.

Since it was another two years before she could file for citizenship to attain "preference" status, continued effort along these lines seemed hopeless. Yet hope dies reluctantly. Mother heard that U. S. residents with an income of $100 per month while awaiting citizenship could file to receive immigration rights for relatives. Sure enough, when Hilde scanned the immigration pamphlet she found a short, nearly unreadable blurb about Form 575 entitled "Application for verification of last entry of an alien for use in connection with the issuance of immigration visas to relatives." But nothing in the paragraph indicated she would actually receive preferred treatment, and the only result of her efforts was a token postcard arriving several weeks later from the Department of Labor.

With quota regulations equally prohibitive, the countries of Western Europe were also turning away masses. Lacking hope for early admittance to traditional sanctuaries, desperate people sought temporary asylum in exotic-sounding places like South America, China, and Africa. Possibly the only thing these countries had in common was an abstruse set of regulations intelligible only to the bureaucrats who wrote them. When Mother complained she was spending most of her time running from office to office, she wasn't exaggerating. "Never in my wildest imagination did I expect such a runaround," she repined.

To insure the émigré not become a liability while awaiting a permanent home, concerned transient fostering nations investigated their financial resources. Most required visas, but all wanted cash deposits. Jewish families did everything humanly possible to acquire sponsorships and money, pooling livelihoods in exchange for cash deposits, visas, and ship tickets for Rhodesia, Cuba, Brazil, Trinidad, Ecuador, anywhere an opening should occur. The result: Mass over-booking in every and all ports.

To avoid frustration, speed was essential, and for Hilde's family nearly impossible. Before anything could be settled, cash on the line was necessary, which meant corresponding with David Kaufmann, explaining situations, obtaining permissions and monies either directly or through Hilde. By that time, ships were filled, ports closed.

Artur had luckily escaped imprisonment during *Kristallnacht* and was presently awaiting confirmation from Trinidad to sail March 11. "Your birthday, Hilde," Lotte reminded her, also explaining how Uncle David had earlier made $300 available for Artur's emigration to Colombia, but by the time he received his answer the border had already closed. Now Artur wanted Hilde to get the money from Colombia released for deposit with Trinidad instead, and additionally Lotte wondered "would it be possible to get another $300 so I could go with Artur? The money goes back to you when we leave the Island, and I would be so happy and grateful."

To save precious time, Hilde thought she could beg $300 from hospital friends and ask reimbursement from David later. Earlier she had tried to solicit funds from Gertrude Borg. Wrote Gertrude, "I feel terrible to have to refuse, but there are so many demands upon me that

I cannot at this time do more. Unfortunately we have relatives who are completely dependent upon us."

While Hilde felt awful placing her good friend in this untenable position, knowing even before composing the letter Gertrude must be buried in similar requests, etiquette and pride counted for nothing when there remained the remotest chance for success. And so, because family was relying solely on her, she continued trudging from bank to bank with David's money, obeying each desperate new instruction as it arrived, praying each time for the miracle which would spring the trap.

Instead, successive letters brought progressive heartbreak: Realizing that each delay also jeopardized the safety of their children, her family now was concentrating efforts on finding a safe haven for the little ones. By December 15, Lotte wrote with some satisfaction that she had been contacted by the Cambridge Refugee Committee, which was in charge of placing children in private homes.

"We would be so happy if our Helmuth could find a good home. It would be hard to let him go, but would relieve us of tremendous worry. We would gladly entrust him to you, dear Hilde, or perhaps one of your colleagues would be willing to care for him. Tomorrow Helmuth will be three years old, and he is a big healthy boy." She postscripted the letter with height, weight, and birth date.

Hilde wept. She, too, was in touch with the Cambridge Committee and every other refugee organization she had ever heard of. Then to make absolutely certain nothing was overlooked, she had checked addresses and written to everyone she had known in England.

Carmel Finkelstein from London was first to answer:

> First of all, worrying or blaming yourself will neither help your brothers nor change the world—nor is there much help in putting one's trust in committees. However, England has been aroused by the plea for the children, who are a universal responsibility. I have sent your Mother a form to fill out, and when she returns it along with pictures, etc., I will do all I can to press it through, as my sister-in-law is secretary of one of the organizations here. If you let me have the address of your sister in Holland we can perhaps work together.

Alice Tallerman claimed she had spoken with people at Woburn House, another organization responsible for bringing refugee children to England who "at the moment have so many to deal with that they will not even accept further names unless I can find private homes to take the children." She was sending forms to Hilde's mother as well as the name of an agency in Berlin which "just might be able to get the children out of Germany sooner than the Woburn House people can." Her first priority would be to look for someone to take all three children, but failing that she would try to get Herbert and Ilse taken together. "I imagine that your family would be glad to send them over here to good homes, even if it meant separating them."

Else

Jewish families caught behind enemy lines were too preoccupied escaping their trap to complain about conditions within it. Mother attended a busy schedule.

"It's so terribly difficult," she wrote Hilde afterward, "the children have a chance to go to Holland, but with the borders closed they can't return here and Selma is being short-sighted and sulky. She says her parents can't bear to think of the little ones so far away. Lotte is more mature. When I visited them, she was paying for a ship ticket for Artur to Trinidad."

Later in the week Mother hoped to see government officials in Dusseldorf about the release of Ernst and Rudolf, realizing chances were slim since "everyone has the same idea." Because postal regulations and orders changed daily she thought it prudent to mail while she could parcels of household goods to her daughters, a few cherished possessions including a box of embroidered linens for Hilde, but mostly dowry to be stored in the States anticipating the eventual arrival of Ernst and Else. Thus in the reflexive completion of daytime assignments, Mother's time passed quickly.

One day, local families traveling to Anrath to visit their men found only empty cells. Mother was beside herself. Custodians of the local prison claimed they didn't know where the prisoners were taken, but one thing was certain, these petty authorities didn't care. Persistent questioning so frayed their nerves that eventually distraught relatives thought it wiser not to ask.

The day's frustratingly painful experiences were magnified by night, but by dawn Mother's wits were sharpened into indisputable logic. Quite simply her sons had to be somewhere, their whereabouts known by someone. If officialdom wouldn't provide answers, she would find other ways to uncover the truth. Women must remain strong to investigate immigration possibilities, so when the men were freed they would have a place to go. She had heard that anyone holding a visa and ship ticket would be discharged from prison providing he emigrate immediately. While his high quota number prohibited early leaving, Ernst's affidavit might be worth something and certainly it couldn't hurt to inquire about its legal value.

Mother proceeded to Dusseldorf alone, there to consult a lawyer about a deposition for Ernst. The lawyer agreed Ernst had legal grounds for release, but by the time the complaint was transcribed, "Guaranteed dismissal for inmates registered at Stuttgart," it struck Mother as antiquated legal gibberish. Some Nazi was sure to be amused by the ridiculous and presumptuous word "guaranteed" and would no doubt enjoy a hearty laugh before tossing it into the trash.

It came as no surprise either when Else confirmed that nothing had transpired in Duelken while she was gone. Another dead end. But already Mother was examining other possibilities, and after supper drew her wrap from the wardrobe proclaiming, "I can't just sit here knitting and waiting. I must find out what has happened to our boys."

"I've been thinking a lot about this. Even though we aren't allowed to associate with Gentiles or go out after dark because of curfew, isn't it lucky, Else, our boys are so well-liked that friends and former business associates are sure to understand what we are feeling when I tell them that Rudolf and Ernst are missing. Farmers and townspeople know me so well I'm certain they will trust and tell me if they know anything."

"What can you be saying? That you are going out now, Mutter?" inquired Else incredulously."

"Ach, dear child, I haven't lived so many years without learning something. Believe me when I say no one will see me. After all, it's not just of myself and you I'm thinking, but of our Gentile friends as well. It would be dangerous for them to be caught speaking to me, and I certainly don't want to cause them hardship."

"What do I say if someone comes to the house while you are gone?"

"Don't let them in, Else. We will devise a special knock so you will know when I return. Otherwise, you mustn't open the door under any circumstances. Do you understand? Stay in the dark until they leave. No one even knows you are here." Then seeing such a worried expression in a young girl's eyes she added hastily, "Oh but Else, you mustn't think anything will happen—nobody ever comes here."

It was dusk when she emerged from the house, pitch dark, nearly ten o'clock, when she returned without information. In succeeding evenings routinely as the sun fell, Mother reached for her winter coat and, as further protection against the stormy weather of late November, draped a large dark woolen shawl about her head and shoulders. Else watched her fussing over a large bag. What did she put in there? But she never revealed its contents, confirming only their secret signal before wandering mysteriously into the night, where she huddled in shadows, shrouding herself in darkness under the eaves of houses.

What were they thinking, these people in lighted homes, seeing a strange dark figure with anxious eyes, whom finally they recognized as a familiar face? None asked her into their parlors. Of course not, it was *verboten,* but anyway she would never have agreed. Instead she remained on their doorsteps, lurking like a beggar in the black of back entrances, speaking in hushed confident tones.

"My boys have disappeared. You remember Rudolf and Ernst. I thought because Ernst and your son did hurdles together, Hans might have heard something. Of course I understand you have not seen Rudolf since he moved to Kempen. Oh, but thank you. Thank you, anyway. And now I have to be going."

These strangely dignified encounters—repeated nightly and always without success—lasted a week, until on November 25 a postcard arrived from Ernst, posted "Dachau, Block 21," briefly assuring mother and fiancee he was in good health. He said he was allowed to receive fifteen D.M. a week by money order, but the address on the outside envelope needed to be exact. Personal communications could only be returned in kind: A postcard could be answered by a postcard, a letter by a letter and so forth. Thus was it signed, "Best Regards and Kisses, Your Ernst."

A few days later, similar words from Rudolf to Selma. And while it was a relief knowing the men were all right and located in Dachau, their release from this distant prison seemed now more remote than ever. Of these days Mother wrote:

One day is like the next. Nothing changes except for the worse. Twice we sent Rudolf and Ernst money in Dachau, but still haven't learned when they'll get out. Selma heard a rumor that all the men will be home by December 6, but you know how that goes. We cling to a straw when it contents us. Anyone who has a visa and ship ticket is automatically discharged but must leave Germany immediately. For our boys I don't see how this is possible. Auguste believes Holland would take people temporarily, but nothing is organized and all goes slowly. The longest wait is always America.

Claims made on me are so great I'm in the process of selling our house. I must try to purchase ship tickets for Artur and Lotte. Selma's financial situation is such a catastrophe that if Salli Rath hadn't given them money they would all be living in the street. When I brought Herbert and Ilse home with me this week, I needed to buy them underwear. They are dear well-behaved children, and I want to keep them here as long as Else stays. It seems to do them good and relieves some strain for Selma. She has to endure a lot.

We've received notification from the hostel in Holland that they can take Herbert and Ilse soon, which means in a few weeks we will soon be taking them to Koln. The difficulty still comes with Selma because she doesn't want them so far away, but I told her she had to. You can understand what it means to me, but I'm strong and will continue to be. Only the thought that it is for the best makes me go through with it.

Ernst

Nothing to indicate December 6 should be different, but on this particular day when the doorbell rang, prompting Else to tentatively open a shutter, there stood her Ernst. Squeals of joy, Mother running from the kitchen, both women fussing, flinging arms around him, and in the breath of moments weeks of anguish disappearing!

Smiles crinkled his eyes, tears of happiness marked his face, yet something was not quite right. Else, too joyful to notice her fiancé straining to keep her at arm's length, didn't see in those few moments a dark warning passing between mother and son. Whatever it was, Mother's whispered answer was very simple, "I'll open the door." Whereupon she quickly passed through the pantry leading to the rear of the house, and after unbolting the big door used for wagons and cattle, entered the adjacent building known as the "wash kitchen" where she began preparing a fire in the water heating tank reserved for laundry.

Else in Mother's footsteps turned for Ernst, but he had remained outside and taken the long way round, only now entering through the cattle entrance. Bewildered, she called into the wash kitchen, "What's going on in there, Mutter?"

"Ernie wants a bath."

"But why can't he do that in the house?"

No answer, but Mother's expression and forbidding hand signs told Else it was so unpleasant, bathing in the laundry tub was a necessity. Was it fleas or lice or something like that? Else knew nothing about parasites but had heard such things were common in prison camps.

For the first time since his unexpected arrival she viewed Ernst with the eye of an examiner, and putting it mildly, her beloved was a sight. Head shaven, bulky athletic frame grown thin, he stooped and grimaced as he moved, holding his lower side pocketed under the great palms of both hands. Suddenly she comprehended. "Ernst, you are injured!" But he merely waved her aside, entering the wash kitchen for Mother to assist with clothing, leaving Else to wait and worry.

Even after bathing he refused to elaborate. "What good does it do to dredge up the past, and besides, what kind of talk is this for women and children to hear?" However, once Ilse and Herbert were put to bed, he hunched himself uncomfortably onto the sofa and began speaking in the desolate tones of an angry man forever grounded after once soaring hurdles.

Yet in describing the march from Dachau to the train station at Munich, his voice retained a certain pride. "I stood always straight as an arrow walking briskly to hide my impairment, the way Dr. Emanuel told me to," he said, adding that it was just plain dumb luck their family doctor was imprisoned at the same time and officially ordered to attend the sick. "He probably saved my life, but not in the way you think."

Back at his prison block, when Ernst had secretly uncovered his injury for examination, Emanuel had refused to treat it, mumbling that he had seen prisoners shot for less, admonishing Ernst to conceal his bulging abdomen under bulky clothing and under no circumstances to report sick. "You must sit, walk, and stand straight—until you drop if need be. Only pray you are released soon, because if you aren't, you are probably doomed. Even now I won't predict how much longer you can hide it since you are in critical need of medical attention."

Ernst continued. "At the train station in Dachau, we were finally treated like human beings again, but I think it was only because so many people there were seeking us out, giving us money and food, that the guards were forced into good behavior. I have no idea where all those women came from or how they knew on this day we were being released, but I took the names and addresses of those who helped me."

He slumped. "Now the only important thing is to get medical attention. Emanuel warned that the wall of my intestine could burst at any time. He got out of Dachau at the same time and is probably scheduling me for surgery in Koln right now. After that, I have no choice but to emigrate. Before releasing us they stood us in line and warned that our discharge is conditional upon emigration, that we have only a few months to get out of Germany before we are arrested again."

Selma

In Kempen, Selma waited for Rudolf. But the optimism generated by news of Ernst's release gradually died as her vigilance stretched from days to weeks. It was not just the loneliness of the watch that dispirited Selma, but the knowledge that Rudolf's safety and hope for discharge depended solely on her own success in obtaining valid papers and a ship ticket when all odds were against it.

Uncle David's affidavit was a step forward, but still she needed bond money, and then there was the matter of obtaining scarce and exorbitant tickets. Ernst and Else were also trying for Trinidad. To Hilde she wrote, "I am still alone. To live through these weeks is terrible, but we have to be strong. Even though sometimes we want to give up, family responsibility keeps us going."

January 4, 1939: a day planned and dreaded. Mother and Selma, each grasping a child's hand and toting a well-worn suitcase—crammed to overflowing with clothing and favorite toys—boarded the train for Koln. Weeks of practicing happiness for the children's sake had steeled them to the ordeal, and even under these painful circumstances their voices remained reassuringly gentle beneath expressions nearly serene.

"You are going to like it in Holland living so close to Aunt Auguste and Cousin Margot. You'll see. They'll be visiting often and have promised to bring whatever you want," said Selma kissing Herbert.

"And think of so many children to play with! Ilse, aren't you lucky to be in a place where you will be able to make so many new friends. But you and Herbert have to remember to share, sometimes I think you tend to forget that," clucked Oma. And so the placating adult prattle continued as the train rattled along its predestined route, while the children, quiet by nature, sat in subdued silence.

In Koln, emotional chaos, as parents and grandparents relinquished children into the waiting arms of the Holland ladies, who whisked them onto the train. A few tots wept openly, others stared back at their parents dazed, while older children, setting the good example smiled stoically, waving to their families.

"Did you know our children are very lucky to be getting the last transport to Holland?" one woman shouted to Selma after surrendering two small boys.

But Herbert and Ilse were crying now, and Oma had reached into the ample bosom, where marvelous surprises are hidden, to pull forth a piece of chocolate for each, while Selma whispered soothingly, smoothing tousled heads, "Father and I will be coming to get you just as soon as we possibly can. Remember we are never far away, not much farther than Aunt Auguste's house is from ours, and you know how close that is. Only they don't let us visit. You understand that. Still we will write and send you things. Then you must ask one of these nice ladies to write back and tell us how you are. Herbert, you are a big boy now and I'm counting on you to take good care of your sister."

Someone had come to fetch away their darlings, mother and grandmother kissing tear-streaked faces greedily, hugging small bodies tightly, "We love you, we love you, remember that. Give Auntie Auguste a big hug when you see her."

The apple-faced woman with the friendly smile took Herbert and Ilse by a hand, leading them into the crowd, while mother and grand-mother stood on tiptoe. Before disappearing, however, she turned to raise the children's arms in a farewell wave so that once more they had a chance to see this boy of six in charge of his sister, who would turn five in less than two weeks.

Failings

The house in Duelken had sold with unexpected ease, leaving Mother scrambling to dispose of household goods to prepare for emigration whenever it should come. Until now, she had been too preoccupied with getting her sons and their families out of Germany to think much about her own exit; but with Erna handling affairs in Palestine and money coming from the house sale, she supposed her situation was well in hand.

Her one secret yearning was to find a way to take her featherbed with her. Certainly nothing else was worth the trouble. "Wouldn't know what to do with most of it, anyway," she wrote Hilde, "but selling things here is hard when nobody is permitted to buy from us. A notice came last week that we can't send things anymore. Two boxes are back in the Viersen Post Office, so probably it is already too late."

Selma spent most of her energies trying to obtain her husband's release. With the children safely in Holland and an affidavit and ticket to Trinidad in her pocket for Rudolf, the situation was gradually changing and belatedly she worried about herself. To Hilde on January 8, she wrote:

> Since Wednesday the children are in Holland in Bergen am Zee. Auguste received the news and plans to visit them. It was terrible giving up the children without their father being here, but there was nothing else to do. Common sense had to win, and just knowing that the little ones are well brings peace of mind.
>
> Rudolf's affair is coming along. He is already eleven weeks in Dachau, but this morning Mother and I went to the government in Dusseldorf and they told us our documents are enough and that Rudolf will be coming home. Of course, we don't have it in writing, but it was a relief and made the trip home much better. You can't imagine how many trips like this we have made, but we can't rest until everyone is out of the country. I have a ship ticket for him leaving March 31, and hopefully he will soon be here to use it.
>
> Dear Hilde, I don't know what is going to happen to me. With the possibility of being together with Rudolf getting closer I would like to find employment in America, but my greatest wish is first to go with Rudolf to Trinidad. If it is possible to go the 31st with Rudolf, could you get me the bond money? Without help from foreign countries it is impossible to leave. Please, please try.

By January 23, Selma's husband was by her side. Other than the frostbite he had suffered during the bitter month of December, he appeared in decent health.

> Yesterday our greatest wish was granted. Rudolf is well and home again. I guess by now you know that Trinidad is closed since the bank returned your deposit. Our plans now are for Rhodesia and we will need 200 pounds. (One quarter of it is assured through the $265 deposit for Trinidad.) The sponsorships of your wealthy friends in the U.S. do us no good because our quota numbers are too high, and we must find a place which will take us soon, otherwise we don't know what is going to happen to us. Hilde, it's not easy to beg, but we need help so badly there is no other way. I have good reports of the children. We sent chocolate to Ilse for her fifth birthday. Herbert was homesick at first, but is better now. It's not easy, but best for the children.

With Rudolf safely out of prison camp, Mother could now in good conscience plot her own exit. Erna's baby was due in two months and Mother was planning to be there for the birth, remaining as helpmate until her quota number for America was called, when she would place herself in Hilde's hands.

Several trunks were bound for Palestine, affairs at home winding down, when she met unexpected trouble. The money from her house sale, instead of being "ready cash," required depositing in a special "blocked security" entrance account. It was no problem obtaining withdrawal permission "for purposes of emigration," but she soon discovered the amount on deposit was not nearly enough to satisfy Palestine's new "capitalist" requirement for an entrance certificate.

Always in their anxious letters, the family reserved space for expressing gratitude to David, knowing without his financial assistance there was no practical hope of escaping. David did not fail them, but eventually the confusion of names and places became too great, and he placed the entire responsibility on Hilde's already overburdened shoulders:

> I do not know whether you with all your diversified knowledge realize that when you say Artur or Rudolf or Ernst or whatnot, all I know is that they are the names of your brothers, but which is which

I have no idea. So just put the money where it will do the most good
and keep it there or use it to your best ability.

It was only when Hilde relayed Mother's request for 1,000 pounds
sterling, roughly $4,000, that David turned her down. "I am not pre-
pared to risk such a sum, since there are many chances that the deposit
will not be released," came the answer, and because David had so often
demonstrated generosity, no one questioned his refusal of this large
sum. But for Mother the setback was devastating, since it meant
starting over, this time without her home for comfort.

Despite protests to the contrary, her sense of displacement began the
day her house sold, as if something of herself were fused into that
sturdy bulwark which had shielded generations from natural adversity,
but now could not weather the transgressions of mankind. Still, hardships were bearable so long as she believed them temporary.
Heartwarming images of Erna and her newest grandchild sustained her
while she awaited sailing orders, and in that same spirit, she had shed
house and furnishings. That she could fail never entered her mind.

Now, instead of confirmation, she had gotten rejection both from
David and from Immigration. The indefinite delay of her reunion with
Erna, along with perpetual worry that her boys and their families also
were going nowhere, combined to set her at loose ends. "I can not take
it anymore being by myself," she wrote Hilde. "I'm giving up the
apartment and moving in with Uncle Andreas. Your next mailings
should go to Kempen."

Others noticed the changes in her. From Kempen, Selma and
Rudolf wrote: "Oma is not feeling well. Maybe you have noticed from
her letters that she is constantly dissatisfied and worried about not being allowed to leave. It wasn't until she got to Uncle Andreas' with all
her junk that she realized she couldn't be happy here and wanted to go
back to Duelken, and because she was so nervous we let her have her
way. Now she is at Uncle Leo's and hopefully will soon be well enough
to return.

The doctor prescribed several medicines, but she is still upset. She
has made up her mind she can never leave and nothing anyone can say
or do will persuade her otherwise. Then she complains about selling
the house. It is a never-ending cycle."

From Auguste: "Mother is always the one who cares and worries about everyone else, and now she is so despondent she waits only for the day she can leave this place."

And from Lotte: "Mother seems to be getting senile. She is afraid the quotas will close again before Artur and Rudolf get out. She is blaming herself for everything that goes wrong and nobody can reason with her. It is terribly sad to see her suffering so—but only the thought she soon can emigrate can truly change her outlook."

CHAPTER V

1939 - 1943

Success

It was definite. Ernst and Else were bound for China. Following tearful farewells in Mayen, they had made connections with the international line in Koblenz, where their train was expected to wind between various cities in Germany and Austria, straddling high the Austrian Alps before squealing for a final stop at Brenner Pass, pausing perhaps for one backward look into the territories of the Third Reich before steaming into Italy.

The newlyweds, somewhat surprised at finding themselves alone in a coupe designed for six, had nonetheless considered future occupants by piling belongings tidily under Else's seat. But as miles continued pulsing by, an unnerving sense of isolation set in, although the privacy was welcomed by Ernst whose dressings needed continual attention and regular changing.

The couple, almost shy with one another, spoke in gentle undertones as Ernst reached for the smallest suitcase to inspect what Else's mother had provided as nourishment, admiring how economically his mother-in-law had utilized packing space by including only what was essential. A large corned beef with slicing knife occupied the middle, while cradling the corners was matzos for the season. Ernst estimated many meals would come out of this suitcase, certainly more than enough to sustain two young people until they boarded ship in Trieste. The corned beef, tenderly wrapped in a white linen napkin once belonging to Else's grandmother, gave off the reassuring fragrance of the Mayen kitchen where it was prepared, and for a moment the young woman's heart ached for her dear parents from whom separation seemed ever more assured with every whistle of the train.

"I know something we can do as soon as we get to Italy," said Ernst. "I have an extra 1.10 D.M. left from our expenses, which I'm going use to buy you an orange."

"Oh," sighed Else, "I'm tasting it already. But Ernie, how can we do that? You know they only allow each of us to take ten D.M. across the border. What will happen if they search and find us with the extra money?"

It was indeed a terrible risk, and Ernst knew it. Their throats were parched, their thirst excruciating, but was it worth imprisonment? Gruesome memories of Dachau flooded his head as he carefully tucked the money into an upholstery niche to direct his full attention to the matter. By now their train was high in the mountains, its sturdy engine climbing, climbing. Already they had crossed into Austria, the Pass now only hours away without a trace of official interest in their where-abouts or doings. Ernst weighed the odds.

Then, without hesitating or showing the slightest hint of regret, he reached into the upholstery cache, opened a window, and flung the money to the winds. "We'll find a water fountain in Trieste."

They were but a few miles out of Brenner Pass when the coupe came under siege. Two uniformed security guards, male and female, ordered them to wait in the aisle while they conducted a search. The pair peering nervously through the doorway witnessed the neatly ar-ranged rows of clothing tossed helter-skelter to the floor. The woman opened a bottle of Else's shoe polish while the man examined Ernst's hair pomade. Since they said nothing about the articles they handled, attacking everything with equal thoroughness, Ernst and Else could not determine whether anything or everything met disapproval. Perhaps it was simply a matter of policy to maintain such dedicated silence while they worked.

The male security officer looked up. "Now your turn," he said to Ernst. The female had already grabbed Else, and both were being es-corted from the train in opposite directions.

Else's heart fluttered frantically when the woman marching behind gave her a purposeful shove indicating she must get off the train. Was this an arrest, and would the train simply go on without her? Where had they taken Ernst? Would they ever see one another again? Desperation gave her the courage to ask. But she might as well have addressed a stone, and by now she was being ushered into the station lavatory where the most thorough search of all was about to commence.

It proceeded in orderly German fashion, top to bottom. First the curls, which only this morning she had painstakingly arranged on the crown of her head, were taken apart and one by one examined, then her clothes were removed and searched, and in a final humiliating gesture, the woman's hands extended into the orifices of her body.

Though examination was brisk, conducted with the impersonal thoroughness of a professional completing an assignment, Else felt violated and weak. Evidently she had passed scrutiny, because now the woman was gruffly ordering her to dress, "Better make it fast if you are expecting to board that train again."

Ernst, wading anxiously through garments and toiletries, every few seconds stretching out the window to scan the platform, uttered whoops of joyous surprise when Else appeared in the doorway. Moments later, two trembling young people were clinging as though nothing could part them again. They would not speak of the ordeal—it was too personal—and only after the train entered Italy did they wonder aloud whether other emigrants were also aboard. Neither had seen anyone else searched at the border.

However, in Trieste when they reported to the hotel where they were expecting to spend the night, there was no shortage of refugees. In one large room consigned to emigrants waiting for ships, at least thirty or forty bodies lay sprawled on couches and chairs or had adapted various sleeping postures side by side on the carpet. The sight of this human sea brought gasps from Else.

"Never mind, I think it's time to find our water fountain," said Ernst, tactfully.

Such a beautiful warm sunny day outside, if only thirst weren't so fierce, the balmy Mediterranean climate itself might have sent their spirits soaring. The acrid salt of the Adriatic Sea (would it were fresh!) had mingled with yet another smell, producing an aroma so sweet and magical that, like children dancing after the piper, they were lured into following the seductive scent. At its source on the waterfront, they dis-

covered a fruit and vegetable mart with oranges by the bushel, producing the overpowering but heavenly jasmine-like fragrance.

"I know we haven't the money for it," cried Else, "but wouldn't it
be wonderful to taste one of those beautiful oranges!"

"You mean you'd prefer oranges to real water? Silly girl. Just you
wait till we find our fountain."

"If only we could speak Italian we could ask someone where to go
for water, or maybe something with sign language and pantomime,"
she added mischievously holding her throat and letting her tongue drag
in perfect imitation of a desert derelict searching an oasis.

Now both were giddy, but by the time Else had regained her composure she was quite serious. "Everyone here looks so busy we don't
want to bother them, especially when we aren't going to buy
anything."

"We won't need to," said Ernst, also recovering. "You know as well
as I do that somewhere in this city there's a fountain spouting water
out of little jugs or cupid mouths or something like that. All we have to
do now is find a central square with the statuary all Italians love."

Still inhaling deeply as though smell alone could quench thirst, they
turned from the flurry of the market place to head for the city. Behind
them a woman called something in Italian. Reflecting that the busy
homey sounds of the water front sounded enchanting in any language,
they continued walking. But strangely, the voice kept getting louder.
Finally they turned to see a woman grasping a sack of oranges, energet-
ically racing to keep up with them. While the dark eyes danced, her
entire body seemed to talk. First she pointed at the bag, then at Else
and Ernst, all the while beckoning them backward.

"She wants to sell us those oranges," said Ernst, hesitantly, "but of
course it's impossible." He began pulling at the linings of his pockets to
demonstrate their emptiness. "See?" he said to her, "No lire."

"Ach!" the woman exclaimed, flinging her arms in mock exaspera-
tion, trying to communicate that reimbursement was unnecessary, that
the oranges were her gift to them. "*Complimento,*" she explained
throwing the sack at Else who promptly returned it. Again and again.
Finally, shoving the bag at Ernst, she turned on her heels and scurried
away, hearing profuse thanks. She recognized these two, of course.
Every day refugee wanderers just like them filed by her stand with
longing eyes reflecting the sorrow of ages, though perhaps not quite

like these young people, who for all their troubles seemed somehow untouched. They were so beautiful, so full of love for one another she felt compelled to reach out and touch their hearts as they had hers.

Ernst and Else greedily clawed the rind and bit into the ripe pulp, letting the drink of the gods trickle down their throats. Oh how they indulged themselves in those sweet fruits! Reluctantly, then, they turned back to the hotel where the bodies had sardined even closer for the night. Else resisted. "Who knows what we could catch in there?" she sniffed, wrinkling her nose in the stale air. But Ernst was ready with his reply: "You might as well get used to it right now, Elsechen. Remember, you're going to China!" And so they were. The little suitcase which had provided two and one half days' worth of meals and adventure was nearly empty, and tomorrow they would be boarding ship.

The plan for getting Artur, Lotte, and little Helmuth out of Germany was proving incredibly complicated. Though the long-awaited domestic sponsorship for Lotte and Helmuth had come through, it appeared wife and child would not be permitted to leave so long as Artur remained on German soil. This latest hitch had everyone going in circles trying to meet the London Committee's request for a facsimile of Artur's immigration papers for Columbia, Trinidad, Cuba, or whatever other port he might be seeking. "I'm terribly confused," wrote Lotte, a message echoed by her sponsor, Mrs. Muriel Parsons, writing Hilde from England:

> For some time I have been in communication with your sister-in-law as we are trying to get her and her little son to our home. The permit is not obtainable as long as her husband is in Germany. Although Frau Bruch writes in English it is not always quite easy to understand what she means, and her last letter, received a day or two ago is rather puzzling. Perhaps you can clarify the situation and give me some idea how long it is likely to be before the visa comes along. Frau Bruch says it may be a few weeks and she sounds pretty desperate and anxious to get her husband out of Germany sooner than that.
>
> She speaks of her husband sailing for Cuba. Is there, to your knowledge, any way in which we can help him to get started for Cuba without coming to England, as permission to do that will take such a long time? We have seen people in London and they strongly

advise against applying for Herr Bruch to come with his wife as a married couple for a domestic post because of the delay. It is likely to take two or three months, although it is incredible that there should be so much delay. The suggestion that Herr Bruch should come in a domestic capacity was, of course, only a matter of form to help him to come here in order to get a boat to Cuba.

I hope you will be able to give me some idea of how we can help—quickly. I am so terribly sorry for them and all the poor souls who are suffering so dreadfully and I am so hoping to make these two happy while they wait for Herr Bruch to make a home for them elsewhere. I suppose that is what they also are hoping for.

But however specific their original dreams, this small family would unconditionally have swapped every one for visas and tickets to England, and for once fortune smiled. Inexplicably, a domestic sponsorship for all three came through, and by mid-May Artur was writing to Hilde not from Germany, not from Cuba, but from Bradford, England. Penniless and insecure, wondering whether luck would hold, he nevertheless made the brave declaration, "I promise to get everyone out and vow I will not rest until it is done."

Ernst and Else eventually arrived in Shanghai the long way round. Knowing they had over-paid for tickets, they reminded themselves that ship line personnel were no different from others taking advantage of the refugee's urgent situation. It was only when their ship became attracted to as many ports as a bee is to flowers, they realized they had boarded a cruise ship. No wonder it had cost so much and they hadn't seen other refugees around!

Here was a very different sort of passenger mix, one which included a bejeweled Maharajah dripping with rubies and pearls, whose current heart's desire was making pretty Else part of his harem. His was not a hasty decision, however, for he spent several days eyeing her critically before approaching Ernst and making the offer. When finally he removed his turban, placing it on Else's head symbolically demonstrating the seriousness of his proposal, Ernst thought he had probably collected all the humorous material he would ever need in leaner times to come.

As predicted, the situation in China was primitive. The majority of refugees waiting for papers to other countries lived in a camp, sharing minimal necessities en masse. The newlyweds did not. Because of his injury Ernst was wary of crowded conditions and the camper's existence, and so for one American dollar per month, he arranged for the two of them to live away from camp in a room all to themselves.

Whether conditions were improved by his decision is perhaps debatable, but certainly the couple considered themselves fortunate. Their room's utilitarian furniture consisted of a cot covered with a straw mattress, a table, two chairs, and a shabby makeshift meant for clothing, which they sarcastically called the "armoire." Later, Else's parents would send a cabinet to hold the various articles their children had taken out of Germany for purposes of bartering. The lavatory outside the building was a pail shared by fourteen others, while bathing was a once-per-week family affair in a tub of brownish water straight out of the Yangtze River sometimes with, sometimes without, a cake of soap.

For food, the pair raided the camp to scrounge "soup of the day," something concocted of whale meat, or peas or beans. Occasionally, in addition to soup, the kitchen offered an egg or bread, all of which despite the non-Kosher preparation, they devoured thankfully.

When cash ran dangerously low they sold articles brought from Germany—crystal and linens belonging to Else's mother and grandmother, since most of Else's own lovely engagement gifts needed to be left behind. Everyone knew that taking new items out of Germany was foolhardy and extravagant, since essentially it meant paying twice, once when you purchased the goods, and again when you were ordered to show receipts to pay duty taxes in the exact amount. Duty officers were well schooled in what was new or old, and Else and her parents had packed carefully, making certain, also, they included nothing on the restricted list. There was a time when such excellent items as Leica cameras could be taken out of the country and sold elsewhere, but Leicas and many other German-made items were now *verboten.* So grandmother's crystal designed and etched by long-forgotten craftsmen, her mother's tablecloths and towels lovingly monogrammed to show off married initials, as well as other sentimental heirlooms which had been in the family for generations were now the salable items which would replenish their larder when it was empty.

At first they optimistically pawned things, expecting to one day retrieve them, but soon realized mere sentiment could not compete with food, rent, and medical supplies. Ernst had a way about him which made parting with the treasures easier.

"Ach mein lieben Frau Bruch," he would begin, leaning toward her confidentially while squinting into an imaginary jeweler's glass, "I think I have discovered a flaw here which is ruining your otherwise perfect collection. See how in this vase my jeweler's eye has detected a chip? Now what can you do with a chipped vase, anyway!" Thus did their "armoire" grow lighter, while a disillusioned husband made the following pledge to his wife: "I'll make it all up to you when we get to America. You'll see. I'll buy you a ton of glass if you still want it, and it's going to be a lot better than this stuff."

War In Europe

Hilde, always in close communication with what was happening abroad, jubilantly greeted news that Artur and his family, after innumerable and frustrating tries, were finally safe in England. She was also gratified to learn of Ernst's and Else's arrival in Shanghai. Progress. If only Rudolf and Mother could be part of the exodus, the family might find peace.

During periods of stress, having Kurt nearby provided tremendous comfort, so Hilde never missed seeing him when the *Niew Amsterdam* was in port. Sometimes he brought with him a fellow worker for free meal and banter. Hilde, not wishing to distill a single second's worth of filial camaraderie, refused to court gloom even when the two were alone.

Weeks without word from Mother, then finally a letter addressed to Hilde and Kurt, posted from the sanatorium where Oma had gone because of her depression:

> You both write such satisfying letters, but I haven't had energy to answer. It was my intention to go home, but I have no home any more. That depresses me more and more. I have no work either. If I had my home, I could be busy. Why did I sell so early? How could I have been so simple minded to think I could go to Palestine that quickly. Now I must suffer for all my mistakes. You, dear Hilde, have sacrificed so much for us, I'm ashamed. The dining and bedroom furniture was well worth sending to you.
>
> When Ernst said "good-bye" before leaving on his trip, he suggested it was best I come here, and I didn't care anymore. But then

when I got here and saw all the suffering I got more disturbed. They gave me medicine which didn't help at all but just made me tired the whole day. At first I insisted on going home, but I was so ill most of the week that the doctor thought I'd better stay.

Now I've gotten used to the place. The food is good, the doctor very understanding. It's just that so many things weigh on my mind that the heartache keeps me from sleeping. Having nothing to do doesn't help. You, dear Hilde, can keep busy, and if I had my home, I could do the same. How could I have brought such misery upon myself?

If only I can find strength to start over again and travel this fall. Sometimes I doubt it's possible. Erna sends lovely pictures of her baby. Viktor is an able man. If only they were in America, everything would have been different for me. How much I would like to be with you, I can't put into words.

Artur is in England, Rudolf and Selma will follow soon. The situation in Shanghai doesn't suit me either, but how to wait alone without money in Kempen is a big question. My trunk is on its way to Palestine again. Even so I go with empty hands.

By mid-June, Mother had left the sanitarium and was back in Kempen:

I'm here again, but since through my own thoughtlessness I sold all my things, I'm very unhappy. I have nothing to do. I can't sleep. The small streets, strange people and the whole atmosphere is so depressing. How could I have sold everything and given up my independence? Blaming myself for my sorrow is self-destructive and you are probably asking yourself: How could Mother do that? But nothing changes the result. It is a burden I must carry alone and how I'll survive it, I don't know.

Lotte, Artur, and Helmuth have good lodgings and through my help live comfortably. Rudolf is working. Selma makes flowers and belts. It shouldn't be long now before they go to England. Salli Rath and family are also going. I'm at wit's end. All these years I have quietly made decisions, but now that I should have a good life, there is nothing but trouble. Did Artur write to you that the brother and sister-in-law kept his deposit for themselves? Can you imagine that? The excitement never stops.

I haven't heard from Erna, and don't know if my trunk arrived.
All my things have got to be somewhere, but I still have enough to
wear if I can leave this fall.

Hilde received few letters from Germany that summer of 1939,
possibly because her family believed little of their drab life worth mentioning. Rudolf and Selma still patiently awaited travel permits to
England while Mother clung to a date in autumn when she hoped to
make the quota for Palestine. In New York, Hilde's state of mind was
as turbid as the oppressive city air. "It's just my work is getting stale,"
she muttered to herself, cranking out the latest Macy Foundation
report and looking to other activities for stimulation.

Vacation time almost upon her and with it the need to obtain that
elusive driver's license, her ambitious plans included buying a car and
sharing driving chores with friends while they motored through the
New England countryside. With renewed determination she resumed
driving instruction, resolved to master the road test she had previously
failed. As further incentive to the successful completion of the driver
exam, she shopped early and fell helplessly in love with a '31 Chrysler,
hoping it wouldn't hold the same appeal for someone else since she
hadn't nerve to buy. Fortunately, all ended well when license and car
became hers. Admittedly, she was not nor ever would be a good driver,
but so what? She had done the necessary, and this time even parallel
parking hadn't tripped her up.

Once out of town, winding along the mountainous roads of New
England, troubles seemed to dissipate as easily as city heat. She and the
ubiquitous Carmel Finkelstein, who had turned up unexpectedly that
June, as well as several other friends from the hospital staff, spent
August motoring through lush hills, valleys, parks, ridges, and towns,
examining every rill and dimple with the zest and thoroughness of ex-
plorers. Sometimes they paused a day or two in one of the park camps
to ride horses, swim or hike. They captured the Old Man of the
Mountain's craggy face on film, expecting to drive over Mt.
Washington when Hilde's car suddenly balked in the unfamiliar rarefied New Hampshire atmospheres.

For Hilde, setback was never more than temporary. Even while her
radiator steamed, she began changing into hiking shoes, advising her

passengers to do the same. She had always wanted to hike Mt. Washington, believing it was a little like walking across the George Washington Bridge, a prerequisite for becoming *bona fide* American. Disappointingly, this potential for adventure needed scrapping when one of the party, surprisingly this time not Hilde, fell and twisted an ankle.

Then it was "so long" to a glorious month of carefree relaxation as their troop, with spirits recharged, turned and headed South. Neither the bumper to bumper slow down of returning vacationers nor the wall of hot humid air extending from City to Saw Mill River Parkway could dampen Hilde's memories of those delightful days. Just as well; they were to be the last happy ones for months to come.

GERMANY INVADES POLAND. Huge letters blackening fronts of newspapers everywhere sent people huddling to radios to hear dire predictions of full scale war in Europe, which, in view of England's treaty commitment to Poland, seemed all but inevitable. Since Hilde wasn't due back at hospital or clinic for a few days, she, too, remained glued, half afraid of leaving for fear of missing something, half afraid of staying for fear of hearing something, but ultimately hearing plenty: ominous reports from the Polish front, ultimatums from England and France, and finally, Hitler's lying, self-righteous proclamation justifying the action.

"Hitler's speech—insane," she scratched in her journal. Two days later, on September 3, her worst fears were realized when England and France declared war on Germany. Most certainly this meant the end of Rudolf's English escape route, and since Palestine was under British control, Mother would be affected as well. What of Auguste's family or Herbert and Ilse, two children left to survive in a tiny country soon to be pincered by war? All of them trapped as surely as if a prison wall had dropped around them.

"Today I'm here five years." Her October 3rd anniversary finally came, the date she had anxiously awaited from the day of her arrival, since it meant she could apply for citizenship and begin proceedings for getting Mother out of Germany. She would file immediately, regretful that regulations did not include quota exemptions for brothers and sisters, that she still was powerless to help Rudolf and his family. Forms needed processing and she could expect further delay waiting for the citizenship examination to be given. Calculated by weeks or months, how long before she would actually have the Naturalization Certificate in her hands? She did not have time, and it occurred to her that with citizenship pending she might finally be eligible for preference under Form 575. If not, what was the sense of the darn thing? She would investigate, reapply if necessary.

While grim reports of war saturated radio waves, personal information remained sparse. She wondered how many letters in either direction were actually getting through. Strict censorship of mails made true communication impossible, and with nothing more than a few nondescript statements to cling to, she put up a brave front, convinced no one at the hospital could possibly understand what she was feeling.

Probably she was right. A World's Fair opening that fall in New York City promised to be the latest popular diversion for a populace wishing to avoid war. Hilde, also craving distraction, was particularly captivated by the exhibition of Old Masters there. But if by such activity she found release, it was fleeting at best, and before long she was consulting Dr. Robert Loeb about "a perpetual and overwhelming sense of fatigue."

While examination turned up nothing, disabling symptoms continued, and as a record for Loeb as well as herself she continued logging them: "Mope along—tired. Sleep practically twenty-four hours—depressed. Tired—get nothing done." Again she saw Loeb and again he found nothing physically wrong, as the year 1939 dragged to a close, with Hilde spending what had now become a tradition of egg nog, New Year's day, warm friendships—all the ingredients of a perfect winter break—at Dorothy Andersen's farm.

On March 25th, with Andersen and Borg as sponsors, she took the citizenship exam, but by April of 1940, her health had so deteriorated she checked into Presbyterian Hospital for comprehensive testing. Ironically, it was the same week Hitler was occupying Denmark and invading Norway. Hitler's campaign proved overtly successful, while Hilde's tests were again negative, treatment unclear. Additionally, she wondered if Loeb might be losing humor with her. "I fear he's beginning to think me a hypochondriac," she wrote. Anxious not to convey weakness or incompetence she headed back to work, but had to leave when an episode of dizziness seized her during hospital rounds.

In May, Holland fell. Auguste's family and Rudolf's children were all under the Nazi net, and she could do nothing but speculate in horror. Telegrams to Winterswiyk asking for immediate response elicited none, yet barely had she time to worry about the state of things in Europe when she became directly involved in an incident in her own backyard.

Following the invasion of its homeland, Holland had declared an "arrest on high seas," in actuality occurring in the nearby Port of Hoboken, where the *Niew Amsterdam* was docked. Saturday morning, early, Hilde got the SOS wake up call from Kurt's friend, whom she recognized immediately as a frequent dinner guest. Not only Kurt, he said, but everyone bearing a German passport aboard the *Niew Amsterdam* was being jailed by order of the Dutch government. Hilde, needing to hear no more, rushed to the New Jersey harbor, where by a strange twist of fate, she was directed to the German Consul. Seeing the state the poor woman was in, the official tried to relieve her anxiety with soothing words. "No need to worry, Fraulein, we Germans always stand up for our boys."

But angry-eyed Hilde was having none of it.

"I've seen the way you people take care of things in Germany, and I don't want anything to do with you here in America."

Then, she explained to the ship's Captain why her brother must be removed from the company of Germans who were either outright Nazis or at least forced to follow Nazi doctrine. And she had it her way. The captain discharged Kurt into her custody.

Though Kurt had not entered the U. S. illegally, he wasn't properly admitted either, and a major concern was to get reliable emigration papers and employment so he could not be deported as an economic liability. With the help of a friend, Hilde located a counseling job at a summer camp, and that is how Kurt would pass the summer of 1940.

News from Holland arrived piecemeal, as Auguste experienced it, or more often described it in letters Mother relayed to America. Gradually Hilde assembled a story. Her sister's little family in their small brick Winterswiyk home were so far undisturbed, although with so many new ordinances concerning Jews, who knew how much longer it would continue? About Rudolf's children: Ilse was presently living with a Dutch family who were so charmed by the outgoing little girl that when orders came from the Reich government to send all Jewish children back to parents in Germany, the family had asked Auguste, as Ilse's kin, for permission to adopt her; but in face of the ordinance it could not legally be done. Soon the Dutch family would be forced to surrender Ilse, occasioning a tearful reunion in Kempen where Selma and Rudolf and Oma after two years without her would ecstatically welcome their darling child—to what?

For news of Herbert, Auguste contacted the ladies of the local Refugee Committee, who informed her that her nephew had been evacuated to England. Prior to that, Herbert had been hospitalized for diphtheria. It wasn't serious, but in order to prevent a serious outbreak among the other children it had been thought necessary to isolate him. Auguste, only mildly concerned, would have followed his progress more closely, except that within days of her telephone call, Nazi planes blackened the skies. Even in Winterswiyk, she could hear the distant drone of bombing, and while she was not positive where these attacks were being directed, she could guess it was Amsterdam. Days would pass before she actually learned of Herbert's escape.

According to a committee woman, only hours before German troops occupied the town, the hostel committee had taken a handful of children to the harbor and placed them on a coal barge. Since German planes were dive-bombing everything in sight, it was nothing short of miraculous that in the midst of continuous fire, this small children's transport had succeeded in averting disaster.

Though Ernst was still in no condition to find employment, Else had found a job waitressing. Between this tiny income and Ernst's bartering skills they scraped together enough to keep themselves going. Love and youth and faith in the American dream had provided strength and incentive, but after fourteen months in Shanghai, Ernst and Else were ready to leave. On July 15th they boarded an undersized Japanese liner with an oversized load of emigrants bound for the United States and Canada.

In order to accommodate huge passenger lists, families were separated and arranged by gender for sleeping purposes. Thus the four berths in Ernst's roomette, which might normally have been shared by a family of three, now were occupied by three other men. The same partitioning of the family unit which contributed to crowded conditions also promoted bickering and occasional fist fights among emi-

grants, who against their will were forced to endure each other's undesirable habits. Even the obliging Else had trouble when the missionaries
she bunked with set an 8:00 curfew and locked her out when she did
not abide by it.

Unpleasant as living arrangements were, a more sobering experience
lay ahead in mid-ocean, when out of shear exhaustion the ship's
engines failed. The level-headed Japanese captain spoke honestly about
their chances. The SOS he had sent was for all practical purposes
useless, since ship lanes here were so wide that likelihood of assistance
or rescue was non-existent. His crew was already engaged in making
repairs, but meantime, if they wanted to keep their ship afloat,
everyone had better cooperate and follow his instructions to the letter.
With the ship gamboling about like a top in a maelstrom, no one
needed additional warning. Sizing people by weight, the captain
marched so many to the left, so many to the right, hoping to produce
an equilibrium. In the dining room, chairs were strategically placed for
people wishing to sit or kneel beside them in prayer. In the next days,
while the ship pitched and rolled, praying continued, arguments
abated, and when finally they arrived at Vancouver and Seattle, it was a
far more appreciative group of passengers who debarked.

From Seattle to New York City, Ernst and Else traveled through the
heart of their new country by Greyhound, delighted finally to be unpacking European clothing inappropriate for wearing in China, only to
discover that now the garments didn't fit. Ernst's suits flapped like an
understuffed scarecrow's, Else's frocks went nearly twice around. They
were an odd pair, these two, who at bus stops preferred not using
restaurants, instead wandering off to find water fountains, butcher
shops, and bakeries where they might purchase sausage and rolls.

Traveling through the rich farmlands of the Midwest, Ernst gazed
upon familiar topography, recognizing in the lush countryside the fertile fields outside Duelken, the Rheinland homeland he no longer cared
to remember but was still unconsciously drawn to. "We shall be coming back here to make our permanent settlement," he vowed.

Hilde had been vacationing when brother and sister-in-law arrived,
but was soon back to welcome them. On the evening of August 22,
following her swearing-in for American citizenship at District Court,
Else, Ernst, Kurt and Emanuels gathered at her apartment to celebrate.
By September 3, the citizenship papers had arrived by mail, and by

September 24, Hilde was seeing Ernst and Else off on a train heading toward Chicago where they would settle in the farming community of Aurora.

Ironically and sadly the day following her citizenship vows, Hilde learned from Berthe Schloss that Jack had died by his own hand. How incredible that a person once so significant in her own life had slipped out of it altogether. Only a few years had passed since her feelings for him were ripe with promise, but because of circumstance now were cast to the ages. Though adjustment difficulties were most pronounced in the elderly, where extraordinary disruptions to lifelines made starting over virtually impossible, its reverse was also seen among the young who couldn't find their beginnings. Had Jack been allowed to complete his degree in Germany, perhaps the new world might have been kinder, but with language and cynical temperament also his enemy, it was hard to predict if he ever would have overcome the odds. Asking no details, Hilde expressed genuine shock and sorrow, telling Berthe she would be calling on her in November during a scheduled medical conference in Boston.

Mother

Year's end found Hilde again at Andersen's farm breathing pristine winter air, cutting wood, and completing other miscellaneous outdoor chores. The new year filled her with a desire for change. Work at the Clinic had become dreary, more a source of fatigue than strength, and she determined that if she could not effectively ameliorate conditions for loved ones in Germany and Holland, she might at least make beneficial changes at home. She resolved to revitalize an old interest with new tools, those of psychiatry, and thus explore the many unsolved problems of obesity.

Originally she had expected to remain in New York close to her clinical studies, perhaps attending the New York State Psychiatric Institute, but Dr. Lambert of the Rockefeller Foundation advised her to apply to Johns Hopkins in Baltimore and work under Leo Kanner of the Harriet Lane Clinic for the best training. Kanner was enthusiastic. "Yes, I like what you have to say, and if you can find the money, I'll be delighted to help. Come to Baltimore and we'll discuss it in detail." Fellowship grant and position at Johns Hopkins, begun as informal inquiries as early as January, were both affirmed in writing by April, and her new career scheduled to begin in September.

"Good-bye, B.H.," she told her journal, June 30, although separation from Babies Hospital was temporary since the whole purpose of studying in Baltimore was to bring fresh psychological insight to her obesity work in New York. Because Mother's emigration was also in progress, Hilde skipped the usual summer vacation to remain in New York awaiting confirmation. Over the Memorial Day weekend, Mother had written she had a ship ticket but still could not leave. More delays, only this time Hilde thought Mother sounded more determined and optimistic than she had in a long time.

The daughter, meanwhile, did not idle, but organized summer with her usual foresight, planning to escape city heat by working on a boat known as The Floating Hospital, which had been organized to benefit sick impoverished children. The vessel made daily excursions down the Hudson, and Hilde noted that since the trip offered stimulating experiences for both mothers and children coming from poor, over-congested districts, it had definite value.

Summer passed with Kurt making occasional visits to the boat, while both worried and waited for Mother. Finally, on August 28 a note: "I will come soon." Three days later, Hilde had completed work on The Floating Hospital and begun apartment hunting for Mother, hoping by positive action to produce positive results, knowing, also, that the classes at Hopkins scheduled for September 1 would have to begin without her.

September 7, a cablegram came from Lisbon requiring additional monies, nothing short of catastrophic to Hilde's finances, yet somehow she managed, her greatest fear now being Mother's reaction to the strain of additional delay. At 65, she was no longer resilient, having already suffered serious nervous disorders. In the unlikelihood that all would now proceed smoothly in Europe, what would happen if her ship were not allowed to dock in New York? The ship she was boarding was loaded with refugees hopeful of eventual U.S. entry, but listing Cuba as their primary destination. Though it was fully two years ago, everyone still remembered the tragic odyssey of the SS St. Louis, which had not been allowed to dock in Cuba or any other port. Some of its passengers had threatened suicide when the ship returned to Hamburg. With worrisome, unanswered questions like these weighing on her,

Hilde became disorganized and forgetful. "I'm not myself," she wrote after spending several restless nights tossing and turning, then missing a dental appointment.

The emotional limbo would continue another two weeks until, realizing how destructive it had become, Hilde canceled all patient appointments and took the train to Baltimore so as to begin work September 15 in Kanner's Clinic. Two days later came a letter posted from Lisbon. Mother would be sailing.

Were daughter aware of the many obstacles mother had outmaneuvered getting aboard the *SS Nyassa*, admiration might have supplanted worry. The right to sail was fiercely earned.

While Hilde's U.S. citizenship insured the waiving of quotas, Mother still needed permission from passport offices in Berlin. Her goal had never seemed closer, but even with ship ticket and papers seemingly in order, she would not trust it. One thing was certain. Under no circumstances would she return to Kempen. After all, she no longer had a home. Leaving Rudolf and Selma and Ilse behind in Kempen had nearly broken her heart. How her little granddaughter had grown those two years in Holland! Was it possible that she, Adele, was permitting those dearest to endure their hell alone? Yet somehow she had done it, kissed each of them "good-bye" promising to be part of the committee welcoming them to America, all the time knowing at least for now chances were zero.

They had made it so easy by their unselfishness. Throughout those nerve-wracking weeks in Berlin while she waited permission, passing idle hours writing postcards or packing boxes for Rudolf containing items she knew would never be allowed to leave the country, the Kempeners, true to their loving and generous natures, had responded enthusiastically to every mention of forward progress, combining thoughts in a note which found her there:

> Now can we finally say: *It happened.* For the parcel: Thank you, we can use it. From your card we assume there is another box you didn't get permission to take which we will also take care of. Everybody here is interested in your trip and is waiting for news from you. Every day you get a little closer to your new home. Your dreams will come true. We wish you the best crossing.

Even so, those dreams nearly met an end in the passport office. She supposed she should not have been surprised that others ahead of her had also fulfilled quota requirements since it had happened so often before. But this time she would not give in, and surprisingly, the emigration officer in charge did not dismiss her in the usually rude manner. Instead, he patiently abided her story, while she inherently sensed a reversion to a past she believed gone forever, especially among those empowered to control lives. This small pause, which she interpreted as respect, endowed her with a boldness to speak.

Rapidly she related a tale of multiple ship ticket purchases come to naught, of a daughter in Palestine who had given birth to a beautiful little girl without assistance from a loving grandmother. Now she was on her way to see her American daughter become a successful doctor. Weren't the papers in order? She had made so many trips to offices in different cities getting them right....

She hardly dared catch her breath or meet his eyes for fear he would cut her off, signal with a single flick of the hand he had heard a million hardship cases just like hers and was ordering her to stop. She knew she had to make her own story different, appear strong and in control of the facts, logical, not weepy, begging or servile. They hated that. Suddenly Adele drew herself to her full five foot five inch height and met the official's gaze directly. Whatever it took, she would convince him logically that she already *had* waited her turn.

"Madam, you know it's not really your turn to leave," he paused long enough to see the snappy eyes drop painfully, "but because you are such a courageous woman I am going to give you my permission anyway."

"Danke schon, danke schon, danke schon," was all she could repeat over and over, clasping the precious stamped permission to her breast.

He continued, "Your valid passport serves as your right to use the rails, but only where space is available for such purposes. Germany is at war and German troops take priority. Also bear in mind that Jews are not permitted to use sleeping cars, dining cars, public waiting rooms or station restaurants. I have set up an appointment for you in this office one week from today. By that time your passport will be ready. Madam, I wish you a successful journey."

The following week she picked up the Reisepass, already stamped with the revealing scarlet "J," signing it "Adele Sara Bruch," though it was not her name. Had she been a man, she would gladly have adopted the middle name "Isaac" to designate her Jewish heritage because such indignities were insignificant compared with the little brown booklet she fisted.

The passport also gave her access to Holland. Three years had elapsed since she was in Auguste's household, which now she entered as an alien in transit. The friendly town of Winterswiyk also looked different. What before was gently curved now seemed coldly angular, like the flag of the Third Reich with its fearful Nazi insignia hoisted in front of post office, bank, and other official establishments.

The little party, reunited for a short time, feigned merriment. As in Kempen, it was painful leaving loved ones coping with intolerable conditions, but with so much travel still ahead, she was forced to concentrate on her own problems. Lucky she had allowed plenty of time to accommodate the unreliable and often impromptu train schedules since she was further delayed in Lisbon, when Portuguese ship line personnel claimed to find miscalculations in the payment of her ticket. They had not charged her enough, they said.

So her final hours dockside were spent wiring Hilde, wondering how her daughter could possibly find so much money on short notice, wondering too what excuse authorities would find next to destroy her only chance for happiness. As it turned out, none. For with cash safely deposited, the gangplank of the *SS Nyassa* magically opened, allowing Mother to join the hundreds of other refugees squeezed into the barn-sized dormitory reserved especially for them.

Pearl Harbor

Hilde's fears dissolved the moment she saw the beloved figure anxiously hanging over ship's railing trying to pick a familiar face from the mass of strangers below. Mother looked exactly as Hilde remembered, though it was not her endearing appearance the daughter would recall in later years but her poignant first words: "I shouldn't be here, Rudolf and Selma should be here."

They celebrated the triumph of her arrival in the newly leased apartment on Ft. Washington Avenue, fastidiously renovated by those two industrious beavers, Hilde and Kurt. Tomorrow Kurt would move in with Mother, and Hilde would leave for Baltimore, returning weekends for visits or to see patients in the "student room" she had rented specifically for this purpose.

Already, she was dissatisfied with work in Baltimore. The reason she had left New York in the first place was to be more than a pediatrician interested in psychiatry, restricted to "always doing things apologetically." Now, belatedly, she discovered child psychology was also a "patching up," its methods directly contradicting her family studies that what goes on between mother and child is too important to separate. Child Guidance Clinics operated on a hard and fast policy: child sees doctor, mother sees social worker, while information concerning fathers almost never surfaced, since most men refused to participate outright. In short, nothing combined, and ironically, in the very field supposed to be a freeing of the mind, Hilde discovered the worst bureaucracy of all.

She blamed much of her disillusionment on the stereotyped procedures of child psychiatry and felt the only way to broaden her scope was to study adult psychiatry, complete with the dynamics of psychoanalysis. Already she had attended several interesting lectures, while John C. Whitehorn, head of the Henry Phipps Psychiatric Clinic had granted her permission to sit in on case presentations at conferences held three times a week. The problem now was how, diplomatically, to get herself out of a year's commitment to the Harriet Lane Child Guidance Clinic and into Henry Phipps and the Baltimore-Washington Psychoanalytic Institute instead. Even supposing it were possible, who would pay for it? Already she had gotten off on a poor footing with the Rockefeller Foundation by reporting late to Harriet Lane, and they had penalized her by withholding a portion of pay she had been counting on and badly needed. On October 3, she tactfully described her unhappy situation to Dr. Lambert at the Rockefeller Foundation:

> Before leaving New York for Baltimore I tried a few times to see you in order to hear your advice concerning some problems which were on my mind. I was sorry that it was not possible to arrange for an interview, and I regret it now even more after an unexpected difficulty has arisen. There are two problems which I felt needed clarification. The one is directly related to my training here; the other relates to

personal problems which arose in connection with the arrival of my mother in this country.

As you may know, the work in Dr. Kanner's clinic is chiefly directed toward a practical handling of the psychiatric problems as they are encountered in children. I am very grateful for having the opportunity to work under the expert guidance of Dr. Kanner. Even after this short period I feel justified to predict that the cooperation will be a most profitable and enjoyable one for me. However, since the aim of my training is to prepare me for further research into psychosomatic problems, I am anxious to widen my knowledge of theoretical aspects of psychiatry, and to get acquainted with different schools of thought. I feel that I should become familiar with the basic viewpoints of psychoanalysis. I discussed this problem with Dr. McIntosh and Dr. Kanner, and they both agree that I should make use of the opportunity to take courses and seminars at the Baltimore-Washington Psychoanalytic Institute. I should be grateful to have your opinion in this matter and to learn also the attitude of the Rockefeller Foundation in similar cases. I have not yet made further inquiries concerning work at the Institute.

The other problem which I was so anxious to discuss with you had been precipitated by the arrival of my mother. After months, even years, of attempts to bring her to this country I finally got word in the middle of August that she would arrive shortly. It was impossible for me to ascertain the correct date of her arrival. I was ready to leave for Baltimore, but felt postponed from one day to another. I am happy to say that meanwhile my mother has arrived, and I felt greatly relieved to find her in such excellent physical health and fine spirits, in spite of hardships of a five week trip from her home, and all the mental anguish and suffering of the last years. I was able to make arrangements for her in New York which, I am confident, will enable her to make a good adjustment in this country. In this way I feel greatly relieved of constant worry and can devote myself to my work full heartedly.

Unfortunately, the financial problems which arose in connection with her arrival threaten to become a new source of worry. I had to pay an additional $257 for her transatlantic transportation. In securing the money I was confident that I would be able to meet my obligations out of income, counting on the full amount of $150 for the month of September. This unexpected demand of money is the reason that I was anxious to receive the fellowship money in advance. However, since her arrival postponed my work here until the 15th of

September, I received only $80 instead of the expected $150. This difference of $70, which may not appear very large to you, confronts me with insoluble financial problems. I hesitated to write about it in the hope of managing in some way. But I find myself unable to do so. Since I have to support my mother (and myself) and I have to make repayments for debts contracted in connection with emigration problems, I am unable to make any curtailments on the running items of my budget. The unexpected change in the September income leaves me unable to meet urgent obligations, obligations which I had to contract without fault or mismanagement on my part.

In view of the exceptional circumstances of my financial embarrassment which on the one hand caused the slight delay of my arrival in Baltimore and on the other confronted me with unexpected obligations, I beg to ask your advice, whether it might be possible to pay me accordingly the full allowance of $150. I am confident that you will be able to arrange a solution which will permit me to devote myself to the interesting work here without restraining financial worries.

Lambert's reply, October 6:

In regard to your program, we prefer that you devote your full time to child psychiatry in accordance with the purpose of your fellowship. There is, of course, no objection to your attending the clinics and seminars given by Dr. Whitehorn's group, but we would discourage your participation in outside courses such as those of the Psychoanalytic Institute. I should think that you could find in New York the opportunity to extend your knowledge of psychoanalysis.

About your financial problem, I have to say that our regulations do not permit payment of stipend beyond the period of actual study. You are receiving, of course, the "full allowance" of $150 a month, and this will be sent you regularly in advance at the beginning of each month through the period of actual study—not to exceed twelve months. You will recall that we went over the financial question last year and you assured me then that you did not have a problem. I would have discouraged the fellowship application had I anticipated a difficulty on this score. I assume that the problem is one that you did not anticipate. I trust that you will find some way to meet the situation.

While not exactly what she was wanted to hear, neither was Lambert's answer unexpected. She knew she would do the necessary as she always had: continue fulfilling obligations in Kanner's Clinic, gleaning what she could from the experience as she had from McCune's lab. Regarding outside activity, she was less positive. Initially she interpreted Lambert's response as "he didn't say 'yes,' he didn't say 'no,'" but ultimately, since it suited her, his words "no objection" became *carte blanche* endorsement for all her psychiatric ambitions. They opened the door to "moonlighting" and, later, with Kanner's approval, soliciting outside supervision in cases she was treating. Eventually she would pay twenty or thirty dollars per month, whatever was required, to Lewis Hill, Harry Stack Sullivan, Agnes Gray or other luminaries for their advice, hoping in this way to broaden her own knowledge and develop the beneficial connections she would need the following year when she applied for another fellowship, this time in psychoanalysis.

While Hilde's aggression sometimes backfired to embarrass her, more often it worked to her advantage, since most people assumed her intentions honorable and forgave her for possessing a superior mind. It was therefore not surprising that this pediatrician with the formidable personality soon captured the attention of some of the brightest names in psychiatry, many of whom were already familiar with her published papers on obesity in children. John C. Whitehorn would later analyze his association with her:

> During her year here we have developed much respect for her indus-
> try, perseverance and intelligent use of imagination in formulating
> and attacking psychiatric problems. Her honesty sometimes outstrips
> her tact. Even in complicated and trying situations her integrity of
> character has been outstanding.

Hilde's most important contact was Dr. Frieda Fromm Reichmann, who practiced psychoanalysis out of her residence at the Chestnut Lodge in Rockville, Maryland. The two women had much in common. Both had been encouraged to pursue their chosen careers by families where mothers seemed particularly influential, though Frieda, fifteen years Hilde's senior, had completed her medical training shortly before World War I. After Hitler's ascension to power, both doctors had left Germany knowing the Nazis would not tolerate their medical ambitions.

Hilde, of course, knew all about the refugee psychiatrist whose reputation glowed in medical circles. Much more surprising that Dr. Fromm Reichmann recognized the young refugee pediatrician through her published papers on obesity. To make the newcomer from New York at home and provide contacts and friendships she would need, Frieda organized a dinner welcoming party with six or eight women psychiatrists from the Baltimore/Washington area in attendance. The wonderfully social evening reminded Hilde of an earlier reception in New York when Gertrude Borg had helped an insecure refugee adjust to life in America. Different circumstances, but the generosity and greatness of the hostesses was the same. Later, she enjoyed a long private talk with Dr. Fromm Reichmann, who graciously invited her to attend her psychoanalytic seminars.

Thereafter, every Monday evening, Hilde queued up with psychiatrists from the Baltimore area to squeeze into one of the cars heading for the Chestnut Lodge where Fromm Reichmann held classes. Frieda immediately included her as a regular, asking her to report on a book written in German concerning dreams. Within a few short weeks she had established a blistering schedule, daytimes working Kanner's clinic, evenings attending seminars or conferences, weekends traveling to New York to see Mother, while at the same time consulting Dr. Booth and attending to her own patients.

It was on one of those hectic weekends that news of Japan's attack on Pearl Harbor jammed air waves. As it happened, December 7 in New York City fell on a Sunday, but when Hilde headed back to Baltimore in an unheated and dilapidated train car, passengers discussing the inconveniences and discomforts stopped short of complaining. "Better get used to it," they commented stoically, "don't you know there's a war on?" For most Americans the sneak raid brought shock and outrage followed by surges of patriotism, but for Hilde and her family, America's declaration of war was nothing short of personal tragedy.

More than two years had passed since Europe first erupted in full scale war, delegating Hilde as the critical communication hub for an entire family. Now, America as depot for asylum and information was also sealed. Getting Mother out of Germany less than two months before her adopted country declared war was the final miracle, years of uncertainty only beginning.

Hilde knew if she were to continue functioning productively she would need help, that only one person could understand a refugee's anxiety, and that was Frieda Fromm Reichmann. The next Monday night during an air raid blackout, two cars made the usual trip to Frieda's seminar, this time driven without headlights. War talk governing conversation in car and seminar stirred in Hilde nearly visual memories: black columns, entire newspapers devoted to listing dead, wounded and missing; the macabre World War I exercise of scanning for a name you recognized.... Suddenly she felt dizzy: Everyone in the room talking about war effort, grandiose personal contributions, and in the midst of it Frieda's humble statement, "I will continue doing what I do best, working with people who need psychological help."

Later when Hilde approached the famed psychiatrist, she was as good as her word, within the month offering regular and continuing therapeutic help. A year later, when Hilde was making her own professional changes, moving from the Childrens' Psychiatric Service into the Henry Phipps Psychiatric Clinic and the Washington-Baltimore Psychoanalytic Institute, her relationship with Frieda Fromm Reichmann changed from private patient to that of analysand, while regular sessions became more restrained and professional in character. Ten years still to the future the two women would acknowledge a close personal friendship.

"I Protest"

Mother embraced her new country with a loyalty rarely seen, openly regretting at the time of Father's death the family had not taken savings and emigrated to the United States. Perhaps it was simply hindsight. Throughout the early 1930s she had stubbornly adhered to a fixed course, becoming increasingly saddened watching her children's plans for the future collapse, but foolishly linking their deprivations with her own sacrifices, when to begin married life with Hirsch she had needed to leave loved ones behind. How naive to have compared the few kilometers of distance between Duelken and Kempen with the thousands of miles separating family today, and how irresponsible to have likened her own insecure beginnings with the terrible hardships her children were forced to bear.

Shortsightedness had cost her dearly, since the joy of starting life in a new country with Hilde and Kurt by her side must always be tempered by images of Rudolf and Auguste struggling to survive the devastation she had left behind.

"I know you won't forget us," echoed the premonitory last line of Rudolf's austere November 2nd letter. Ten days earlier an Order Banning Emigration of Jews from the Reich had ended the final flickering hope of escape, and now there was no shielding Mother or anyone else from truth. Auguste had written about evacuations to Poland while anxious relatives around the world shared bits of information insuring that the uncertainty and misery would be equally borne by all.

Most cruel were Artur's words: "Now can I speak freely to tell you that if the war in England had started four weeks later, Rudolf would be here. I had everything in order. He would be here, but Selma and Ilse would still be in Germany. Many emigrants still have wives in Germany. I know someone who managed to get his wife and children as far as Belgium but then could not get them any further."

Mother received her own heartbreaking evidence of Rudolf's evacuation when the latest letter to Kempen came back stamped "SERVICE SUSPENDED / RETURN TO SENDER. Then, in June of 1942, came news from Erna that she had received a message from Auguste through the Red Cross. The note sent from Lager Westerbork, Holland, Barache 59, where the family were interned, didn't detail living conditions in the camp, but Auguste complained about being quartered in separate huts where "children communicate using English, Hebrew, and Dutch."

Following months of silence even this tiny piece of information had tremendous impact on family members, who were urged to write immediately. More distant relatives were also given the new address, and soon a fleet of letters begging reply were crossing the oceans, though whether they ever reached their destination was unknown since not a single answer came back.

Eventually an equilibrium of unspoken despair settled on those outside the pale of Naziism, as though sequestering the dark thoughts might stunt their reality; even so, Mother would not shirk her duties. Once upon a time she had wondered if it were possible to emigrate to America on a work contract, worrying how potential employers might view her advancing years. "I have no fear I can still give a full day's work," she had assured Hilde, and though ultimately emigration was not conditional upon employment, she now happily honored that earlier promise.

First she enrolled in English classes, then, looking for ways to utilize her sewing talents, discovered an industrial home scheme where she could earn the minimum wage of thirty cents per hour. Through the United States Department of Labor, she found work with the Elgin Handmade Novelty Company on 25th Street and dutifully recorded her labors and earnings in The Home Worker's Handbook. Once war was declared, she also volunteered these same services to the armed forces, knitting warm sweaters or other articles of clothing for America's fighting men.

With her talents in constant demand, Mother felt completely independent, and loneliness, which had always been a major part of her existence, became a thing of the past. Widowed relatively early in life, she had thereafter attended weddings, funerals or other functions important to the Jewish community, always alone. But unlike social arrangements in the old country where friends and relatives established themselves over a fifty mile radius, Jewish emigrants to America colonized within five city blocks of one another, and so it was with great joy Mother welcomed long lost friends she never expected to see again. Thus Mother's generation, bound by common language, became the nucleus of a tight-knit, self-help, German Jewish community in the Washington Heights district, existing apart from but in proud cooperation with the much larger surrounding metropolis.

By sharing an apartment with him, Mother saw a lot of Kurt, yet Hilde also checked up on her nearly every weekend. The daughter was again taking charge as she had in childhood, giving orders, rattling off prescriptions for patient and family alike, now more awesome than ever. Though Mother had never doubted her success, she was truly impressed Hilde had made so many gracious and important friends. Every weekend brought new activities, more names for Mother to remember. Next weekend they were invited to Dorothy Andersen's farm.

As exciting as life was in the new country, Mother could not for one minute forget her dear ones abroad, and though communication with occupied Europe was no longer possible, she did write Palestine and

England often, sending special treat parcels to her four grandchildren, Ayala, Herbert, Helmuth and Geoffrey. Geoffrey, the child Artur and Lotte had successfully planned to bond them to England, was born little more than a year after their emigration, at about the same time Artur was joining the British Army. For a few months Herbert also lived in the household, but with air raids and bombing a constant threat, it was soon thought wiser to return him to the hostel, reserving get-togethers for vacations.

Regarding his present situation, Artur wrote Mother:

> I'm here on furlow, but Geoffrey doesn't know me—only wants "Mama." Herbert is also here. He is a quiet, sweet boy with many of Rudolf's features. We were sorry after the Coventry bombing we had to send him back to Lymm because he is like a son to us, but he is in a wonderful place.
>
> When he first got here after the Holland invasion, he looked like a skeleton, but now at the hostel he eats everything they put in front of him and seems a changed boy. One curious thing, though—he has forgotten all his German except for the word "rabbit," *Kaneinchen*, and otherwise speaks English entirely. The three children playing together today reminded me of our own childhood, and Lotte and I spent the whole day talking about you—especially your garden. Today we planted seeds. It's really too early, but by the time I get another leave it will be too late.
>
> I'm happy, Mother, you are proud I am a soldier. I should also add that I'm an army cook and a very good one. While it doesn't look like the war here will be ending tomorrow, some day the Nazis will get what's coming to them.

In February Kurt reported to Fort Dix. The army had accepted him without emigration documents and would soon send him to Fort Bragg for eight weeks of basic training. Mother, in a quandary over her large apartment without Kurt to share rent, found a solution in the German classifieds under the heavily printed heading, "Gesucht Dame." The ad called for an older woman to provide companionship, light cooking, and no housework. Proudly she sent the clipping to Hilde in Baltimore with the explanation, "I answered the above announcement and will soon work for a Mrs. Apte at 50 Central Park West. Just came back from taking the position."

To which Hilde replied, "Congratulations—it sounds good. But until you know if you like it, we will leave the question of your apartment alone. You will first have to find out if there is room for your personal things. Normally you would need a room to yourself."

Brushing aside these daughterly reservations, Mother reported, "I've been here only two days and have to say that I'm getting along very well. The lady is 72 years old and can do quite a bit for herself, although she needs my help with dressing. I bring her coffee in bed, and while she rests I prepare my own breakfast. At night I sleep in her room, but am not disturbed. There is also an unmarried daughter who is a nice lady. She is a fugitive from Belgium where she hopes to return later."

Unfortunately, Mother's latest show of independence would not last. After barely a week on the job, she began showing signs of failing health, which in the second week interfered with work. Bitterly disappointed by this show of vulnerability, she complained to Hilde, "I was happy in this job, but for me trees don't grow to heaven. I had to go home today because I didn't feel well. Had to lay down a lot and make damp compresses."

After an examination by Dr. Emanuel revealed a swollen liver, she explained, "I have to change my eating habits. In the morning my mouth is dry and I have a headache. That's not what I need right now, but I suppose it all comes out in the wash. Sorry to worry you so much."

Upon her return, Hilde recognized the seriousness of Mother's illness and immediately had her hospitalized. She also learned Mother had consulted Dr. Emanuel about an increasing waistline as early as September, though symptoms were indefinite. By February, however, he had no doubt that Adele, like so many refugees of her generation, had cancer.

The end occurred rapidly when Mother's liver burst, although for a day or two she remained semi-conscious, mumbling disjointedly, realizing, perhaps, she had become incontinent. While uncertain what she was saying, only that she was complaining, to soothe and quiet her, Hilde whispered in her ear, "I agree. Nobody should be sick like that."

But Mother heard and responded clearly, "Yes, nobody should be sick like that. I protest!" That the forceful German words, "*Ich prostestiere,*" should become her last, seemed an appropriate memorial to the strength of the woman who had spoken them and of the courageous way she had conducted her life.

In his condolence letter, Hilde's old friend and nemesis, Gotthard Booth, said it best:

> At least it was a good end that your mother had been allowed to give such final proof of her independent spirit, having established herself in a job after having lived with Kurt until he was inducted. I admire such a clear cut and purposeful life. Along with many problems, she has also given you the strength and the sense to deal with them.
>
> Wishing that as time goes on more and more of her strength and less and less of its problems will live and grow with you.

CHAPTER VI

1941 - 1946

Latvia

In early December of 1941, Rudolf and Selma received orders to make themselves "travel ready." With six other Kempeners, they spent their final week in Germany conserving food supplies to pack in knapsacks and sewing what few valuables they still possessed into linings of garments to be worn along the journey. Of the nine, only a single young man refused to be routed to the Krefeld rail station where his fellow sufferers gathered. The exception was Selma's brother, Leo, who simply preferred suicide to deportation.

On December 10, following the rail trip from Krefield to Dusseldorf, evacuees were marched to the local slaughterhouse where, with some 1,000 others, they passed the night as Gestapo searched and "lightened" luggage. The train was scheduled to leave promptly at 9:30 the following morning, so at 4:00 A.M. they were ushered onto the loading ramp and forced to abide cold and rain until railroad personnel could ready cars for boarding. Already behind schedule and with a strict timetable to meet, loading was haphazard. Often sixty-five people crowded a single car, others receiving half as many. Resulting disorganization was to plague guards throughout the trip as parents and children continually sought each other, while those squeezed into crowded cars searched for emptier ones.

In order to avoid future mishap, the conscientious Captain of Police, Salitter, suggested in his secret report that railroad personnel "prepare trains at least three or four hours before the scheduled departure." He also believed it wise to schedule at least sometime during the trip a one hour break when Jews could drink water, since "if we do not supply them with water during the trip, they try to get out of the train at every opportunity, even when they are forbidden to do so."

Discomfiture of guards notwithstanding, the train arrived late and without further misadventure at the military ramp of Skirotava, some seven km northwest of the city of Riga, sixty-two hours later. Since the unloading ramp had glazed with ice due to temperatures well below freezing, it was decided to leave the unheated train standing in the station, saving unloading for morning and allowing the cold tired German guards gratefully to turn their cargo over to six Latvian policemen.

But what of those who huddled for warmth inside the boxcars? Were they not imagining what lay ahead? Back at the slaughterhouse, when told of the relocation to Riga, such information seemed of little value since few put stock in what Nazis said, and even were it true, there was no way of informing loved ones. Getting in touch with relatives meant death, yet despite the warning, whenever their train pulled into station, many hands reached into the night trying to press notes into hands of passengers from other trains. Most attempts failed, but one woman trying to contact her mother was told by a sympathetic hometown soldier that she had already been deported to Theresienstadt.

Rudolf and Selma were not among those clamoring to send word of their whereabouts to anxious relatives. Of the immediate family, only Selma's parents still remained in Germany, and what comforting words could they have offered? Despite endless stretches of darkness, daylight arrived too quickly when those inside the freight cars were again confronted by unfriendly German and Latvian SS warnings, "Whoever tries to escape will be shot." Allowed only knapsacks and one small piece of hand luggage, the baggage which was separated from them at the start of the journey now disappeared for good.

The unwilling travelers fell meekly into line, Ilse walking between her parents, stretching coltish legs to match tempo with the adults. Nearly eight years old, she had lost the cherubic blush and pudginess of childhood along with much of its carefree innocence, though she hadn't lost so much juvenile curiosity she did not now wonder where they were headed. Still she knew not to ask, not to whine or complain, not to be sick, not to be conspicuous in any way. Her short life dictated entirely by safety and survival had taught her to accept authority without question. More than anything she feared Nazis, the powerful uniformed men who had once sent her father to prison. They were why she and Herbert were sent to Holland, and why she was returned to Kempen while her brother was being smuggled to England. Now she was uprooted again, only this time with beloved parents beside her, Ilse felt nearly content.

One thousand and seven marchers put up a brave front. Determined to make the best of circumstances, they could not possibly imagine the reality. What little the German Jew knew of ghettos came from pictures and descriptions in history books which most believed were relics of long-eradicated barbaric civilizations. Yet despite poverty and discrimination, these ghettos of their reading were not entirely impoverished, for within their boundaries inhabitants were autonomous. The ghetto dweller had religion and tradition to sustain him and understood personal contentment. Nor was he cut off or without protectors in the outside world.

But this newly created twentieth-century ghetto in Riga, heavily guarded and surrounded by barbed wire, was unique. It differed from its centuries-old counterpart not merely in bruising outward appearance, but by intent, since its "architects" had construed the barbed enclosures as holding pens for prisoners whose labor might prove useful to the German war effort before their exhausted bodies gave out.

The ominous purposes of the Riga ghetto, however, were not immediately apparent to members of the Duesseldorf transport as they trudged through ghetto gates to be told by SS Obersturmfuehrer Kurt Krause that they were specially selected for their knowledge of German. Krause's stern and wordy speech appealing for hard work in the cause of Germany seemed logical and appropriate to people long grown accustomed to Nazi jargon, and afterwards, when he assigned a Jew to form and head a labor detail, the action appeared to confirm his words. Thus, uncomfortable and unhappy at finding themselves abandoned and friendless in a frozen desolate land, the Duesseldorfers "fell in," reassured that so long as they remained compliant and useful, at least they would remain alive.

Living quarters were in dilapidated abandoned houses where pipes had frozen solid. Space inside was so limited that as many as sixteen crowded a single small room, although mercifully, families were allowed to remain together. Dried blood on floors, walls and ceilings boded ill, and the Dusseldorfers wondered who had preceded them. Whoever these mysterious people were, they had departed frantically, leaving important personal items such as eyeglasses and dentures behind, while the most precious commodity of all, food, still sat frozen on plates. The weary travelers reached into knapsacks to draw upon dwindling supplies which now they supplemented with frozen food from the apartments; and to the famished, this unexpected bounty appeared as nothing less than manna in the wilderness.

For eight grueling days, the men of the Duesseldorf transport joined with Latvian Jews and German Jews from two earlier transports to work at the Riga harbor unloading ships. As they were given nothing to eat all day and the food in their knapsacks was gone, they were forced to survive their four hour march and hard labor by eating turnips which they discovered, frozen rocklike in abandoned fields along the way.

Then on the morning of December 22, they were told they would be building a camp and to ready themselves for relocation. Heavy-hearted to be leaving parents, wives and children behind, unprotected in the harsh environment of the ghetto, the men selected for this duty remained skeptical, unmoved by captors' brisk pep talks, "Hurry, the sooner construction is complete, the sooner your relatives will follow and you will be together again."

Five hundred marchers guarded by Latvian SS tramped through heavily drifted snow to a desolate clearing in thick woods some seventeen km. away, where primitive huts made ramshackle ghetto housing by comparison seem nearly elite. Crews from earlier transports had begun erecting barracks, and now their grim post and beam frameworks sprang starkly from the snow like pathetically lean rib cages. Gravel atop dirt served as flooring where frozen earth prevented foundations being dug, but most obvious and serious of construction flaws was the absence of roofs.

Prior to arrival, the SS had demanded their watches. Those few unfortunates hesitating to part with these last vestiges of civilized existence were seized, marched into the woods, and shot. The hideous echo of gunshots still rang in the ears of survivors as they entered camp.

At forty-one, youth had passed Rudolf by, although middle age had not deferred his selection to the Salaspils convoy. Health wise, the first born of Hirsch and Adele Bruch had never completely recovered from incarceration in Dachau. Finding no specifics worthy for honest complaint, he nevertheless surmised his body wearing down, growing old before its time like an engine overused or mistreated by the owner, and knew under such harsh conditions he would not last long. What singularly intrigued him was that the approach of his own death aroused none of the fear or alarm he would have expected, only rock determination not to let the slowdown show. He was, of course, acutely aware his captors, rather than abiding idleness, would sooner shoot him, yet this he thought improbable, since it was not in his own makeup to malinger.

To meet grueling demands of the SS, he fabricated little mental exercises for private play based on remembrances of the Kommando games of childhood. As the exercise proceeded, Rudolf felt heady in the strength he commanded, alert as never before. Yet had he witnessed his own reflection, surely the aging image would have shocked him, the once powerful fleshy frame reduced to bony hulk, shrunk by several inches through a perpetual stoop. His face, with melancholy expression always too craggy to be called handsome, had from rapid weight loss grown austere, while the taut skin pinching his facial features announcing the extraordinary importance of his nose, widened and brightened his gray-blue eyes which appeared owl-like above the hollow of cheek bones. Only the sensitive lips, revealing his gentle nature, remained serene and unchanged.

By night, under coarse horse hair blankets, he huddled searching for warmth against wintry winds blowing from the Baltic, dreaming of Selma and Ilse safe in the ghetto. He had not seen Herbert since the cataclysmic night of November 10, when he was hauled off to prison, and now the boy remained tenderly fixed in memory as a child celebrating his sixth birthday, although it might have been another lifetime when he secretly built the hutch and bought pet rabbits to celebrate his son's special day. Now it was impossible even to construct an image of his son, much less imagine what life must be like for the lad so far away in England. As a matter of fact, except for the comfortable feeling it brought Rudolf to know of the boy's safety, he rarely thought of him at all.

By day, Rudolf concentrated on mind games, his labors demanding all his energy. In Camp Salaspils, where Hunger was King, the daily ration of 180 grams of bread supplemented by soup made from cabbage leaves and potato peels insured a constant gnawing of the innards. Injury and disease were common, the only cure for either, shooting. Occasionally the SS offered to truck the ill back to the ghetto for recuperation, but Rudolf never for a minute believed transports got further than the deep woods, where Nazis could shoot with abandon, unconcerned about alarming inmates of the camp.

His skepticism was born of logic. Where dying had become so commonplace that often eighteen or twenty men per day succumbed, it was constantly necessary to reinforce the workplace with fresh manpower. Unbroken bodies were supplied from the ghetto which, except at Christmastide, continued to receive trainloads of Reich evacuees several times a week during the months of December and January. Rudolf, knowing that these supplemental forces came from the ghetto, made a practice of contacting anyone who might reassure him about conditions there. It was while learning his wife and daughter were adjusting well, that he also received the disillusioning information that none of the hospital vehicles from Salaspils had ever arrived.

To avoid unnecessary panic, particularly where large numbers were involved, the Nazi overlords manufactured plausible explanations to cover their actions. In practice, however, individual and hasty execution of orders was often so crude as to give the show away. Andreas Mendel, Rudolf's fifty-year-old friend and neighbor from Kempen, had been promised space in one of the hospital recovery transports but was already so weak that he staggered and fell on his way to the bus, where an SS promptly ended his misery by shooting him in his tracks like a mad dog, ultimately sparing him the unnecessary trip to the forest.

Smuggling was a means for staying alive, as well as a mode for dying, since the penalty for being caught was hanging. To be successful, it was necessary to procure goods and establish a network of contacts both inside and outside camp. The best opportunity for acquiring vendibles was through the camp depot, where clothing taken from dead and murdered Jews as well as from Jews newly arrived at Riga was dumped and sorted. It was here the Duesseldorfers' luggage had been taken from Skirotava, contents assessed, and the best items made ready for shipment back to Germany.

Because Nickel and Teckenmeier, the two German Commandants in Salaspils did not like or trust their Latvian SS counterparts, certain Jews were favored with positions of responsibility, one being to sort goods at the clothing depot. From here it was possible to smuggle articles to fellow Jews whose jobs outside the compound brought access to the Latvian black market, where goods could be exchanged for bread. Often clothing workers and "middle men" paid dearly for this opportunity. Searches for contraband were constant, hardly a day passing when some unfortunate wasn't caught, while his own comrades put the rope around his neck.

Though conditions in the barracks were worse than those of a dog kennel, each passing night brought increasing comfort, making confrontation with dawn more difficult. This morning Rudolf could not shake the jitters from his bones, and the night chill followed after him. While waiting in line for his morning slice of bread, his teeth continued to chatter, his body tremble; and, later at the lumber mill, he had trouble concentrating above the knocking in his head. Legs, too, felt weak and wobbly, first from intense heat generated from hauling heavy loads, then from insidious cold freezing his sweat.

With supreme concentration he outlasted the day's assignment, but for the first time he could remember, the evening slice of bread and ladle of soup held no interest. Only one thing mattered: crawling under the horsehair, locking eyelids to seal himself once more in a private world. The straw atop the wooden pallet felt extraordinarily comfortable, as he plunged into those familiar realms where warmth surges even to the toes.

He was surprised to observe how it was Friday night, and gathered around the family dining table were his sisters and brothers playing *Komoedschen*, Father with baby Kurt on his knee, Mother cajoling Herbert and Ilse and offering chocolate from her secret but well-known hiding place. How could it be? Yet there they were together, all his loved ones, once more laughing and happy in the familiar parlor. And seeing them like this, Rudolf swooned until his heart broke out of sheer joy.

The following morning the body was removed, another victim of typhus, statistically not worth recording. It was taken by the Jewish burial detail to the gigantic gaping aperture which had been dynamited out of frozen ground to accommodate huge numbers of dead, and there like others whose mass demise no longer claimed grief, dumped unceremoniously.

Since the hierarchy of Salaspils contacted Ghetto administrators at regular intervals, reporting the dead in order to solicit replacements, it was not long before kin also knew. Wife and daughter so long dry-eyed, wept quietly against each other, marveling they were still capable of so much feeling. Some of their emotion was obvious release from the terrible haunting fear which had stalked and burdened them all along, that Rudolf in his weakened state would suffer silently and stoically, eventually and inevitably succumbing to the deplorable conditions which had been described as Camp Salaspils. The rest amounted to the loss of a cherished dream, the prayer that they would ever again be re-united whole, all of which had perished along with their beloved husband and father.

A household of fellow-sufferers, who understood too well the pain of losing loved ones, comforted Selma and Ilse, pledging to help any way they could. In truth, Rudolf's death caused barely a ripple. Life commanded Selma concentrate on two things only: staying healthy and protecting Ilse. Yet even on pessimistic days, Selma admitted chances of survival for both seemed good. Her sewing skills had landed an important job managing a clothing distribution center outside the ghetto, where she was responsible for sorting and salvaging, mending pieces herself, or instructing others to make necessary changes. Ilse attended classes in one of the newly formed ghetto schools. Ironically, the girl whose early childhood was so often interrupted by illness had not suffered a single serious asthmatic setback for over a year, and in defiance of all odds, appeared healthy and fit.

A Mother and Daughter

Selma put grief in perspective to look ahead. Her job was "safe," her daughter thriving, and winter with its terrible cold nearly over. Pipes had thawed and houses finally had running water. Ilse was happy about that. All winter she had been hauling the sloshy stuff from the central well, located beneath the dreaded gallows on Tin Square, but no matter how carefully she balanced her pail, most of it spilled as an icy trail behind her. Reprieved from well duty, she still spent much of her time on the dreary Square, where now she kicked a soccer ball, imitating young people who would soon participate in sporting events there. Her mother sighed, grateful for the adaptability of children.

"Operation Duenamuende," which began on February 15, 1942, involved the ghetto's two largest contingents, Berlin and Vienna. Those holding regular jobs were dismissed, and often whole families with one working member were excused. Those remaining were told they were being trucked for relocation to Camp Duenameunde, where work conditions would be easier. Instead, like their Latvian predecessors, some 1,500 were taken to Rumbula Forest and shot. The entire operation was so clandestine that only the twenty Jewish policemen in charge of preparing mass graves knew what was happening, and they had been isolated in jail with a recording that played two hours every day warning them not to talk about their work. Thus, on March 14, the procedure could be repeated with no one the wiser.

Again, the mandate called for 1,500, and labor leaders from individual houses were requested to provide lists. Ill, elderly, and parents with young children were to be the beneficiaries, since working inside fish canneries was sure to provide extra food and relief from cold. Those selected were not the only ones wanting to go, so an additional 400 volunteers were also accepted, while to enhance the ruse the Nazis included doctors and nurses "to care for the sick." No maps were available to check out the fictitious city, and because the Duena River was well-known to harbor-working Jews, and "Duenamuende" when translated meant "Mouth of the Duena," it had about it a diabolical ring of truth.

Whether intentional or merely absent-minded, deceit abruptly ended when victims' clothing was trucked back to the ghetto and dumped in the *Gewerbebetrieb*, a factory-like building bordering on Tin Square. Selma was one of those chosen to sort the newly arrived clothing, and what she saw made blood run cold. Amid the heap of undergarments caked with mud were familiar outer garments. Recognizing a neighbor's coat, Selma reached into the pile to retrieve the gold wedding band she had earlier helped sew in its lining. Worst were the tiny sweaters carefully hand-knitted, bright balls and expressionless stuffed animals worn out from over-loving. They might as easily have been Ilse's.

Kaddish that night was recited in many houses, yet despite being forced to acknowledge the grim realities of Duenameunde, most felt truth a poor exchange for hope, and life soon returned to normal. Once it became apparent no new actions were pending, Selma, too, settled back to work with renewed confidence.

For one thing, spring made a difference. People traded raggedly outer garments for smiles. The ghetto was softened by greenery. Earth, fertilized by formerly smelly cesspools, was transformed into neat rectangular plots where vegetables could be planted using seeds obtained through barter.

Soccer season in Tin Square had begun, and informal concerts featuring singing, and more formal concerts performed by an orchestra with talented artists from both sides of the ghetto, continued throughout the summer. But what Selma and Ilse liked best were the dramas performed nearly every weekend at the *Gewerbebetrieb*. When the beautiful curtain lifted to magnificent scenery and talented actors, it was possible to forget that this majestic theater was only a shabby building housing the clothing remnants of mass murder. Lessing's *Nathan the Wise* and Goethe's *Faust* held universal appeal, but it was in the closing words of *Jeremias* by Stefan Zweig that Selma heard despair crying out and recognized her own identity.

Inevitably summer became autumn, and soon winter came, except the winter of 1942-1943 wasn't so cold. Pipes stayed unfrozen, and by burning remaining furniture from abandoned houses, living quarters remained relatively comfortable. It was no secret Germany was taking a beating in Russia and favorable war reports also served to boost morale. Ghetto inmates who had come this far and whose working value seemed increasingly important, felt they were likely to remain alive.

Another spring, another summer, and more encouraging news from the front. Even Selma dared speculate about "after the war," when she and Ilse would take Herbert and go to America to live with Oma in that grand city of skyscrapers.

The first signs of change came in July, when a contingent of workers reporting at the gate were told to return home and pack for "relocation." Remembering what similar orders had meant in the past, hearts sank, and it was with great relief they marched away from the forest and toward the suburb, Mezapark, with its concentration camp, Kaiserwald. First into Camp were single men and women, and then, because the SS intended admitting only strong working Jews, the ghetto gradually emptied of everyone except the old and infirm, children, their teachers and parents, and certain ghetto functionaries.

Perhaps their fate should have been obvious, but for those left behind, summer and autumn passed peacefully, almost leisurely, the elderly or ill sunning themselves behind homes or outside the hospital. Routine remained the same, Selma reporting for work outside the ghetto while Ilse's schooling continued in consolidated classrooms, since "Duenamuende" had depleted the ghetto of so many children. Both mother and child drank deeply these final warm days of autumn, while they awaited liberation.

On November 2, work crews returning from outside details were detained from entering ghetto gates. Orders were to allow no one in, but the guard, unprepared for a mother's hysteria, grudgingly allowed Selma passage. Inside, she witnessed familiar queues, the old and ailing, yet so many children, too. Some stood beside a teacher or parent, others like Ilse, somberly waited alone. When daughter saw mother, she sobbed happy relief, while the mother, gently grasping her daughter's hand, took her place in line waiting to be counted with the others. On November 6, 1943, for all practical purposes, the Riga Ghetto was permanently closed.

Westerbork

Though topography of the Netherlands makes clandestine activity virtually impossible, Holland herself unwittingly aided the Nazi cause in 1939 by establishing the refugee camp, Westerbork, to house the many emigrating and stateless Jews from Germany. Not until summer of 1942 were Dutch Jews evacuated here, but Auguste and her family were among the earliest arrivals. While it wasn't exactly where she might have chosen to spend endless days waiting for war to end, the camp itself was bearable.

Craving normalcy, people mimicked former lifestyles by pursuing favored hobbies, grabbing pleasure wherever they could find it. Parents could be seen sitting in front of huts entertaining children with party games or Monopoly, while older men and women played Skat,

Dominoes or Patience. Serious bridge players lived in a world of their own. The sports-minded jabbed or danced through jujitsu or tumbling routines, while inside huts musicians practicing singly or in concert filled the air with beautiful familiar strains, Schubert, Sibelius, and Haydn.... It might have been possible for this mass of humanity to forget they were living on a dusty plain behind barbed wire, were it not that every Tuesday a transport train snaked in to collect its retribution.

Those whose names appeared on the latest list understood how illusory were their little freedoms. Some few resigned themselves, others hoped by continual deferment to outlast the war. It was somewhat humiliating when a Dutchman maneuvered for exemption, since it was not to the SS he pleaded his case, but with that oligarchical clique of German Jews who had been in Westerbork from the beginning. Berlin had in mind the identical solution for all, but the SS discovered that by designating the German Jews "Long Term Residents," they could rely on their unconditional good will to make selections; and thus with minimum fuss and a skeleton staff they could deliver the weekly "transport material" with nearly unsoiled hands.

Non-interference by the SS made life more pleasant for everyone. In this Jewish-run operation, where shootings or hangings were unknown, escapees were merely tracked down by henchmen of their own ilk and assigned to the next transport; thus, transgressor and entire family could be added to the transport list with no one feeling guilty.

Beauteous May, Auguste's favorite time, purple lupines lending color to drab surroundings, nature's way of compensating human failing, and so the glorious deception might have continued, except that on that final Tuesday three names from Winterswiyk are tallied to the fearsome transport list. Postponement no longer possible, Leo, Auguste, and Margot feel fortunate to head a line when a car opens so they can claim a quiet corner near a small barrel with a bag of sand. Even now, after all she has been through, Auguste wonders if she can bring herself to use it.

Occupants of the boxcars are told not to worry since they are being taken to labor camp where work will be easy, and when they arrive at Sobibor they are immediately reassured by what they see. A kindly doctor in a white coat walks along the platform asking, "Is anyone sick? Does anyone need assistance? We will see you are escorted to our hospital."

Perhaps Poland is not so bad. The ill are apparently in good hands, taken away by ambulance trucks, while camp workers, Jews in smart uniforms step forward to tag luggage and offer claim checks. It feels good to breathe deeply fresh country air, shake out cramped muscles before winding along a sandy path past picturesque officers' homes and gardens to an adjacent camp where another cordial speech awaits them: "Have no fear, families will be housed together. But you understand this is a work camp, where you will be living in close quarters and where we *do* fear disease and epidemics. For everyone's comfort and health long hair will be shorn, and we ask that each of you shower."

Ever since she can remember, Auguste has worn her dark hair in thick plaits folded to the nape, a special mark of elegance she has taken for granted. Now, unpinning and smoothing the familiar tresses, she feels a throb, but quickly rebukes herself for the uncharacteristic vanity. "How silly, when it can always grow back." Mercifully, the brisk shearing allows no time for mourning, and she and Margot are ushered to another room where others are already undressing. Auguste folds her garments neatly, marking them, admonishing Margot to do the same, "otherwise it may be difficult to find them later."

Even in this crowded room, the two might have been alone, so private and endearing are Auguste's thoughts toward the delightful child whose mere existence makes her own and Leo's worth living. Nearby, rustlings of hastily discarded petticoats as women gently aid children or aging relatives in tying shoes together or unbuttoning frocks, and since nakedness runs counter to a natural sense of modesty, there is an anxiousness about it. That was why when the female guide at the doorway signals it is their turn to shower, Auguste and her Sunshine, like all the others, unknowingly race for the death chamber.

Herbert

In May of 1945, seven days following Hitler's suicide in a Berlin bunker, Germany unconditionally surrendered, leaving relatives of the persecuted still tortured by uncertainty. Throughout the war, family and friends had remained stubbornly hopeful one day to be reunited with loved ones, behaving in this respect not unlike the victims themselves, constantly embracing hope in order to repel its unthinkable alternative. But once Soviet troops entered Auschwitz in January of that same year, describing the appalling condition of the few thousand prisoners surviving the atrocities practiced there, most of that sham world came crumbling down. In April, when U.S. troops liberating Buchenwald and Dachau and horrified British army personnel arriving at Belsen made similar discoveries, few had reason to anticipate anything but the worst.

Still, for the Bruch family, the final thread of hope was not severed until July, when Artur wrote from England: "Today I have sad news which really isn't much of a surprise, that Rudolf died in concentration camp. It is unclear what happened to Selma and Ilse because they were transported outside the camp and no one is sure where they were sent. I got the full story from Salli Rath in Cambridge, and Salli got his from Arthur Winter, who spoke to some survivors landing in Sweden. Salli's sister managed to hide these many years in Utrecht, and because of terrible suffering from hunger and cold now weighs only seventy pounds. She was able to verify that Leo, Auguste, and Margot were transported to Poland."

Not until July of 1954 would Hilde learn the details of Auguste's fate, through L.J.M. Claessens, a Dutch attorney from Arnhem researching reparation funds for surviving family members: "Your sister, her husband and their daughter were deported together, and it is absolutely sure that they died at Sobibor (Poland) May 28, 1943. As you know, perhaps, the camp at Sobibor had a better registration about the murders than the camp at Auschwitz. The date of death could be fixed rather well out of the Sobibor camp administration."

Information concerning her brother was readily obtained through Arthur Winter, Rudolf's expatriated neighbor now living in Sweden. Upon request, Arthur sent Hilde an eighteen page typed report, including the rationale for undertaking the research:

On May 19, 1945, I read in the Swedish newspaper that 43 liberated Jews, deportees of the Riga Ghetto, half originally from Rheinland-Westfalen, had arrived at the refugee camp, Holsbybrunn, in Sweden. When I saw the name Heinz Samuel from Huls (near Krefeld) listed amongst survivors, I hoped to learn something from him about the people of Kempen. From the Jewish Congress I tracked his address, wrote him, and later received a detailed report of his experiences as a deportee. I also went myself to Camp Holsbybrunn to get further details from his wife, Ruth, and some of the other deportees living there. I was interested in the destinies of nine people, nine out of six million, nine average human beings of ordinary intelligence and ordinary moral views. I had known them since we were children, had gone to school with them, eaten cheese cake with them, and carried the black, white, and red flag through the synagogue with them. What I discovered was not much. I could not even learn the exact dates of their deaths. What I did find out was how they spent, along with 13,000 others, the most terrible time of their lives.

Hilde scanned for names. Rudolf Bruch, dead of typhus. Selma and Ilse Bruch, transported November 2, 1943, believed by survivors destined for Auschwitz. With tragic facts like these confronting her there seemed little doubt that Herbert, now a young man of thirteen, was the miraculous lone survivor of her oldest brother's family.

Throughout the war years family members were in touch with Herbert either through Lotte and Artur or by writing him directly. In this way, they hoped the youngster would retain a sense of security through broadened familial ties, though the fortunes of war had separated him from those he held dearest. To further demonstrate auntly concern, Else and Hilde from America sent packages of treats designed to appeal to the lad's sweet tooth, as well as hand-knitted garments to warm him against raw English winters.

Herbert remembered little about his past, certainly nothing of the aunts and uncles in England and America presently fussing over him. His previous life seemed best forgotten, anyway, having little to do with the present, which had gotten so far out of his control that obeying whoever was in charge was all that mattered. Privately he vowed to continue saying and doing in England exactly what was expected, just as he had in Holland.

His final remembrance of that earlier world was when he and some of the other children from the hostel were rushed to a barge and shoved somewhere below. He worried why the Committee had not thought to collect his sister from the family she was living with, but sensing he might not like their answers believed it wiser not to ask. Instead he huddled nervously against a similarly terrified youngster, concentrating on the vibration of engines to blunt the blast of explosions above. Copying the older children, he squinted his eyes closed, poking fingers into his ears to block out cracks of thunder followed by little metal pebbles pelting across the deck like sheets of rain. While it hardly seemed possible, the see-sawing flat-bottomed hulk continued to hold him up, gradually threading its way out of the harbor so as to leave the fury of his other life behind.

They landed in Liverpool, where he was placed in an emergency house in Wigan, Lancashire, for orientation before being moved to the Jewish Convalescent Home on Pepper Street, Lymm. It was in Cheshire that Uncle Artur and Auntie Lotte came calling. While he did not remember who they were, he thought it pleasant to see them, even nicer to visit their house in Coventry where he was allowed to play with Cousin Helmuth. He sensed the two of them got on famously, though Helmuth was only a wee lad three years younger than himself and would soon have a brother who was just a baby. So when Auntie Lotte asked if he wanted to come live with them instead of at the hostel, he said he wouldn't mind.

The nightly air raids made Auntie Lotte nervous, especially with Uncle Artur away in the army. She told Herbert and Helmuth to keep away from cities whenever possible, and so for a whole week they went visiting Auntie's lady friend in the country to get a good night's sleep for a change, except that while they were getting this rest, their house in Coventry was being bombed.

When they returned, there was nothing left but a pile of rubble. Over and over Auntie Lotte reminded them how grateful she was no one had been at home when it happened, since now they would all be dead. Except she seemed more worried than ever, because they needed another place to live, and where could she find something like that for three children on a soldier's meager pay? Uncle Artur and Auntie Lotte suggested he go back to Lymm, where he would feel safer and happier, and he said it did not matter, because, of course, it didn't.

From "Rosebank," Lymm, the hostel Matron, Esther Blooman, described her impressions of Herbert to his aunt, Dr. Hilde Bruch, of New York City:

> I am replying to Herbert's letter, as he does not write very well yet. He is rather a quiet, shy little boy with a quite definite sense of humor. His English is not too good yet and I am never quite sure just how much he has understood when I speak to him. However, it is improving daily.

He lives here with twenty-four other children, four of whom are refugees, of which he is the eldest. He goes to the local school which is only a few minutes walk away. The house itself is very nice and we have a lovely garden and big playing field. He has plenty of good nourishing food, and is gaining a great deal physically.

As we are not far from two big cities, we get quite a lot of air-raids, and when these are bad the children sleep in an air-raid shelter below the house.

Where are Herbert's parents and sister? Have you their address? With love from Herbert.

Sincerely yours,

Esther Blooman

Hilde Bruch, Psychiatrist

Several years would pass before Harry Stack Sullivan, President of the Washington School of Psychiatry in the District of Columbia, would confer on her a Diploma, but already in 1943 Hilde Bruch, M.D., under the title Associate in Psychiatry, College of Physicians and Surgeons, Columbia University, had returned to Manhattan to exercise her new skills. Physically and emotionally, she was never far removed from the Island where nearly ten years earlier Liberty, guarding a famous backdrop of skyscrapers, first captured her reverence and imagination. Weekend visits with Mother and colleagues, and the maintenance of a small private medical practice in New York during the years at Hopkins, had kept her in frequent touch. Although she had missed stimulating art lectures at museums within walking distance of her apartment, or concerts and lectures performed on stage a dime's subway ride away, she considered her return strictly professional, a follow-up to the "scientific investment" she had left behind.

Unfortunately, during her absence, her fat children had not fared well. Lacking her own supervision and interest, programs at the obesity clinic had all but folded, leaving those in charge frustrated and bewildered, fully convinced nothing is quite so boring as motivating a group of uncooperative fat patients. To reactivate former files, Hilde sent survey forms and letters, discovering many of her fat kids were now "grown up." Although response was poor, it was obvious from those answering that most had relapsed into obese young adults, weighing proportionately the same or even more than when she had originally seen them. Perhaps their complacency was just another indicator of overall apathy toward dieting. This seemed borne out when one young man, after being asked why he had fallen off his diet, replied, "The clinic forgot about me, so then what was *I* supposed to do?"

Worse, her newly acquired knowledge in psychiatry was proving useless in understanding the problems of the obese, and she was angered by her own naiveté. Whatever had made her believe fat people, simply by "gaining insight," would follow curative steps toward better general adjustment and weight loss?

On the contrary, it became plainer with every session that her more gifted adolescents already displayed a remarkable knowledge of psycho-dynamics and had amassed enormous psychoanalytic vocabularies. These neophyte lay practitioners, briefed in past therapy sessions about "real" or "unconscious" feelings and what influences these feelings should or should not have upon their psyche, now proceeded to spout useless, though not necessarily incorrect, jargon back at her. Quite aside from her own pique, it was obvious that had that approach worked to begin with, these precocious over-analyzed patients wouldn't be here with her now.

Time had come to rethink the validity of traditional therapy, though her major peeve continued to be with so-called "authorities." Psychoanalysts were suspect, because she had observed their tendency to blame personal failings on poor cooperation, claiming obese patients either "resisted" or "engaged in power struggles." Obviously, if she were to accept this excuse herself, blaming either the "unanalyzable" patient for stubbornness or his previous therapist for not having done a "real analysis" on him, no one would benefit.

Meanwhile, she noted dryly, the personalities of her kids remained passive as ever, the psychoanalytic blurb having fostered a kind of intel-lectual arrogance, though ironically not an iota of confidence and self-esteem. Essentially, she was seeing the same "helpless" children she had seen years earlier in a tiny pediatric office, where the presence of a sin-gle chair insured a mother be left standing.

Nor had Hilde changed her basic philosophy—that development of obesity involves child and family within total environment, and that the key is to identify which forces have gone awry. Now she was adding another essential ingredient to the formula: recognition must come from self-discovery, not be superimposed by some "expert."

It sounded misleadingly simple, but to locate "culprit miscues," signals gone haywire through years of self-deception or outright lying, was no easy task. Her role as scientist would be to assemble facts in close collaboration with her patients, at the same time remaining alert to the most minute discrepancies or confusions in how the information was being presented or misrepresented. She would be the attentive *listener* and *receiver,* they would be the *conveyers* and *initiators* of all important information. By emphasizing her patients' importance as reporters, she would be acknowledging their value as people, reversing past experiences when mother or therapist was perceived as active, dominant forces in their lives. Thus, more than actual words passing between them or interpretations arising from the words, it was the spirit of the procedure itself which became the critical link to success.

In later years, studies and observations would lead to a formulation of hunger awareness, in which she would advise parents to approach current trends with a skepticism culled of common sense. Whether to offer breast or bottle, whether to rely on baby's demands or schedule feedings by the clock, are not prime issues at all, but these "bags of tricks," harmless of themselves, dangerously undermine a mother's confidence in determining how and when to feed her infant. This *is* critical since it represents the earliest and most repetitious interaction between mother and child.

The all-important mother-child relationship, beginning from the moment a mother first receives her infant for nursing, also marks the beginning of individuation in the child, for despite physical dependence, the newborn is far from passive. On the contrary, crying, though difficult at times to interpret, is from the start quite definite, and hunger is only one of many instinctual needs.

It is therefore critical a mother learn to differentiate her child's cries in order to make appropriate response. An alert, confident mother soon learns to recognize *clues* in her baby's crying, so that the decision to feed, change a diaper, or merely offer the support of a comforting hug, is entirely appropriate. On the other hand, a confused, over-anxious mother who turns to "experts" for advice rather than relying on her own competency, is likely to continually misread cues, masking insecurity by indiscriminately offering food. Over a period of time this behavior is likely to produce a perplexed, overwrought child who cannot differentiate hunger from a multitude of other discomforting sensations.

With increasing loss of body control, sense of self also disappears, and the child becomes increasingly passive, while emotional tensions, having nothing to do with food deprivation, are mistakenly experienced as "I need to eat." In this state of anxiety and depression, food becomes the temporary refuge, often resulting in binge eating. Though faulted by the world for not exercising more will power, the victim of obesity is guilty only of lacking hunger awareness, a critical deficiency which makes it virtually impossible to control a function which cannot even be recognized.

How does the concerned therapist proceed in unraveling this mess of conflicting information? Hilde would begin at birth, when essential patterns are forming, being careful not to recreate the mother/child role by acting dictator, realizing that for therapy to awaken in her patient a sense of autonomy the patient must actively participate in treatment. In the end, patients must themselves learn to make distinctions: understand that there are differences between bodily sensations and emotional states which they cannot be helpless about, since only by becoming initiator and discoverer will they truly become master of their own house.

Such concise formulation regarding eating disorders and their treatment was as much in the future as the books she would write two decades later. From 1943 throughout the postwar period, Hilde concentrated on becoming a skilled psychiatrist, gathering clinical information which would later furnish material for her writings. Data regarding obesity being inconclusive, she put pen aside in favor of practice, especially adult analysis, in order to gain the broad-based foundation in general psychiatry she felt necessary for therapeutic application.

Despite external changes in career, her philosophies remained constant. Most recently, she found herself at odds with the Sullivan group practicing in New York, whom she regarded as pale imitators of the "real" thing. Of the many prestigious people Hilde had met, Harry Stack Sullivan alone seemed worthy of unqualified admiration. The degree to which she had been impressed by his uncanny ability of communicating with the complex mentally ill cannot be exaggerated. He visualized things in a stream of images so process-oriented, she swore at times he could literally envision words even before the patient spoke them. This same sensitivity also made him an outstanding supervisor.

Specifically, she remembered one particular case concerning a certain catatonic schizophrenic from student days. As usual, she had detailed specifics of her case for Sullivan, including the fact that although the patient was listed as mute, he had actually talked to her. All the while, Sullivan listened solemnly, giving no indication she had said or done anything unusual, except that when she finished he made this puzzling reply, "I take it for granted, then, you had a schizophrenic episode."

She was flustered because it sounded suspiciously like an insult. Vaguely she shook her head to conceal discomfiture, waiting to consult Frieda.

"What does he mean by that schizophrenic stuff?" she blurted during her therapy session, while Frieda laughed good-naturedly as a parent does when her child says something amusing. "Oh but Hilde, you must know this is highest praise since it means you have tuned in correctly."

Afterwards, she was the cream floating atop a pitcher, exulting in the knowledge that she was one of Sullivan's favorites because she could understand and converse in "schizophrenese." The catatonic schizophrenic patient, also the benefactor, later thanked his therapist when she left the service by presenting her with a carton of Lucky Strikes. It was not the brand she usually smoked, but when Hilde frowned and pointed the fallacy out to Sullivan, he laughed heartily, "On the contrary, he communicates what you and I already know, that he was *lucky* to have you as his therapist."

Those were glory days alright. How appalling now to be affiliated with the New York Branch of the Washington School of Psychiatry, with its rigid disciples who, in choosing to follow the master, retained none of his greatness or methods. Utterly obsessed with interpretation, by quoting and requoting, examining text in order to unveil purest meaning, this bunch had succeeded in losing all concept of the most important thing, the fluidity of ideas. To describe Sullivan's approach as open-ended was an understatement—the man was process itself. Yet here at this "factory" his ideas were being canned, labeled, and conventionalized until they gleamed with orthodoxy.

Eventually, when she could bear it no longer, she decided to resign in favor of a group associated with Columbia University, who in her opinion were "more psychoanalytic" in character. Before it was over, however, the exit was messy and noisy, and had she been completely honest, she would have admitted her disagreements with the New York branch of the Washington School were as specific as they were philosophical in nature.

Times had changed since the war years when serious, qualified students were at a premium in classes small and cozy, when vivid discussions were encouraged in private residences by teachers larger than life because they were uninhibited by the guidelines of mammoth institutional psychiatric bureaucracies still in their growing phase. The situation had been ideally suited to Hilde, meeting all her standards for academic freedom.

Unfortunately, wartime benefits had come tumbling to an end with the war itself. Servicemen returning in large numbers required psychiatric counseling. Understandably, the demand far outstripped the supply of adequately trained therapists, and to bridge that need, various analytic societies, including the New York Branch of the Washington School, proposed training lay analysts for therapeutic assignment.

When Hilde was scheduled to teach a classroom of students with non-medical backgrounds, whom she felt were lowering the standards of instruction, she balked. Outrage literally exploded when she was assigned to jointly teach with a social worker a course ironically designed to instruct and train even more unpedigreed psychiatric social workers.

To circumvent her displeasure, she tried stressing the psychiatric and interpersonal aspects of social work, in this way hoping to avoid transforming every dissatisfied agency worker into a psychoanalyst. But when her fellow-teacher, the social worker, arrived back from vacation joyous and excited because she had resigned her agency job to devote full time to private work as a psychoanalyst, Hilde, the psychiatrist, had had enough.

Complaining that the school bulletin clearly defined standards for psychiatrists: "Graduates of a Grade A medical school who have completed a one-year accredited internship and psychiatric residency for three years," she snorted her rebuttal: "Who are these lay people, anyway? Certainly it's hard to envision any educational background that can be considered adequate equivalent for admitting non-medical professional workers into clinical courses."

As further ammunition, she sent letters to Harry Stack Sullivan and Frieda Fromm Reichmann. A rather long letter to H.S.S. pulling no punches about the way things were being handled in New York still managed to sound diplomatic, if somewhat self-serving:

> I wish to state…that this disagreement concerning the training of lay people for the practice of psychiatry has in no way influenced the high admiration and regard which I have for the teaching program and psychotherapeutic principles developed by you, Dr. Fromm Reichmann, and the other teachers of the School…. In case this disagreement should lead to my withdrawing…I would like to ask you whether I might continue working with you on a private basis.

But Sullivan, as Psychiatric Advisor to the Navy, had more on his mind than the grumblings of a former student. Interest in veteran's affairs begun during World War I had only increased his responsibilities during World War II. Now, effectively, he brushed her off.

> I wish I could say something in reply to your letter that would express sympathy and hope of something constructive. I am driven to the point of mental incoordination by last-minute details of the White Memorial Lectures for this fall, and I cannot find time to talk with anybody further before I leave for the Army School of Neuropsychiatry where I give the first lecture tonight….

To F.F.R. vacationing in Santa Fe she wrote on August 7, 1945:

> All the newspapers are full of the new atomic bomb, and I feel a little bit foolish to tell you today of my own private little bombshell. But I am afraid you will hear about it anyhow, important or not, and even more regrettably, vacation or not.
>
> I made no secret about my reaction and misgivings about the training situation here in New York. I felt I could keep quiet as long as I could maintain an "I don't know" attitude. That became practically impossible when Clara asked me to do control work with "Miss K." …I cannot think of a more contradictory situation than my giving the course with her…. It would mean a public demonstration of my approval for training of lay analysts and openly belie my real opinion in the matter. I therefore requested having my name taken

off this one course. I agreed to give the course in Washington but made it clear that I could not continue to teach if I were left in the dark about fundamental policies of the school.

But Frieda's tactful reply left little doubt where her own sympathies lay:

Please, Hilde, sleep over this several nights and think about it. I am a little disconcerted about your attitude. Please, reconsider it carefully, and don't undertake any definite steps before we have talked about it.

Some of us think it may be one of the future duties of the school to work out and offer a specific curriculum for non-medical training of psychotherapists. We can't swing the gigantic job we are facing in the next decade without the help of lay people—everybody knows that; so we may just as well help to train *good* lay therapists.

Reasonable sentimental statements like these were emotional wishy-washy so far as Hilde was concerned, but because they came so highly-charged, to take the offensive against them was to sound the opposite, completely unreasonable. Coming from Frieda, the remonstration seemed not unsuitable, but what she read next left her trapped and bruised and angry as a bull: "'Miss K.' has also asked me to control a case with her next winter and I have accepted without hesitation."

In the end, unable to rally support from a single corner, she resigned as inconspicuously as possible, since it would not do to burn any more bridges behind her....

Hilde Bruch, Parent

Being the eye of a storm did not diminish Hilde's effectiveness in per-forming duties, medical or personal. She, in fact, prided herself on being able to arrange the variables of her life into well-disciplined pla-toons organized for battle. In the midst of the latest fray, for example, she had strengthened independence, while simultaneously building a thriving psychiatric practice now producing a decent income.

Having depended on grants or handouts as long as she could re-member, it was hard to imagine the implications of her new earning power, yet she recognized its importance if she were to give Rudolf and Auguste and their families the financial support they would require after the war. Alas, when that dream crashed, the only question remaining was her nephew, Herbert, how best to mend his young life and serve his future needs.

She did not doubt as pediatrician-child psychologist she was qualified, that her small but adequate savings account made her a logical choice, but the actual decision of guiding an adolescent to manhood took some reflecting. For one thing, she had never occupied more than two rooms, part of which was partitioned as office space to treat patients. It was an arrangement she had never thought about, since it represented all she could afford. But as a matter of fact, she had always felt proud and comfortable in her surroundings, devoting time and thought to furnishings which she considered not merely efficient but charming and attractive.

A thirteen-year-old, of course, would change all that, requiring a room to himself for privacy, yet needing the ample attention and supervision adolescents always want from parents. While she yearned to provide the material and disciplinary comforts which were the fruits of her labor and experience, she was also perplexed about how to fit the many emotional demands of parenthood into her own demanding schedule.

Soon she discovered she was not alone in her desire to rear Herbert. Ernst and Else wrote from the farm community of Aurora that they would be delighted to have Herbert share with their son, Harvey, the joys and benefits of family life. Such a warm and loving invitation, offering the very essentials she could not, left Hilde uneasy, but also facilitated her decision. As a New Yorker of professional standing, she, too, had a unique contribution to make. Certainly the cultural activity of a large city would enrich a young person's life in ways that living out in the sticks could not.

Lotte's letters indicated her nephew to be an excellent student. Presently he lived in Manchester attending the Burnage High School on scholarship, where he consistently placed first in his class. Remembering her uncles' generosity where her own education was concerned, Hilde sent additional money to the Refugee Committee for Herbert's personal use.

> I would like very much that you let Herbert have the money without any strings attached to it. My main concern is that he does not develop a realistic attitude about money—it seems to me essential that

a boy of his age learns to spend without having to account for every
cent.

In a follow-up letter to Herbert she wrote:

I sent the money to the committee and I hope that it works all right.
If you have difficulties let me know. I wrote to them that it would
probably be difficult for the other children if you had more money,
and it therefore might be wiser to send to Aunt Lotte some money
for herself and the children and also for little extras if the guardian is
too stingy with the money I did send for you. Don't feel cheated if
you don't get it just the way you planned it. After all, the committee
has given you a home and taken care of you very nicely for such a
long time.

If you get the money I do hope that you get the little things
which a boy likes to have. Fountain pens are very hard to get here,
too. In case I can get one here, would you rather I send one to you or
buy the one you heard about. I also was wondering whether you
would need a compass for mathematics, or don't you study that in
your grade? Anyhow, don't hesitate to let me know what you need,
and I hope you can use the money for whatever you feel best, probably some nice books or shows that you haven't had a chance to enjoy
freely.

It turned out Hilde had guessed correctly, that "pocket money"
would only create problems among children who must be treated more
or less equally. The committee denied her request, and thereafter she
sent funds directly to Lotte, who, because of her own needy circumstances, was likewise frugal in their disbursements.

Concerning the adoption of her orphaned nephew, Lotte advised
Hilde, "The main thing is that the boy gets loving tender care and
enough good food. That's what he needs. If Else and Ernst take
Herbert, he would have family life. Even if Else is still as orthodox as in
Germany and expects it from Herbert, it wouldn't make much differ-
ence to Herbert so long as she is good to him."

Lotte's main concern was that the continuing war with Japan would
cause additional delays:

Even if you have everything ready for Herbert, it still will take some
time to get passage on a ship. Right now war transports to the Pacific

are first. Children are on a danger list. Every child must be accompanied by a male adult who will assume responsibility—just in case the ship should sink.

It would be disappointing if the boy has to wait a whole year for departure to America. Next week when he comes to us for fall break I will tell him that he'll be going to Uncle Ernst's. But I doubt I'll find the courage to tell him how long he'll have to wait.

Since Herbert's emigration, fare, and papers were Hilde's responsibility, so too, if she chose it, was his guardianship. While the situation wasn't perfect, she believed she had reached a satisfactory compromise regarding domestic arrangements. By renting a separate room in her apartment complex and enlisting the after-school guidance of a male teacher-friend, she believed Herbert would find the privacy and companionship he needed during the time she was occupied with patients. Evenings and weekends she intended devoting herself exclusively to the boy. Thus it came somewhat as a surprise when her sisters-in-law reacted negatively.

Else's response was immediate:

> I don't agree at all with the pattern of life Herbert will have in New York as you described it in your last letter. I should like to mention that it does not sound very "expert" placing Herbert in strange hands again after promising him that he shall live with you. You will have an "emotional problem" by not keeping your promise and I don't think one can hurt a child more than by breaking a promise.
>
> Herbert needs a home, not a "shelter." There is quite a lot of time after school when a boy needs companionship or wants to engage in sports. The feeling of belonging to a family unit, no matter how small it is, and having a home where he can bring his friends will help in establishing a sense of security. And certainly security is a very important part of any age. One is not an adult at thirteen, but you make it sound very much so in your letter.
>
> You don't have to fear any interference from us. If your plans should fail and you should decide to let Herbert live with us, we shall be ready to welcome him at any time. We hope you will not object to our financial help where Herbert is concerned.

She recognized her mistake immediately, though it had sounded sensible enough when she proposed it. Nevertheless, she felt guilty only

of inexperience and haste. The only rooming experience she even remembered had failed miserably, but she was willing to try again.

Lotte's reaction, milder than Else's, was also plainly disapproving:

> I can quite understand why you have given so much thought to
> Herbert's move, but he is not a problem child at all and can adapt
> himself very quickly to new surroundings. In any case, I should ad-
> vise you to take a room for Herbert in the same house for the first
> time so that he sees you care for him and that he can trust you. He is
> just coming into a difficult age when he needs a motherly friend. He
> surely will enjoy the Friday evenings in the homey atmosphere of
> Tante Therese's. Let's hope he will be with you soon.

Yes indeed, let us hope, thought Hilde, and in the meantime I'd
better be looking for a larger apartment. Curious, but true, once an
alien notion was firmly planted it germinated and grew as if hers from
the beginning. Some of this newly sprouted enthusiasm spilled over in
a playful letter to her good friend and colleague, Jerry Frank, recently
returned to Baltimore after "holding the line" abroad:

> My personal life is dominated by the need for a new and larger
> apartment. There ain't no such animal. Just the same I need one.
> When I went back to New York two years ago, my inborn pessimism
> made me look for the least that would do—and it was from the
> beginning just marginal. Quite soon my practice was on the big busi-
> ness line. Of course, I would not do anything—until now there is a
> real emergency. I have my home and office together, which is all
> right for bachelor women psychiatrists. But now I am adding a fam-
> ily and need either a very large apartment, or separate office space—
> both on the impossible list or nearly so.
>
> The only surviving member of my oldest brother's family is a boy
> of thirteen, who, through one of those miracles, was evacuated to
> England during the bombardment of Amsterdam. I have applied to
> have the boy come and live with me and hope that it will not take
> too long. I have been in correspondence with the boy for three years,
> and he seems an awfully nice fellow. It will mean quite a change in
> my way of life, one to which I am looking forward with pleasure.

It was Hilde's most energetic self whipping Herbert's papers into
shape, affidavits of support from herself and Kurt, as well as character
references from Rustin McIntosh and Kurt's commanding officer.

Immigration visa and travel reservations came harder. The Jewish Refugees Committee in Manchester politely thanked her for supplying necessary documents but warned that "shipping accommodations are non-existent at present...neither the U.S. Consulate nor the Ministry of War Transport takes into consideration individual cases."

In December of 1945, Frieda Fromm Reichmann was granted compassionate leave to visit her aging mother in London. The flight was scheduled to return January 13, and if Herbert could obtain a visa and seat reservation on her plane by then, Frieda would escort him back to the States. It was a stroke of luck not likely to recur, and Hilde jumped on it. To the Secretary of the Jewish Refugee Committee she wrote:

> My friend, Dr. Fromm Reichmann, is traveling by air and I would like Herbert to do the same if there is a chance that it might speed up his coming. Through a personal friend of mine, someone from the State Department is going to inquire, in a very private way, of course, whether special consideration could be given the personal aspects of Herbert's case. Such personal attention might help us. I should appreciate if you keep this confidential.

The "personal friend" was none other than Harry Stack Sullivan, who had written Howard K. Travers, Chief of Visa Division, Department of State inquiring into "probable causes of delay in the issuance of a visa to one Herbert Bruch, age thirteen, of 9 Wilmslow Road, Withington, Manchester:

> I would of course assume that the matter was proceeding with the customary dispatch consistent with regularity, had I not been told that no visas for this purpose were being issued. This seemed to me sufficiently improbable so that I am imposing on your good nature to inquire what the facts may be.

After listing enclosures of affidavits and references, Hilde made a personal plea to the Consul General of the United States of America, in London, England:

> Although I have not seen my nephew since 1934 (when I came to this country) we have been in active correspondence for several years. From his letters I have gained a good impression of his developing

personality. Herbert seems to me to be a very warm and considerate boy who always had good relations with his foster parents in the hostels and with his peers, an all around "good sport." As he grew older I recognized the expression of an unusually good intelligence. My impression has been confirmed by the fact that he received in 1944 a scholarship for High School education from the British government. Within a very short period he managed to be among the top students of his class. I am very anxious to help this gifted and ambitious boy to continue his education and follow a professional or business career in this country. In doing so I fulfill not only a general human obligation toward a deprived but promising young person but I am also expressing some of the gratitude which I owe Herbert's father, my oldest brother, who supported me in a generous and unselfish way when the early death of our own father made it seem impossible for me to follow my chosen career of becoming a physician.

In addition, I beg to be permitted to express here a personal problem. Due to the tragic events since 1933 with all the upheaval in human relations, I have been denied the happiness of having children of my own. My professional work, which is devoted to the physical and emotional well being of children and adolescents, is probably the best testimony to my sincere interest in children. It fills me with pride that my research work has found wide audience amongst physicians, psychiatrists and educators and that in this way I have been able to contribute my small measure to the progress and welfare of American youth. But this professional success is no valid substitute for the desire of a woman to have children of her own. I beg you to consider that Herbert will find in this country not an aunt who fulfills a duty, but a woman who is desirous to experience the joys and obligations of motherhood.

Within the last week a situation of which you can help me take advantage has developed. A friend and colleague of mine, Dr. Frieda Fromm Reichmann, of Washington, D.C., an internationally renowned psychiatrist-physician, is planning to visit her mother in England in December and has volunteered to look out for my nephew and bend her efforts to secure passage and have him return to the United States with her in January, 1946.

It is because of all of the foregoing that I have presumed so much on your attention in the hope that the necessary visa can be granted to him so that whatever proves the most opportune passage can be secured for him to come to me soon.

Like pieces in a jigsaw puzzle, suddenly everything fitted. The day after New Years, the Committee informed Hilde, "Provisional booking arrangements have been made, but the airline reserves the right to cancel, if necessary." Then, at last, the cable saying he was on his way....

She scolded herself for getting to La Guardia so early, but in her present state there was no holding back. When finally the plane landed some seven hours behind schedule, there were still more disappointing delays. An unidentified rash was uncovered and the entire passenger list placed under quarantine. Hilde, anxious as any new mother, felt grateful Frieda was aboard. That way, at least, the boy would have companionship and someone competent in charge.

But the child who eventually disembarked was hardly what she was expecting. She had sighted Frieda from a distance holding his arm, talking and urging him along, both momentarily hidden by other passengers pushing to either side. When they emerged, she was shocked to see how fragile he looked—no bigger than a puny eight-year-old toting a shabby suitcase. As she rushed out to greet them, she was suddenly aware of her towering size, what a giantess she must appear next to Frieda, who in heels stood no more than five feet.

It was 9:00 P.M. when they got to her apartment, the big day so slow arriving already at an end. Still, she found time to coax the youngster into a warm bath, while she returned to the kitchenette to prepare her chicken specialty. Afraid his enthusiasm would be slightly dampened by the fact that he had already eaten chicken twice on the trip, for added celebration she poured wine while they drank a toast to his new life. It had been hard getting the bananas for dessert, but well worth the effort, since he had never seen one before. Then it was time for bed, the living room couch, which would do until she could find a bigger apartment.

It had gone reasonably well, except that while he seemed reluctant to speak a single full sentence, she had been chatty as a magpie. When harmless questions consistently drew long pauses, she retired into a monologue about life in America, which seemed to make both more comfortable.

She let him sleep till noon the following day before steering him to a clothing store to properly outfit him for an American school career— *long trousers* being most essential. He seemed fascinated by the new image in pants, admiring himself at length in the department store mirror, at the same time flatly refusing to try the checkered sport shirts and loud socks she was also urging on him. Here was a boy with a mind of his own, a Bruch characteristic Hilde understood and admired, though she disagreed with his conservative English tastes, which in colors ran from gray to beige. Finally she persuaded him "a little red is nice" and he agreed to accept a tie with a thin red stripe.

Hilde had never considered any other place for Herbert than Elisabeth Irwin High School on Bleeker Street, which was known for its progressive curriculum and academic excellence. On the way home from enrolling, she asked what he most wanted to do in America, and when he said he wanted to see an opera, she rushed to the Metropolitan ticket office to fulfill the wish, her own heart nearly bursting with joy.

One week later, she was sending appreciations to England. In a letter to Miss Baruch, Matron of the hostel in Manchester where Herbert had last lived, she described her nephew's early experiences in America:

> We have spent a good deal of time looking over old family photographs and he is very eager to learn about his background and people. During the next few days, when I had to go back to my work, he kept himself busy with a number of new books and my typewriter. We also had visits with a few distant relatives and several friends of mine, with all the excitement of having dinner on the outside. Then the Big Event came, a performance of *Tannhaeuser* at the Metropolitan. It really was exciting, everything, getting dressed, going there, seeing the red plush and lights, the people in the audience, the orchestra and performance. He enjoyed the second act best and made a classical remark about the third act, "They sang so much that this took up all the time," as a contrast to the action in Act II.
>
> Herbert is so full of all the new impressions that he has not yet found time to tell me much about the previous life; but he was very confident and at ease with me from the beginning, and in spite of the long trip, full of eagerness to learn about the new life. I have written you in such detail because Herbert's whole development shows that he has been living with people who were genuinely interested in him.

CHAPTER VII

1946 - 1949

Camp Riverdale

A domestic Hilde, trying to recoup advantages for a nephew long deprived of them, moved from a tiny three room apartment overlooking Central Park into spacious quarters with separate bedrooms on 84th Street, where patients followed a long corridor to reach an adjoining waiting room and office. Herbert, occupying a different part of the complex, enjoyed separate entrance, albeit originally intended for a maid.

The youngster was proving himself a fine student. True, a superior English educational system had put him well ahead of his eighth grade American classmates. On the other hand, his ignorance of social skills and American history tended to equalize things. The school suggested he work on "the development of social and economic ideas" during math class, a move which did not call forth great enthusiasm but which was considered necessary if he were to become as proficient in naming U. S. Presidents as Kings of England.

Social progress was probationary:

> During the first four weeks, Herbert tried to make contact with a small group of boys that he had very quickly recognized as leaders in the class. As they are much more mature emotionally than he is, they did not respond to his tentative advances as he would have liked and he withdrew. Other boys sought him out however, and although he was not overly receptive to their advances at first, he has gradually ac-

cepted their overtures and has become integrated with the group in this way.

The report, while mildly disheartening, came as small surprise to Hilde, who had encountered Herbert's reticence the first day they met. Even now, though claiming ease with her, he showed extreme difficulty initiating conversation or sharing activities and feelings, no doubt feeling happiest alone listening to broadcasts of the New York Yankees. She told herself it was natural "English reserve," the same that governed his conservative tastes in food and clothing, and like any perplexed but conscientious mother set about finding simple and obvious remedies.

Though impossible to reclaim his lost childhood, she was anxious to expose him to "American" experiences, regenerate boyhood in a new land. She also intended changing his pale complexion and puny appearance to one of ruddy and robust health. How better than through the youthful activities of summer camp? After investigating several, she settled on Camp Riverdale in the Adirondacks, proceeded to meet "Official Camp Outfitting List" requirements by going on a buying spree, then laboriously completed the process by sewing name labels or penning adhesive identifications on everything from canteen to tooth brush.

By June 24th, a trunk containing most of his clothing plus such oversized items as sheets, pillow, and tennis racket had been mail-expressed so as to be there well ahead of the "Middler" camper who would arrive with only a day's supply of clothing but well stocked in postcards and writing paper. When the day came to see him off, Hilde was worried, watching the tiny figure board the huge Trailways Bus...was she doing the right thing?

She soon felt reassured. Even the normally non-verbal Herbert under pressure by a "thoroughly fine lot of counselors" to write home, was surprisingly detailed describing his first two days at camp in terms any mother will understand:

> Arrived at journey's end, seven o'clock. Took boat ten miles up to camp. Made slight friendship with some boys. Was taken into Middler camp and shown Cabin. My counselor's name is Uncle Bud. Cleaned up, had supper consisting of soup, eggs, salad, milk, and ice cream (vanilla.) Went to bed 10:15 P.M. later than usual. Had no sheets and pillow. Made my own with towel.

Woken up 7:10 A.M. Cleaned up. Had breakfast at 8:00 A.M. consisting of cold or hot cereal, bread, milk, butter and apple butter. Made beds and cleaned cabin. Then had doctor's examination who said I could not go into water until today. After that boys took swim test which I could not take because I couldn't swim. Cleaned up. Lunch of corn beef, cabbage, fried potatoes, plum. Field day consisting of Indian wrestling, dashes, three-legged race, basketball shots, and tug-o-war. Then there was general swim. I did not swim. Cleaned up. Supper of hamburger, mashed potatoes, peas, peach pie. Then we had an evening of song in the play room plus the band of the camp. Then I cleaned up and went to bed, again without sheets and pillow.

Love,

Herbert

Following this first promising verbal spurt, camp news trickled to finally dry up altogether, but by mid-summer Hilde herself had visited to observe the trunk in his cabin and Herbert swimming. She was full of high spirits when she arrived, accompanied by brother, Kurt, and new bride, "Skipper."

Kurt had met Catherine Bell in 1940 with his first American job as counselor in a summer camp where she also worked as a counselor. The relationship flourished even after both entered the armed services, Skipper as part of Intelligence, Kurt, cleverly, as a guard in an American camp for German POWs. Married less than a month, their visit with Herbert was primarily a "good-bye." Shortly they would be packing their Willys Jeep and seeking fortune in California, the state Kurt had grown to love during his army stint in San Diego.

The outing was fun for everyone, especially for Herbert, who for the first time all summer felt deliciously unshackled of camp restrictions, touring beautiful New York State with this ebullient trio of adults. The remainder of summer passed quickly, while September reaped the usual inflated evaluations from a director anxious to recruit next summer's campers.

Academically and intellectually more mature than most Middlers, Herbie has nevertheless been able to learn a great deal from his associates this summer. The first and most important lesson was to overcome his shyness; to assert himself as an individual living among individuals. The give and take that is such an important part of American boyhood has been very readily assimilated by him. Special exercises have helped to remedy posture defect. Always neat and clean, Herbie has consistently displayed the right spirit in doing his share and more in the cabin.

Pitts

He represented the love of her life—also her best kept secret. He said he wished it otherwise, but family and profession dictated his life and obligations. He was father and grandfather, he was teacher, practitioner, and administrator.

She was mature, a professional herself. She knew how to conduct herself with grace, to rein in a romantic heart bursting to shout his name from atop the Berkshires, where love had first called out her name.

He was her "Pitts," the pseudonym he adopted to mark the city where their tryst began. She teasingly called herself "an Anaerobe," for indeed that's what she was—a micro-organism existing without air or free oxygen. The melodious term pleased her, not only for the pretty tune it played upon her lips, but for all the beguiling myths it recalled to her imagination. She the goddess, Anaerobe, was by love to Orpheus bound, but completely dependent on human love for existence, was doomed by the rules of society into keeping tormented silence.

Oh well, maybe not so torturous as all that, she laughingly told herself. Though not her style to be mute about anything, she did discover in it certain subtle satisfactions. While he was conducting class, for example, she could feel pride swell as quietly she feasted her eyes, all the while knowing that whether she performed brilliantly or remained dumbly unresponsive, she would still be his student of choice, the one he most admired. Should she chance upon him in the dining hall exchanging information with a colleague, the look which passed between them was the electric charge which powered her entire day.

Though he expressly warned her not to commit such feelings to paper, a heart in love is one not easily muffled:

> I know you don't want me to write letters—and I can promise this
> one won't get into the mail or into anyone's hands. Maybe this is just

a safeguard for myself, that I really write down things I had on my mind during the past few days. It isn't that they bother me. On the contrary, I seem to be walking around with a secret smile on my face, as if I were guarding a great happy secret. Maybe writing down these things will help to get them out of my mind, and thus make them safer.

I was sorry you could not come on Monday after the lecture. I left with the conviction that you would be able to get away. It was nice that you called me later. I remember the call, only I was so sleepy that I do not remember what I said. I hope it did not shock you. It sounds foolish, but I'm still concerned about that. I wanted you very badly—I had been so proud and happy during the evening—and I felt there was no other way to express my admiration.

That Monday night I could do something that had eluded me thus far. For the first time I could see you all in one—the man whom I had known and respected and liked for these many years as friend and teacher and boss and scientist and what have you—and the man I had come to love during the last two years. The division had troubled me a good deal in the beginning, though it had become less and less. Our private life was something apart from seeing you in the dining room or discussing a paper. On Monday night, I finally could make the fusion and I am very happy about it. I had wanted to express all this in a more direct and meaningful way, so we'll have to catch up on a missed opportunity next time.

I am sometimes quite amused about the things I am too shy and bashful to tell you, even now. I don't know whether you noticed—you usually do notice such things—how happy I was that you wanted me to be just quiet and passive. I had been dying to ask for exactly that for some time—not always, but sometimes. But you expressed satisfaction over my participation quite often, and the other only once—quite in the beginning—and I did not want to disappoint you. Something else that makes me glad—although it might sound paradoxical—you speak more often and with more affection of your family. I have a feeling that it has to do with your better feeling over our relationship. You sometimes say you feel guilty toward me. I don't understand it, and I wish we could talk about it quite openly. I had started to write "often" and I mean that, too. You must know that you have made my life richer and warmer—and many things I don't dare to write down. Somehow it isn't fair that I am getting so much more out of it, but I am not so sure whether we really experience this in such a different way.

You scare away from the word "love." It really does not matter what you call your feelings. I am completely happy about what you show and express, no matter what you call it. Maybe we mean different things when we use the word. Possessiveness, domination, imprudent behavior do not belong to it, nor does being committed beyond the time of a meaningful relationship. I am against all that, too. What remains is in my feeling sufficient to deserve the term "love," and what I have experienced from you in tenderness, consideration and true respect and interest looks very much like it according to my usage of the term. The few things you told me about your earlier years seem to contain the clue why you have to remain more detached than I am in verbal expression. Let's talk about it next time.

This looks to me like a pretty long letter that is earmarked not to be sent off. I hope that my *Hausfrauen-instinkt* which does not permit work and effort to be wasted will not kick up and make me give it to you unless I really feel you want and should read it.

The letter, so uncharacteristically revealing of Hilde's inner feelings—such is the nature of love—was far too personal to be sent. Only one other shared her secret, definitely approving it: Frieda Fromm Reichmann, her analyst and closest friend. Frieda's passionate and unconventional views regarding love developed out of the Germany of the 1920s, when the sensitive young student, Erich Fromm, came to her for analysis and they sampled Freud's concept of "transference" firsthand by falling passionately in love. While Erich, her junior by ten years, searched for a more objective psychiatrist, they conducted what Frieda characterized a wild affair. "We weren't married and nobody was supposed to know about that and actually nobody did know," she confided to Hilde.

Now, she was overjoyed that her protégé and "Mr. Pitts" would experience similar rapture. "Society still pretends adherence to monogamous marital sex consummation only. Yet everybody knows that that is no longer it. Of course, there are some promiscuous fools who take advantage of this development. Should that be a reason to hold it up? Or will the time come when society changes its official standards?"

Nice to have Frieda's approval, even more, a friend to share truths with, but so far as needing professional or social sanction, it was neither solicited nor necessary. Lightness of foot and soul were more than adequate compensation.

Strange how with Pitts she first found it easier to share her bed than to part with intimate thoughts. But since he was an eager talker, she encouraged him to speak, at least until he teased her that this must be what it's like to be in "analysis." Following that remark, she grew even more deeply silent, because for all his talk of admiration, she knew he felt uncomfortable with her psychiatric training, even though as a pediatrician he still remained her mentor at Babies. Then when he asked whether she felt in danger of getting personally "involved" with patients, he unwittingly touched upon the precise reason for her reserve.

"My therapeutic usefulness depends on not getting involved or allowing a patient's personal experiences to affect my personal happiness," she explained with all the professional demeanor she could summon, because suddenly she found herself wondering whether the same might apply to her relationship with Pitts, for whom she felt anything but detached. The idea was sobering, but already by their next meeting she was willing to part even with the soul she had always controlled.

"I know I've kept myself somewhat divided, and I hope that didn't disappoint you too much…. You were half-joking when you referred to 'analysis,' but the truth is I was afraid I would be forced into a position of psychiatric detachment, or whatever you might want to call it."

"By now, you must know that what concerns you also concerns me, and that my happiness and security and peace of mind are very much affected by what is going on between us. If we can share these thoughts and feelings as intimate friends, then I won't have to hold back, and certainly there is no need to get mixed up with any analytic concept."

Following that understanding, they settled into a somewhat patterned existence, meeting whenever they could, Hilde refusing to pout when he was unable to get away. The flame that flickered and tortured her while she waited for the phone to ring or envisioned meetings which never transpired, was alternately rewarded when the fire burned dazzling bright and minds and bodies became one.

Before Herbert joined her household, they sometimes rendezvoused in her apartment, because she loved the comfort of attending his needs in a homey atmosphere. Surely it was a labor of love which motivated her to sample recipes all day so at night she might delight and pamper him with gourmet preparations served upon Royal Copenhagen place settings for two. She had discovered the appealing single iris pattern at a conference abroad, specially selecting additional pieces to complement their candlelight occasions.

An endearing formality attended these soirees, where brandy and conversation gave way to meaningful pauses, while both stubbed cigarettes into the separate Royal Copenhagen ash trays and she excused herself to slip into something feminine and lacy designed to arouse his senses. It seemed so terribly important to create an image of perfection now that she was in her lover's hands, since his assessment was nothing less than a reflection of herself.

Following Herbert's arrival, things grew increasingly complicated, their meetings more restricted. She adjusted. If not privately, she could still see him at social gatherings, and there were always those scheduled out-of-town conferences when she could anticipate more. But after he announced he was taking a new professional position in another city, her temper flared. She wondered whether she could survive the void and briefly considered following him, even discussing the possibility of moving with Herbert.

The plan was impulsive, totally impractical, something she already knew, and Pitts was at pains to convince her of it also. He reminded her that what was for him an important career step was unlikely to be the same for her. Besides, they would stay in touch. Whenever prudence permitted, he would write or call, and there were still the conferences....

Remembering Karl Orzech with his worthless promises, she once more felt betrayed, then immediately relinquished. Not only were the times different, so was the man and the relationship. Her beloved was a man of honor, theirs a mature modern relationship. All this she understood. At the same time, she could not stay the flood of feelings gnawing at her heart. He must have sensed it, too, and worried, because from a distance he found courage to speak:

The Drake, Chicago

Dear Hilde:

I have delayed slightly in penning this in order that your next "personal" letter might come from a different city. Frankly, I was a bit "bewildered" by the course of events at our last meeting—

"dumb" is perhaps a better word though it does not, as you know, do justice to a complicated emotional situation.

I have tried in the past to be honest about my feelings, but at the same time I have chosen to cast this honesty to the winds during the moments when I have been with you. From an intellectual standpoint, I know you would not wish me to do otherwise. Nevertheless, such moments do engender tensions and a yearning within you, which I am not too dumb to understand, for more than I am able (willing, if you like) to give.

If our meetings, which do yield both social and physical enjoyment, are to continue, they cannot be construed as the building up of an obligation which must be met in the future. Such a feeling of obligation in either party would spoil the whole affair. Either you or I must be free to stop the meetings if events enter our lives which change existing circumstances.

In writing in this way there is the intent of firmness with no note of harshness. I have enjoyed all our contacts and gone hog wild over some of them. As a male of the species, there is periodically within me a violent need to bend the bow until the string is taut, then send the pulsating arrow deep into its wanted target. Please excuse the poetry. This being so, each occasion has been more than worth while for its own sake alone. Of course, I should miss it in the future if circumstances should stop our meetings, but I could never regret so much fun and so much physical relief.

I do not feel that I should encourage you to come to Stockbridge if the reason is solely one of being with me. If I am unable to see you or can see you only at five o'clock tea, there would be too many regrets. However, be assured that failure to see you would not at all result from willful neglect. It would merely mean that I was a victim of circumstances. The people coming to Stockbridge represent the world in which I live and work, and while there, in large measure, I belong to them. I know you understand this, and I hope you will believe that I shall be looking all around expectantly to see if you are there.

As ever,

Pitts

Given no choice, since the impossibility of accepting the situation on his terms was exceeded only by the more devastating thought of losing him altogether, she retreated to other distractions, relying on time and distance to heal the hurt. Patience wasn't easy, but there were plenty of other things to keep her busy until he chose to make the next contact.

Domestics

The lad from Germany/Holland/England had by necessity become expert in assimilating new and varied surroundings. In America, he gravitated to professional sports, especially baseball, adoring the Yankees, tolerating the Giants, and hating the Dodgers. He kept abreast of his team's winning ways through newspapers, sports magazines, and a portable radio which became his regular after-school companion for late inning broadcasts. Hilde deemed his preoccupation with keeping scores and tabulating statistics intelligent but unworthy, and more importantly, another excuse to procrastinate.

Not that he needed excuses. Years of adult supervision, of being told exactly what to do, how and when to do it, had resulted in a peculiar kind of apathy which stifled initiative, sometimes interfering with the development of natural abilities. He had learned to live encapsulated in a present severed from its past and having little connection to a future.

As Hilde gradually recognized the depth of his problems, she sought psychiatric help, making certain he reported for regular therapy sessions. Physical appearance was another worry. At thirteen years of age when he came to live with her, he weighed only seventy-five pounds and was far below average in height. Concerned when growth and puberty continued to be delayed, she consulted colleagues, who found only a mild nutritional disturbance and put him on a high protein diet; by the time he entered college, he would stand at a lanky six feet.

Despite what would seem to be a tangled assortment of medical problems and differences of temperament, Hilde and Herbert developed a lighthearted and playful rapport. It was true the go-getter, Hilde, would never feel entirely at peace with Herbert, the sleeper-procrastinator, who constantly challenged her powers of psychological persuasion, yet no one would ever doubt her love or willingness to understand and tend his needs.

One of their favorite places to visit was Dorothy Andersen's farm on High Point Mountain near Port Jervis. Hilde, of course, was no stranger to the ramshackle hut where chopping wood and hauling water from a nearby stream were considered part of its rustic charm. Since her return from Hopkins, she was no longer affiliated with Babies Hospital and was therefore out of professional touch with Dorothy, but now that the relationship was strictly personal, they saw even more of one another.

Inside the well-weathered shingled exterior, warmth and friendship awaited anyone who entered. Dorothy, orphaned early in life, understood companionship in very concrete terms, and her tumble-down lodging embodied simple household pleasures such as having a place to stay, of having good family meals, of having fun together.

The stocky woman with mannish features, whose lips were never without a cigarette, soon discovered she had much in common with her colleague's nephew. Both loved games—any games: cards, chess, match it, pick up sticks—whatever they knew or could invent, they did with fervor. More for company than true involvement, Hilde sometimes joined in, but could never boast their seriousness.

Another of Dorothy's hobbies, wood working, also appealed to Herbert, and Dorothy was convinced Hilde would enjoy it if only she would try it. Though Hilde invariably arrived well-equipped with reading and writing materials, especially when spending a week or more at the farm, at Dorothy's beseeching she agreed to swap the tools of intellect for tools of trade in order to make a table. But when days passed and she did not lift a finger, it became clear the table would not get done, so Dorothy politely suggested she make a small cabinet instead. A few days later, the cabinet became a foot stool, until eventually Dorothy brought out a finished piece of furniture for sanding. "It's not that I don't like working with my hands, the reluctant carpenter protested, but I prefer soft things like knitting, not harsh things that give me splinters."

The place was unheated, a fact which hadn't fazed Dorothy's guests who were a hearty bunch. Indeed, late fall and winter was prime time, culinary tradition time, when friends brought favorite recipes accompanied by plenty of cheer to celebrate Thanksgiving, Christmas and New Year's Day. It was here, during holiday time, that Hilde further refined her tastes for turkey, hubbard squash, and eggnog.

But even in mid-summer, the large barn-like structure seemed impervious to sun. A Franklin stove in the kitchen ran constantly, replacing dampness with warmth and radiating heat immediately upward.

Those not lucky enough to be assigned the toasty upstairs bedroom, at nighttime pulled a heated brick from the oven, wrapped it in a towel, and carried it to bed with them. The simplicity, the congenial gatherings in the kitchen, card games, regularly assigned chores—all these things that meant so much to Hilde—quite possibly reminded her of another time and another family, in Duelken.

Within two years of Herbert's arrival, and likewise with Hilde's financial aid, Erna, now estranged from her husband, emigrated to the U.S.A. The Civil War in Palestine had left her destitute, fearful, and uncharacteristically melancholy. Accompanied by eight-year-old Ayala, she would spend only a few weeks with Hilde in New York, before leaving for Aurora, where she would live with Ernst and Else while seeking work for herself, schooling for her daughter.

Brief though the visit was, Hilde felt her sister's pain, but a brighter change for Erna was her new name. Just as Hilde had very early dropped the "Brun" out of "Brunhilde," and without officially changing it watched a gradual demise, so Erna freed herself of the High German heroic, "Flying Eagle." She was now calling herself "Ester," spelling it like the Hebrew, without an "H." Barring a few practice slips, Hilde and Herbert successfully made the exchange.

The College Experience

Nineteen hundred and forty-nine was the year Herbert became a senior, and Hilde, like parents everywhere, was caught up and traumatized by the "College Process." She believed, and Herbert somewhat agreed, he would be happiest in the personalized setting of a small college, and following what seemed an interminable period of procrastination, he applied to two: Swarthmore College in Pennsylvania, and Wesleyan University in Connecticut.

Because it was coed and had the reputation for being liberal, Hilde preferred Swarthmore, but knowing the final decision must be Herbert's, she was at great pains to appear objective. Not that she intended leaving anything to chance by allowing events to play their course; not that she wouldn't weight the scales in her own favor:

Dean Everett L. Hunt
Swarthmore College
Swarthmore, PA

Dear Sir:

This letter is intended as an addition to the application of my nephew, Herbert Bruch. Herbert is the son of my oldest brother, Rudolf Bruch. Herbert's father, mother, and younger sister were killed by the Nazis. My brother was a merchant and the family lived in comfortable, cultured circumstances when Herbert was born. After the pogrom in 1938, during which his home was demolished and his father taken away to a concentration camp, he and his younger sister were sent for safety to Holland, in the hope that the parents would soon follow, so that the family could be reunited abroad. Herbert and his sister lived in Holland until May, 1940, when the Germans invaded Holland. Herbert was taken to England on a children's transport. His little sister was left behind and was later sent back to her parents in Germany, where she was eventually deported and killed.

Shortly after the war ended, I received word that Herbert's family had been killed and I made arrangements to have him come to live with me. I had anticipated that he might suffer from the effects of the vicissitudes of his early life and I was surprised that he had done so well in spite of all the hardship. Nevertheless, the readjustment to a new country and new school system offered quite a number of difficulties. I chose the Elisabeth Irwin High School for him to attend because I was impressed by its public-minded and tolerant spirit and also by its sound teaching program. Herbert had some difficulty in adjusting to the much freer educational system after the more traditional English schooling, under which he had done exceedingly well.

In his social development Herbert was handicapped by the fact of not having lived in a real family and being puzzled by the ways of American boys. He was also handicapped by retarded growth and slow puberty development due to malnutrition. Only during the last year did he make up the growth deficit. This slow development, however, had the advantage that he spent part of his childhood in this country. During this time of adjustment Herbert and I enjoyed the help and encouragement of many friends.

In choosing a college for Herbert I considered both academic and social aspects. Herbert's best gifts are in the fields of mathematics and science and he works well on individual programs and under personal direction. The teaching program of Swarthmore seemed best to meet his needs. I felt, too, that a coeducational college would be desirable for him. I also hope that the tolerance of the Quaker tradition will offer a social atmosphere which will counter-balance the early experiences of persecution and prejudice.

It might be desirable to discuss Herbert's educational needs in a personal interview and I should be very glad to come with him to Swarthmore. Since I have many professional and teaching obligations I should like to make an appointment in advance. I would be able to come to Swarthmore on January 10th or on January 17th. Kindly advise which day would be convenient to you.

One week later, at Dean Hunt's invitation, they made plans to visit Swarthmore, some weeks following that, to investigate Wesleyan. On April 18, a telegram for Herbert: CONGRATULATIONS YOU HAVE BEEN AWARDED THORNDICE SCHOLARSHIP SIX HUNDRED DOLLARS—HOPE AWARD MAKES WESLEYAN POSSIBLE FINANCIALLY—MANY QUALIFIED APPLICANTS ON ALTERNATE LIST SO PLEASE REPLY WESTERN UNION YOUR DECISION ACCEPT OR DECLINE AT EARLIEST CONVENIENCE AND NOT LATER THAN MAY FIRST.

It sounded fine to Herbert, who was ready to accept, until Hilde pointed out they had not heard from Swarthmore. To buy additional time, she telephoned Dean Eldridge at Wesleyan, and one week later was rewarded when Herbert was accepted to Swarthmore with a $300 scholarship award. Once again Herbert felt honored, but faced with an alternate choice, confusion diffused some of his pleasure.

Hilde suggested he discuss the matter with a professional who would understand his personal needs but remain unbiased. Then she composed the following letter to Richard Frank, his therapist:

Dear Dick:

I am very glad that you take the time to see Herbert. He has been talking about wanting to see you for quite some time but procrastinated in his usual way. Right now he is confronted with the final decision about college. Last year, when applications were being made, he felt that he wanted to go to a small college and he applied to Swarthmore and Wesleyan. He was accepted and granted a freshman scholarship by both these schools. He really wants to go to Swarthmore, but he has heard that some people consider it a too strenuous college. He is all prepared for you to talk him out of it. The advantage of going to Swarthmore would be that several boys from his school are there, and there are also quite a number of people in and around Philadelphia whom he would have as "family."

Wesleyan is, as you know, an all men's college and Herbert feels rather warm, because they gave him a feeling that they really wanted him when he went for his interview. I can see a potential problem in the fact that it is a "fraternity" college and I discussed this aspect frankly with the Dean of Admissions. He agreed that my questions would have been very pertinent about ten years ago, but that the general experience has been considerably liberalized during the post-war years. There are fewer than one hundred Jewish students in a college population of nearly eight hundred and he does assure me that they were well integrated. The College had turned down the formation of a Jewish fraternity because they felt it would tend towards segregation. To be frank, I did not know that Wesleyan was a fraternity college when Herbert made the application. Although I might have all kinds of objections, on principle, I can see a number of personal benefits for Herbert to have the feeling of "belonging to a house." I assume that he has some other things on his mind and whatever arrangements you make with him are agreeable to me. By and large he has been much freer and happier during the past few years and he recovers more quickly when he gets into an occasional "stew."

With best personal regards,

Hilde had her way. Herbert chose Swarthmore.

CHAPTER VIII

1950 - 1960

Margaret Mead

With Herbert away at college, the next four years allowed more flexibility in professional and social schedulings. What writing she did was delivered to conferences of other pediatricians anxious to benefit from her newly-acquired psychological wisdom. Ideas flowed freely, but were still vague enough that most papers went unpublished, for without the broad and varietal experience of private and clinical practice to back them up, she was reluctant to put them in print. As always, her powers of observation spilled out of the workplace: file cabinets bulged with newspaper and magazine clippings, literary references shared space with laboratory statistics.

While the full implications of psychoanalytic training remained un-formulated, earlier studies and observations were indeed brought to fruition in the book, *Don't Be Afraid of Your Child.* She worked on it during the late forties, dedicating it to all parents, specifically to Mae Enselberg, mother of "Chuck," Herbert's good friend, and, of course, to Herbert, "who helped me overcome my own fears." Not a hand-book, but a guide for perplexed parents, it contained practical sugges-tions without offering "cook book" recipes, since there is no magic formula for parent instruction. It was the common sense answer to experts who trick and intimidate parents with prescriptions of psychological jargon. This time when the girl from Duelken bred on fairy tales declared the emperor naked, she revealed a fabric of dishonesty, pompousness, and fad which shrouded the entire field of child psychology.

The writing was as fresh, lively, and free of literary conceit as the message it conveyed, namely that resourceful confident parents will likely raise psychologically healthy children. Since social, economic, and cultural changes are historic fact, part of an ongoing process in which family, too, is dynamic, "parents must learn to use methods appropriate to themselves, their children and their circumstances." Curiously modern, this sweeping philosophy seems as appropriate in today's very changed family structure as in 1952 when it was published.

The book drew critical praise with one notable exception. The lone dissent came from Margaret Mead, whose stature and popularity as an anthropologist rendered her review disproportionately weighty. But the damaging article appearing in the book review section of *American Journal of Orthopsychiatry*, April 1954, curiously missed the point. It attacked Hilde for being authoritarian in her attitude towards parents, the very opposite of what was intended and which was apparently correctly understood by everyone else.

Couched among harmless generalizations, ironic slurs ran like a malicious undercurrent throughout the article, but it was the more specific second part brimming with what one could only imagine were Mead's own biases that kindled Hilde's fury:

> Just what is the responsibility of members of another culture, who still share the values and attitudes of that culture, when they set themselves up as authorities for the mothers of their new country? The dust jacket tells us that Dr. Bruch was born and educated in Germany and did not come to this country until 1933. But when the dust jacket is discarded, there is no indication in the book itself of this pervasive German background, with its insistence on the single authority and its terrible fear of the consequences of giving in to children.
>
> I gave this book to a colleague who has been working with contemporary German child-rearing materials and, after she had read the first three chapters, asked her to predict the end of the book on the basis of her knowledge of German attitudes toward child rearing. She wrote: "Last chapter will be about how to be 'natural' with one's children; how to be oneself, then the children will be 'naturally'

good, because parents will be 'honest' with themselves and their children. Then parents will be *parents* (not slaves), children will be children (not tyrants)—and there will be no need for the 'expert' outsider."

The anthropologist will be the first to acknowledge the importance of cross-cultural criticism, and to point out the invaluable contributions which German and Austrian psychology and medicine have brought to this country. But these contributions should be labeled. The reader should know how deep is the German preference for a single authority, how different their conceptions of childhood, how distrustful they are of the kind of awareness which has become an integral part of the American character.

That she had been misunderstood was curious, disagreed with disappointing, but what Hilde interpreted as a slanderous personal attack on her ethical and educational background sent her into a rage. She refuted by sending numerous typed carbons of the heinous article to friends and colleagues who were equally incensed.

They answered with sympathetic letters, or by corresponding directly to George E. Gardner, editor of the periodical, declaring "foul." One of Hilde's staunchest advocates, German-born Frieda Fromm Reichmann, considered Dr. Mead's sentence, "Just what is the responsibility of members of another culture when they set themselves up as authorities for the mothers of a new country?" as a direct attack on all foreign-born psychiatrists as well as others working in related professions.

In angry rebuttal, Hilde's anthropologist friend, Florence Powdermaker, chastised the editor:

Dear George:

I really was quite shocked at Margaret Mead's review of Hilde Bruch's book. I was surprised in the first place that she was asked to review this book since her tendency to be an expert on practically every professional subject except possibly mining and engineering has made her opinion of little value to many scientists.

Dr. Bruch has been in this country for twenty-one years, during which time she has, as you know, been an intense student of individual patients and of our culture. This is in contrast to Dr. Mead's authoritative attitude on cultures which she has studied for a year or two.

The book has obviously been misread with Dr. Mead's own prejudices and pre-conceptions as to child rearing. I have read Dr. Bruch's book carefully and nowhere is there any "insistence on the single authority and its terrible fear of the consequences of giving in to children." This is, at best, a misunderstanding, because the relaxed attitude, which is so much a part of the book, is the very opposite of that which would engender "terrible fear," "insistence" or "single authority."

How on earth the two sentences that Dr. Mead quotes can be interpreted as "German and/or Austrian" psychology and medicine is beyond me. The obvious assumption is that the German psychiatrist, psychologist, teacher, etc. now practicing in this country, even twenty years or more, carries with him a background which makes him unsuited to carry out his work.

While Powdermaker queries the wisdom of asking Mead's opinion in the first place, it is quite explainable: When a young specialist collaborates on wartime projects with a famous author/anthropologist, later becoming an author herself, what better way to insure recognition than through the agreeable commentaries of this already established writer?

Hilde was still in psychiatric training assisting Leo Kanner in Baltimore when her participation in a nutrition study was sought in early spring of 1942. At that time, Margaret Mead headed the National Research Council's Committee on Food Habits and was trying to determine what effect wartime food rationing might have on the possible deterioration of American morale as a whole, or at least in selected sections of the population. Hilde's method of study, her extensive investigation of patients together with family members in their home environment, seemed ideally suited to the project.

Hilde jumped at the opportunity, since "it coincides with work I had planned after my return to the Babies Hospital in New York." In retrospect, she felt the wartime nutritional studies insignificant except as additional histories for reference and evaluation, though she did consider the association with M.M. beneficial. Dr. Mead, during their first meeting, confessed surprise that Hilde spoke with an accent. She claimed to have read all of Hilde's publications never guessing she was foreign-born, because the whole obesity study showed such insight and awareness of the American family structure. What irony that she now was making derogatory comments about her background.

Shocked and angered by Mead's assault, Hilde wrote editor George Gardner requesting that two papers being held for publication be returned to her along with written permission to publish them elsewhere.

"I do not care to publish in a journal with such a lax editorial policy that it permits under the heading 'Book Review' a personal attack on an author, expressing the lowest type of anti-foreigner prejudice. You will agree that under these circumstances I can no longer publish my observations in the *American Journal of Orthopsychiatry*."

The editor was apologetic:

> I want to assure you with all sincerity, Dr. Bruch, that we in the Editorial Office did not construe the critique by Dr. Mead as a personal attack upon you.
>
> In the light of your reaction and your suggestion that you withdraw your papers, I would like to suggest the following. Would you like to select another reviewer in your field who would prepare another critique of your book and who you feel would be more competent to judge it? If so, we will be very happy to present this in the book review section as "an additional review."

In the end, Hilde did not withdraw the papers. Eventually she reasoned there was no advantage in backing off and allowing evil to go unanswered. However, in a sarcastic response to the editor, she countered M.M. with a few digs of her own:

> The fact that Dr. Mead raises a nationalistic issue makes it difficult to propose another reviewer. I do not think that it would be appropriate that I myself write a rejoinder in which I justify myself as not being authoritarian, etc. As a matter of fact, I would hesitate to suggest anybody who is not native-born. If one carries her argument to its absurd conclusion I would have to hunt for a pure-blooded American Indian who also is a psychoanalyst and child psychiatrist. I've started some inquiries but I haven't heard of anybody who fulfills this requirement.
>
> I just saw Dr. William Langford. He told me that he had communicated with you already. He hesitates to do the review because he feels he isn't quite native enough. Will says that he was "started" in Europe. He feels that might be cause to object against him—that he

might have gotten the wrong cultural influences before he was born. If this blemish on his background is no objection, he would like to do the review not for the June dateline but for the October issue.

Additional to the Langford review, Hilde requested her paper "Parent Education or the Illusion of Omnipotence" be published as a reply to Dr. Mead's attack, because "it happens to have as its main content a discussion of the dictatorial authoritarian attitude of the experts who superimpose their theories on parents."

When the October issue of *American Journal of Orthopsychiatry* came out, Hilde Bruch was its special feature. Besides the flattering Langford review, two articles by her own pen were included. The issue also served as an amnesty, for while feelings of betrayal and distrust would never be entirely eliminated, Hilde was able to mask them well enough to correspond civilly with Margaret Mead in the future. It helped that the book was successful and could stand on its own merit, but it also did not hurt that Dr. Mead's status was too formidable even for Hilde to crack.

Hilde proceeded to shun and then "forget" the incident, but that did not prevent Frieda and other colleagues from poking fun:

Take Heed, Take Heed
("My Bonnie Lies Over the Ocean")

(Frieda)   Oh, Hilde, in ten easy lessons
You've given us all that we need,
Mothers don't fear of your children,
Just love them and don't overfeed.

(Chorus)   Hilde, Frieda, watch out for your accents,
Take heed, take heed,
Hilde, Frieda, be careful of Margaret Mead!

(Frieda)   But people our side of the ocean
According to Margaret Mead,
Can hardly have any real notion
Of what gives with her and her breed.

(Frieda)   From Germany's culture and custom
To the home of the brave and the free,
Is a damn sight lot closer and then some
Than from here to the pagan South Sea.

Reverse of the Coin

While Mead's attack engendered "righteous anger," Hilde was not above harboring prejudices of her own. Presently engaged in recovering restitution for surviving family members, the pain of Nazi persecution throbbed like an open sore. Though outwardly she offered no sign of the affliction that had branded her for life—as surely as if she bore the tatoo of a concentration camp prisoner—she continued "business as usual," disguising anguish behind a fine "American" smile. Instead of healing, the wound festered, rendering an emotional state so fragile even trivial incidents triggered exaggerated reaction.

At least part of the problem was ambivalence toward her heritage. Vocally she denounced Germany along with everything German, but it was not so simple. Ties ran deep, while every day brought fresh exposure. Herbert was not merely an adolescent deprived of childhood, he was an adolescent deprived of a happy German childhood. No *Butterbrot* packed in fancy tournisters for him, no memories at all, in fact, for in what constituted the most savage deprivation of all, the youngster had deliberately voided all links to his past.

For Hilde, however, reminders of the old life abounded, forcing comparisons with the new. Even as she renounced such memories as "outdated" or "sentimental," she recognized the dishonesty, but could as easily have parted with representations of happy earlier times as with the precious photographs of family members who would never smile on her again. She had rejected the land of her birth, purposefully clawing it out by the roots, but in some respects she remained more German even than the stereotype. She cherished German education for its thoroughness, especially valuing her medical training, which had been accepted without qualification by the State of New York. Her personality radiated Teutonic pride and confidence, the same that had driven her to achieve and distinguished her even in childhood; only her analysts, Booth, Fromm Reichmann, and later Kubie, would recognize the disparity of its trembly foundation.

Harry Stack Sullivan also witnessed this vulnerability when he was commissioned by Trustees of the William Alanson White Psychiatric Foundation to accumulate facts and recommendations regarding postwar control of Germany, and Hilde used his poll as a sounding board for private pain.

After first announcing her bias, "because events in Germany have hit me personally during my days in medical school, hospitals, and even after I left Germany, when several members of my immediate family were lost," she felt justified in speaking plainly, especially since she was well acquainted with "good Germans." The scientist, Karl Orzech, was one. Another was a former school chum become a Ph.D., who prided herself on open-mindedness and a knowledge of current politics, yet hadn't the slightest clue why Hilde would uproot a "successful" private medical practice to leave for England. "This little matter of the April Boycott had entirely escaped her attention as being of any practical importance," Hilde declared, at the same time pointing out that Germans who were truly sensitive to events would not have survived them.

"The so-called liberal Germans of the postwar period are much more likely to be represented by those who had the lucky faculty of closing their senses to what was going on around them, and who then became fellow-travelers of Hitler, although they will be quite justified to point to their past liberal ideas. From the point of view of trusting postwar Germans, these people seem to represent a more dangerous type than the frank, outspoken, brutal Nazi. There is nothing the matter with them except their selfish, calculating coldness of heart, which is willing to drop all alliances whenever it appears to be opportune and who now will be just as ready to seek shelter in the promise of democracy."

Several years later she had the opportunity to express these sentiments more sarcastically when a letter addressed to "Fraulein Dr. Med. Brunhilde Bruch, Unsalaried lecturer at Medical University, New York," managed to find her.

It began, "Do you remember me? During the war I thought of you often." The fellow graduate of the Studienanstalt, now a dentist, went on to explain how after becoming a French citizen like her physician husband, they returned to the Rheinland to set up individual practices on properties owned by the husband. Soon they were blessed with three lovely children, and life seemed good: "We had six lovely private and practice rooms, and my wish to have a music room also came true."

After Hitler came to power, her husband didn't join a Nazi Physician Fraternity, since as an alien he hadn't needed to. This allowed him to treat persecuted Jews, many of whom expressed gratitude.

Yet despite open opposition to Hitler, they had suffered hardships. While away on vacation in 1943, the center of Gladbach had been flattened by bombings, their home and practice ruined. Presently they were living in a small village in the Westerwald where they had milk, potatoes and bread. Her husband was pessimistic about the future.

"And now, dear Hilde, I hope you can give us some information. As French citizens, is it possible to emigrate? Would my husband, a specialist in nerve disorders, need to take a medical examination or only one in English? What about me as a dentist? My husband wishes to do studies on blood in a modern lab. Could you show us the way and ask in the right places?"

The letter closed with gossip about mutual friends, inquiring whether Hilde still heard from anyone in Duelken. "How are you? Hope to hear from you soon."

From Hilde, a purely satirical reply:

I remember you very well. Your letter was less of surprise and shock to me than you probably imagined. It was the first of this type from someone of the old *Studienanstalt*. But on the whole it seems that our old colleagues and associates suddenly—after many years of silence and non-interest—remember some Jewish "friend" who has been successful on the road to a new life. My University career seems to make me a little bit more conspicuous. Unfortunately, you know from your own experience how little one can do for someone of a different background under changing political conditions.

You inquire concerning medical and dental requirements. As far as I know, and there is little or no chance that conditions will be eased, a State Board Examination is required for the practice of medicine in New York State—and in all other states. These examinations are not easy and not a mere formality. I think they are well justified because the difference in the progress between German and American medicine is enormous, it was so twelve years ago and must be much more so now. From all reports, and I have seen quite a few of the doctors who had been over there, German medicine has just stagnated, or even degenerated, so that a newcomer to this country has to learn a good many new things. As far as dentistry goes, not only examinations but a new course of study is required. I am not sure whether the complete course, but it means several years in a dental school. Right now it is practically impossible, even for an American, to secure a place in a dental school because the main training is given to the returning servicemen. That will probably ease within a few years. This news may not be very encouraging, but we had to do it when we came here—and without funds and other securities.

On the whole it may be well for you to know that public opinion is not very friendly to new converts in the field of anti-Nazism. That is the big puzzle here, how Hitler ever had any supporters if one tabulates the large number who claim to have been against him. Your husband may find it exceedingly difficult to explain to anyone how a French citizen with outspoken anti-Nazi feelings could and did survive in Nazi Germany through two wars, and not only survive but prosper, according to your description. The first person who will ask questions in this direction will be the American consul before he gives the visa. You may have cleared that problem already, but you will run into it here amongst intellectuals.

This long letter probably does not contain much news that is of help to you. It is an expression that I have read your letter with attention and sympathy. But as far as "giving help" is concerned, I have never found that one can give more than the inquirer has been able and willing to give when hardship befell us in 1933. One seems to live in peculiar circles, and if no contact of thinking and interest existed during those years, nothing much of common ground can be discovered now. One has to work out one's own solutions according to the possibilities which one can develop oneself.

Status Quo

With Herbert's letters assuring her of a fine adjustment to campus life, Hilde thought it high time to examine her own. True, accomplishments were piling up. She was busy with writing, patients, and friends...busy, busy, busy. Yet life with its whirlwind obligations and achievements was lacking something vital. She had not lost track of or forgotten what that elusive something was, nor would she settle for becoming its memory. Geographical distance had merely put into focus everything deficient in her life.

Pitts had warned that they must retain autonomy if their relationship were to succeed, and she, loving independence herself, had happily agreed to embrace a world of secret messages, accept the clandestine pleasure of being "his Anaerobe." But during the next years she had grown resentful of a role which, far from encouraging autonomy, was completely dependent on his whims. Now that he had physically removed himself, she felt even less free, since he had taken the most important part of her with him when he crossed those borders to set up practice in another state.

He told her she should stay in New York, not risk losing friendships and career interests. She knew differently. Careers moved all the time.... Hadn't he just moved his? Friendships survived great distances with only an occasional letter or visit to sustain them. Could love survive such odds? But if love desired wholeness, which is truly how she felt when she was with him, then even the *question* of separation was incongruent.

She would need to study hard to pass the medical examinations required by his state. Perhaps it worked to her advantage that she could not follow immediately. This way he would have a chance to get used to the idea; but, whether he approved or disapproved, she had a perfectly reasonable explanation for her action—action which probably should have been taken long ago. She was making herself flexible for the future.

Thus, between patient appointments and writing assignments, between sending food packages and letters to Herbert sympathizing with the student's lot, she settled for the tedium of preparing for medical board exams. What kept her spirits up was the certain knowledge that Pitts' faltering marriage was beyond resurrection, that when he also realized this truth by pronouncing its demise, he would send for her.

She passed the exams, but there it ended. He had apparently made peace with his situation, reveling in the new administrative position, which carried great responsibility and little free time. He acknowledged that the added workload was probably a good thing since domestic life was beyond mending, but he was doing what he could to accept his circumstances—for everyone's sake.

His nonchalant tolerance scared her, yet always when he managed to steal a few hours to be with her she felt so grateful that most doubts faded. They met at conferences, North, East, South or West, but always with such prolonged intervals between, that their rare encounters fostered less a sense of happiness than of bitter-sweet craving for what she was being denied. It was springtime in beautiful Virginia when she finally dared break the enchantment, and it drew immediate response from him:

> I am writing this letter with an understanding of and belief in a promise you have not given. After you have read it and absorbed its content, destroy it. After the happening at Old Point Comfort it is only right that I should write it.
>
> Just after the moment of supreme ecstasy you asked what plans we could make for the future. Aware of years of frustration along this line and being entirely relaxed and happy, I declined to discuss the matter at all. You seemed to understand and acquiesced at once. Indeed, you said yourself that you were happy, too, and content with the events of the present. As I write these lines I am convinced that this was so and am more optimistic than ever before about a relaxed and understanding future. I have a deep fondness for you and a deep appreciation of the unrestrained way in which you have met my problems and in which you have revealed your problems, too. I can never answer your problems in the way your soul and your body cry out to have them met. Nor can you ever give a full answer to my problems.
>
>> Doubts and misgivings must always arise.
>> When in doubt, play the hand, be secure!
>> Convention & custom are not lightly passed;
>> Opposing we may not endure.
>>
>> The soul that is sensible, prudent and strong
>> Will always attempt to conform,
>> And only when torn by conviction of right
>> May defy both convention and storm.

You must try to comprehend the life I have to lead. The "must" springs only in part from the needs of fulfilling an ego but also from a realization of the ambitions and hopes of many young men who have given me their faith and who are helping me develop a department. I cannot do things which might let them down. You have surmised a major problem I have to meet at home, and indeed your clear perception of the problem has been an important factor in a resolution to meet the problem as best I can. I know the problem can never be resolved completely but the resolution and what has been done in consequence thereof have helped. Because of the effort and because of children—and grandchildren—I know the family will hold together. It must hold together. None of this must be construed to mean that I have regrets over what has happened between you and me. My superego says,

> Now let the real exception come—
> Conviction born of trust;
> He who dares his peers defy,
> Gains glory in his "must."
>
> Gains glory for no wrong can be
> When mind has seen the light,
> With conscience clean and soul serene,
> Through the still small voice of right.

I am surrounded by and engulfed in departmental problems as well as by those at home. I am not free to travel when and where I will. I am not able to respond to insistence by you that I do so, and will be frustrated if you do not understand. But, believe me, the warmth and fondness remain. Old Point Comfort will not be forgotten. I shall call you when I can and want you to know I shall understand if you accept or reject in accordance with your own needs and problems.

Love had not incapacitated her wits, nor was she deaf or blind. She knew what he was saying. For all the oblique poetic gallantry, she knew that time unspared meant time unshared with her. If after that anything were left, it probably was crumbs. Still she patted the illicit letter into its ribboned folder marked "Personal," tucking it away, so that despite his admonition to destroy it, she might later draw from it exactly what she chose.

As always when things were out of her control, she retreated into work, that citadel of solace and most reliable of cure-alls. But this, too, was fast losing effectiveness, the sinking feelings gnawing ever deeper, and soon she realized that even things formerly considered "good" in her life were contributing to the pain.

Amazing, how huge the apartment had become with Herbert away. Her book, *Don't Be Afraid,* object of so much attention from colleagues and special recognition from Pitts, "I'm proud of you," had left her feeling accomplished yet curiously empty. Certainly, the passing of the medical board examinations was not the achievement hoped for. At best it was another humdrum exercise successfully overcome, come to nothing.

Still, she dared not rock the *status quo* with Pitts. There were better ways to attract his attention while redeeming self-worth. By now she had accumulated enough experience and data to write another book, this one focusing on her specialty, eating disorders. Another provocative challenge also lay ahead when Dr. Kolb, the newly-appointed Director of the New York State Psychiatric Institute, offered her directorship of the Children's Service.

Dr. Lawrence Kolb had arrived from Minnesota's Mayo Clinic intent on reorganizing things at P.I. and particularly the Children's Service. Like Hilde, he was one of Fromm Reichmann's protégés, and it was through the famed psychiatrist he first met Hilde. In Santa Fe, New Mexico, Frieda's summer retreat, he noticed a large-boned powerful woman who charmingly, but somewhat awkwardly dodged tables and guests to set out food and drink for a garden party. Later in conversation, he was attracted to her ideas and forcefulness of presentation. Surely this woman, whose concepts were as formidable as her appearance, would make an ideal choice for the job of reorganizing the Children's Service.

Hilde found the proposition enticing. It had the potential for being highly productive if personnel would work as a team, and while she supposed one project might draw valuable time from another, she also saw no reason why researching a book and researching records from the Children's service could not reinforce one another, especially if careful notes were kept. The biggest drawback was that in order to coordinate programs she would need to collaborate and cooperate, and from past experience she knew it was not something she did well. Thus it was important to have a clear understanding of what was expected of her:

> You want me to continue with my responsibilities on the Children's In-Patient Service at the Psychiatric Institute and also to work towards building up an Out-Patient Department. The work would involve the supervision and training of the residents at the Psychiatric Institute and later on, also of the students at the Psychoanalytic Clinic.

When Dr. Kolb agreed, or at least did not disagree with her version of the job description, Hilde decided once and for all to find out whether she had supervisory talent.

The Children's Service

What happens when important details such as making notes are handled by amateurs? For that matter, who decides the scheduling of nurses, so that anything resembling a coordinated program becomes more than pure accident? "There is a very peculiar system that nurses rotate their time of duty," she informed Kolb. "It is confusing to me not to know which nurse I will meet at ward rounds, and there are many indications it may be even more confusing to the children. In my opinion, the person who is the director of a service and is charged with the responsibility should have a say on such important matters as the type and quality of the nurses of the ward and the scheduling of their time and changes. But I have given up because I feel I lack authority to do so."

Complaints varied, but the concept of "authority" was always at the center:

> I take it for granted as part of my responsibility as director of a service in a hospital which is part of a medical school, and in addition represents a research institute for the state, that every clinical step should be the object of critical evaluation. On the basis of all my past training, at Babies Hospital, Hopkins and abroad, I would consider it neglect not to make observations on a drug that I am using for the first time, regardless of what I have read about it, or how well established its use is. When we prescribe new drugs for the first time to the children, I discuss at rounds in great length that separate notes should be kept on these children. (It would involve copying the ordinary nurses notes into a special book and writing weekly summaries on these children.) Both the head nurse and the residents were asked to keep this information. I was not able thus far to get any meaningful material, but the main fault lies with the fact that nurses notes are kept by student nurses and are, except for dramatic events, completely useless as far as recording observations.
>
> My comments about the drugs are a very minor example of the failure of the ward. In spite of my efforts to make the total milieu of the ward the essential aspect of treatment, I have not been able to get

234 UNLOCKING THE GOLDEN CAGE

chief nurses to come to conferences. More serious is the fact that even the residents who are on the service have not shown up at all or came late to the ward rounds. It is my feeling, although for this I have no proof, that the lackadaisical attitude of the residents is related to the nurses not showing up. I feel if I am responsible for a service and for the training of the physician who works on this service, I should have the authority to expect them to be there.

Also, my feeling is that no progress can be made until the chief social worker is on firmer footing. The response to the improvement of the social service set-up on the children's service has been objection from the rest of the social service department and a yearning for "the good old days." All I can do is repeat that I feel that I do not have the proper authority to do a job as it should be done, without any perfectionistic expectation.

As a matter of fact, the "perfectionist" in Hilde could not be ruled out. To do a job "right" or not at all, to pursue uncompromised truth, these, her greatest strengths as an individualist, were sadly unrealistic when it came to supervising others. Unfortunately, the high expectations she had of herself could not be transferred to coworkers who came across as incompetent, indifferent or both. Most likely they were neither, but mere human beings working for a superhuman and demanding boss. When nurses, residents, and social workers rebelled, as each invariably did in his own fashion, Hilde demanded even more authority to cure what she interpreted as a malfunction of team work. This vicious cycle spawned on the children's ward, affected many other work areas as well.

I've been "trapped," she grumbled, "because I have scrapped personal and professional plans for a job that I do not feel free to discontinue. In the future, I shall do my best to do only as much work as I am asked and paid for. I shall make an effort to see how it works out under these reduced conditions, though I realize that this is probably an unfair test because I know from past experience that I function somewhat along the all or nothing principle. If the work makes sense to me, I automatically put a great deal into it. I have never been good at doing an indifferent job; nevertheless I shall try."

Ironic, yes. Callous, certainly not, since she was incapable of giving less than 100 percent, and her patients—the children—came first always, as evidenced by this memo to Herbert:

At the hospital things have their ups and downs, but the overall feeling is that of progress, and I still feel that I enjoy working with young doctors more than merely seeing patients. One of the decisions I will eventually have to make is whether to give up private practice altogether. Meanwhile the children improve—or don't—and we try to learn how to treat them. Yesterday they had a dress-up party for Halloween and, if you remember, I told you about a little schizophrenic boy who had been the peppermint stick at the Christmas play and then began acting like a tiger and zebra, gradually becoming more communicative. He was dressed up like a witch and very happy to be a witch and insisted on having a broom, and throughout the party he cleaned the radiators.

It was Herbert's senior year when Hilde abruptly faced an old worry which had nothing to do with the natural ability her nephew had demonstrated by qualifying for the Honors program at Swarthmore. But it *was* Honors that exposed his vulnerability all over again. The sophisticated program, designed to encourage personal initiative and intellectual development, meant that two years of unsupervised, unstructured free time had been granted someone who understood only how to live day to day.

Distress did not strike until spring of senior year, when he telephoned Hilde that the college physician was advising him to see a psychiatrist in Philadelphia. Two of the medical schools he applied for had already turned him down. Perhaps in his present state of indecision it might be better to go into the army after all. His friends seemed pretty well set with their own plans. "Saul has a Woodrow Wilson Fellowship to study at Harvard next year. John Forsythe has an assistantship in psychology at Yale. Dave Dennison has an opportunity to take assistantships in biology at either Cal Tech or Minnesota and is planning to get married this summer! Frank Breckenridge has been accepted at M.I.T. and will study mathematics there next year, if he gets an assistantship. Chuck, also, plans to go to school."

Wound of yore reopened, familiar woe never quite eliminated, only misplaced. Hadn't she a right to hope her nephew had outgrown his own turbulent past? Had she ever really believed it or merely buried it to preserve her own peace of mind? No time to think about that now. Immediately she was on the phone asking Dean Everett Hunt about

Honors, how exams were conducted, what was the penalty for failing them.

The Dean, of course, was familiar with Herbert's special situation, yet having so often witnessed springtime honors traumas, he could only offer Hilde the same advice he had given other anxious parents in the past:

> I have consulted Herbert's instructors about his work and do not have a very positive assurance from them. They say he has not partic- ipated very actively in his seminars but they have no intimate knowl- edge of his state of preparation. This is a time of year when many Honors students get panic-stricken about the examinations and it is possible for anybody to become extremely nervous if he starts thinking about all the things he does not know. Unless you think that his physical and mental state is such that it would be harmful for him to continue, our advice is that he should do the best he can with it and that if he should fail it would probably be better for him to have made the attempt than to have given up now. I know how difficult the decision is, and I wish I had as much wisdom for you as I have sympathy.

> Dear Dean Hunt:

> Many thanks for taking the trouble to inquire about Herbert and to write to me about it. I feel like you that it is probably better for him to take the examinations, even at the risk of not doing too well, than to pass on it. He seems to have been doing quite a good deal of work during this week and I hope his ability to work continues.

Commencement at Swarthmore College, and among the thousand or so friends and relatives attending, three proud ladies: Dr. Hilde Bruch, Dr. Frieda Fromm Reichmann, and Mrs. Ruth Stansky. Happy students, happy parents, happy day, and for all those wonderful hours forever frozen in time, a future temporarily at rest.

Summertime found Herbert studying Comparative Anatomy at Boston University in a last ditch—but unenthused—effort to retrieve a career in medicine. When it did not work out, he resigned himself to the draft:

Fort Dix, New Jersey

After spending almost a full day at the Induction Station in N.Y. just waiting and sitting, we finally were brought here by bus. Of course I brought too much stuff (no need for pajamas and three books!) and forgot essentials (towel and soap.) Feel awful. Got only three hours sleep last night.

Private, Herbert Bruch

It was something of a relief having Herbert safely in the army, because Hilde was battling her own wars on several fronts. Still she found time to visit Kurt and Skipper in Palmdale, California, where the two former veterans, having invested their money in homesteading, had begun a chicken ranch. Twelve hundred pullets with the same number of baby chicks amounted to about 300 dozen eggs daily, enough to keep even the "keepers" hopping, but now there were three children as well, and Hilde, always drawn to little ones, described Ronnie, the youngest:

He comes up and hugs you (one of my dresses is full of stains), and then he runs off again. His greatest friends are the goats—they had baby goats last summer and though they are bigger than he, he still plays around with them and likes to stay in their pen—as if he were a little goat himself—only he says "hi-hi" when he sticks his head through the fence.

But just one week later, descriptions to Herbert were more serious:

I finally have settled back and come to a few "decisions" after my California visit, because I felt I was running around in a three or four ring circus. I have decided the obesity manuscript is the most important thing I am doing right now, and so that is the thing I am going to concentrate on. My private practice has gone down to a very small trickle, and I shall leave it that way until a lot of things are clear. I have also cut down on the hospital work. I actually wanted to take a leave of absence so that I could concentrate completely on the book, but Dr. Kolb did not like that. He felt we would lose what progress we had made during the past year, so I am going along on a "play hookey" basis. As usual, the Service gets me rather cranky, but if it isn't too bad it acts as a stimulus for work. However, if I get too frustrated I get depressed and can't do anything. Anyhow it is a situation where to keep one's balance is of greatest importance, and I try to do it.

Under normal circumstances, she balanced things very well, but anxieties were mounting. Herbert's army stint had taken him to Germany and now she wondered how he would react to this familiar, unfamiliar soil. Perhaps this explained why he had reverted to his poor communication habits:

> It is exactly one month since you arrived in Germany and I still worry about your doing all that KP. What is against your letting me know how things have been going? You know the way I am—I start worrying, and by now I am making plans whether I can't come over to see what you are doing. It would be so much simpler if you would write, because as you know, I am sitting here with the grim determination of finishing the obesity book. It has been very hot this year so that it really takes a lot of wanting to finish it. You know how good I am at finding alibis, so do your part and stop me from using you as a reason for going to Europe.
>
> I know that it is bewildering to go to a new country and maybe doubly so for you because it is an old new country. Usually things are more the same and not as different as one had hoped.

When Herbert finally did write, she had her answer:

> I have been in a terrible passive state as you have no doubt gathered from the lack of correspondence, but maybe I will be able to shake it.
>
> Last night Bernard, my Swiss friend, and I decided to go to an orchestra concert in the courtyard of the Heidelberg Castle. Dim lights reflecting off old ruined castle walls, couples sitting under trees up above and behind the orchestra platform. I have a difficult time describing it. I guess I have to practice. Among other works the concert consisted of the Bruch Violin Concerto and Haydn's London Symphony. It sounded very good to ears which haven't heard much classical music for about two months.
>
> But afterwards I was depressed, as I usually am when I am out in public and see so many young couples and I am there without a girl. There must be a lot of nice German girls around but I don't know how to go about meeting them, nor would I have an easy time talking to them because I don't know enough German. What to do?

I hope all goes well with the book, and there is no need to make plans to come over to Europe!

The latest manuscript was subdued compared with *Don't Be Afraid of Your Child*, where writing flowed as easily as a case history, and where she interacted with ideas in true Sullivanian fashion to become one with a process which incorporated her own humanistic philosophy. "Anyone superimposing ideas on another offends me," she declared, "since he interferes with the development of self-identity and authenticity of personality." And with that theme reverberating like a breath of fresh air, she freed not only author, but reader.

By contrast, *The Importance of Overweight* seemed earthbound, as factual as *Don't Be Afraid* was philosophical. What *is* overweight? she asked, and answers were not simple. Not merely an anatomical problem, its roots were part of a complex cultural and psychological conditioning, where "to reduce" was probably oversimplification and actually contained the potential to be harmful. Years of treating this multifaceted disorder had not made its description easier, but if a single theme is to be found, it is the overall common sense approach to overweight. How thin must thin be? Shouldn't realistic attitudes rather than cultural pressures guide our self-perceptions?

Long hours of laborious researching had increased frictions on the Children's Service where she could not spare time for problems. If ever she were to finish writing with sanity intact, she knew she ought to resign. The book had taken so much longer than expected, it had already outlasted her "hunches." Now she must live with the disheartening realization that many of its ideas were already outdated.

After two years on the service, resignation was more disturbing than she let herself believe, though she had already decided it was not her fault. After all, she had fulfilled an executive's duty by delegating work orders to others, yet still was being plagued by picayune details, things nurses and residents were supposed to handle to keep the Service running smoothly. She rationalized it wasn't personal failure, but a frustratingly intolerable waste of time, from which she must take necessary steps to find release:

Dear Dr. Kolb:

It is with sincere regret that I hereby request to be released of the duties of Director of the Children's Service at the N. Y. State Psychiatric Institute. Your concept as I understand it now, differs greatly from what I had understood you expected me to do when you asked me to take over the reorganization of the Children's Service in an executive position.

In spite of many delays and handicaps I tried out a few of these ideas, and your response was so encouraging that until quite recently, I felt that there was good agreement about the basic goals and direction. When I expressed impatience, it was about what seemed avoidable delays. Even now you are quite generous in expressing that you feel I am doing a good job. I am glad you feel that way; unfortunately I do not. I cannot see how I could possibly carry out the program as I conceive it under the practical conditions as they have finally been clarified.

In resigning, she asked to be retained at P.I. in some other capacity, "because my intimate contact with the Institute has shown that there are many unfulfilled needs where my experience could be used," and was awarded the title "Psychotherapeutic Supervisor" for the duration of her years with the Institute.

Interestingly, two years later she received the following memorandum from Lawrence Kolb:

At the recent staff meeting of the Psychiatric Institute the suggestion was made that all therapeutic supervisors have their residents bring to the supervisory session their own written record and the nurses' notes. Apparently, it has not been customary for the residents to provide these records, nor have the supervisors insisted that they be available.

This recommendation seems much more pertinent in view of the fact that in the case of a serious incident involving a patient under therapeutic supervision, it might have been predicted on the basis of a review of the nurses' notes.

Pitts

No matter what her disquietude on other fronts, relative to affairs of the heart everything paled, since it was thoughts of being with Pitts which kept her going. When he first announced he would be moving, her greatest fear was losing his attentions, and certainly their meetings during the past three or four years had become few and scattered, verifying those fears. Either he found reasons for not attending a conference altogether, or else he was too busy while there to spare time for her. Under the circumstances she felt angry and helpless, but because she so desperately wanted to believe, she accepted the excuses *ipso facto*. Now, with his painful letter confronting her, it appeared she could no longer do even that.

Dear Hilde:

When I saw you last on the evening of Columbus Day you asked when I would see you again. The question was direct and proper and I was not able to give a definitive reply. Since the situation still holds, I am writing merely to let you know that you are not out of mind. I often reflect how easy it is to change the entire environment when one comes home in the evening by turning on the lights. All one has to do is press a button. If pressing a button would do the trick, I should be with you this evening.

I know it is unsatisfactory, and since this is so, I know you will also understand when I express the hope that you are finding happiness and relief from tension in some other or in many other quarters. Both of us are grown up and know the facts of human life and the intensity of human desires. Each of us with respect to the other has played an important role as an outlet for intense desire. Each of us is leading a life of great professional activity, and knows the meaning of the word, "success." The circumstances have brought a deeply rooted feeling of mutual respect. I hope, therefore, you will not misinterpret my hope that there is for you happiness in other places.

My life is no longer my own. Rather, I have become the servant of the jobs I hold and there seems to be no decent way of escaping the responsibilities of servitude. I am now multiple times a grandfather, and the need for maintaining the security of the homestead is therefore greater than ever. Regular trips from home bring the need for a social hostess. My wife has come to know the group, to enjoy the trips, and to become indispensable in fulfilling the social demands of the job. These are the intellectual reasons for hoping you have found happiness in other outlets. Just the same, please remember, that what has been has neither been forgotten nor relegated to a place of personal unimportance.

You will hear from me when I do have a chance to be free. This note will merely say that I do regret the neglect and reaffirm what you know about not being forgotten.

Affectionately,

Pitts

How dare he pass her off with a few glib phrases? Fury surged through her veins only to fall stone-heavy in her gut, where it proceeded to gnaw her innards. So many sensations, rage, betrayal, humiliation, melded into a single painful lump. Still her mind refused to believe:

Your letter of Jan. 20 was waiting for me when I came back from a brief vacation in the sun. Although I am used to reading between the lines, this is one I cannot figure out, or more correctly, I do not like what I understand it to mean and I feel hurt.

I do not know whether you expected this or whether you assume that your invocation of understanding does away with feelings. Your hope for my happiness through other outlets is really an insult and comes some ten years too late. It seems as if it never entered your mind that my needs and happiness deserve as much consideration as that of the rest of your family.

It is time for you to know I am not willing to be shelved when it suits you—and to be available when you desire it. I know I have contributed to your confusion by having complied with your demand for secrecy and by not writing how I felt.

From now on I shall write regularly whether you answer or not. I need you—just as you insist that you need me. I am no longer willing to be treated in the interval as if I did not exist. I do not know how we will work it out, but you cannot just walk out on your obligations toward me.

It is possible that I misunderstand your letter, but this needed saying for a long time.

Love,

Hilde

He phoned immediately. Could they meet somewhere? He would be conferring at Babies next weekend and would she be free for dinner later? She agreed. Afterwards they stole back to her apartment to hold that final private conversation, the gist of which she already knew.

Ten years' worth of dreams needed shedding, but where could she find enough distractions to fill the ache? She could not write, she could not concentrate, yet in looking for ways to speed the process, she felt dizzy with a peculiar sense of energy. She told Herbert:

> Today I have news that will make you want to come back soon. I got fed up with all the uncertainty and worry and undecidedness about this apartment and suddenly decided to look for a smaller place. That brainstorm came to me over the weekend, so I started looking on Monday morning and today I rented something that will make your mouth water. It is a 12th floor apartment on the corner of 89th Street and Fifth Avenue and it looks toward Central Park—that means it looks right into the reservoir.
>
> The best part is a roof garden to which I can just walk up and which has very comfortable furniture. I think it is mainly used by ladies who have the time to sunbathe during the daytime; that means that at the time when I go up I will have it all to myself. I have a feeling that I shall make real use of it—if only for ten minutes of a breath of fresh air before dinner.

Similar to the breakdown she experienced some twenty years earlier when only Mother experienced her honesty, now Frieda was its lone recipient; and, like Mother, her dear psychiatrist-friend expressed deep concern. Presently on sabbatical at the Ford Foundation in San Francisco, she urged Hilde to drop everything and come to her:

> I was *thinking* of you! And here comes your distressing letter with the sad news with which I can commiserate whole-heartedly....
>
> Listen, Hilde, why don't you have your secretary pack up your writing material, put one or two dresses, many sweaters, warm nightwear & a raincoat in a suitcase and come on out here. You can visit your sister in S.F. (35 miles from here), and you can stay at a nice little hotel near here. You can work in my little house while I am at the "center," and we can spend the evenings together, working or not, with or without friends. And we could even consider the question whether or not you would like to have some talks with a real human being, a friend, Jungian trained, since we Freud-Sullivanians have not done the trick.

Come out here! Except for the barest necessities and your writing material you can buy things here when you feel better. If you want me to, I'll get you the ticket here with the help of my secretary; all you have to do is let me know when you want to come. *Send a wire!*

Unfortunately, hospitalization would come first, because for all her fevered denial, the familiar malaise had overcome her. Characteristically she made light of it::

Dear Herbert:

You are probably surprised that you get a letter from me from New York and not some picture post card from California. Just when I was getting ready to leave for my vacation I discovered that I did not feel well and was running a temperature. Since I had not had a medical checkup for a long time, I took myself to Harkness Pavilion and I asked for Dr. Aranov, the same doctor you had several years ago. I thought it would be only for a day or two, but I stayed a whole week, and as you can imagine, I made the best of it. It really is amazing how much doctors have learned and how many more tests they do now before they declare you healthy. I consider myself now as good as certified in this respect because all the tests were embarrassingly normal.

I came back home two days before Thanksgiving, and I now plan to go to California on December 20. I shall visit with Kurt first because I think it would be fun to have Christmas with the children. Then I will go to San Francisco and visit with Dr. Frieda and Ester and family. I do hope that this time I can go through with my plans.

End of a Decade

Herbert's career as an army private was ended and the mails were picking up. Would Hilde temporarily store things he had accumulated during the past two years until he could rent his own apartment in the City or at least until he could get back to school? He had purchased two watches, one for her and one for Harvey, and was sorry not to be joining her in Aurora for his cousin's Bar Mitzvah. Unfortunately, he was expecting separation at Fort Dix to take four days, but hoped she would enjoy visiting Ernst and Else and nephews, Harvey and Mark.

As a matter of fact, Herbert would not return to New York or to school, but two months later in Philadelphia, he still sat all day at a desk doing homework, trying to get a working knowledge of UNIVAC programming. Waxing somewhat philosophical: "I suppose I can't expect any more at the start. The people in my department are a pretty good bunch, friendly, but of course I am slow getting to know anyone."

He had caught up with his old friend, Chuck Enselberg, who was taking courses at Penn preparing for medical school, and offered to share rent in West Philadelphia. "Chuck and I are getting along alright in his apartment. I have to leave at about seven-thirty in the morning and more often than not Chuck doesn't waken in the process. In the evening when I return we settle down regularly to a drink, thanks to your provisions. Sometimes we cook and have a friend in or else cook at a friend's apartment and eat there, but half the time we eat out. Then Chuck goes to the lab to work and I come back to my UNIVAC problems. To bed between twelve and one and up at seven-fifteen again!"

Sounded pretty dull to Hilde, not her style, but since routine was what Herbert felt comfortable with and needed, she accepted it. The semi-breakdown at Swarthmore had thoroughly frightened her, forced her to realize his emotional limitations so that she hadn't pushed medical school. There had been a few minor triumphs. She had managed to change his taste in foods ("which ranged from 'A' to 'B' when he arrived"), had even succeeded in enlivening his selection of clothing, though here he resisted experiment, and given a choice would wear the same comfortable sweaters and trousers day in and day out. Such trifles mattered not a whit. It was his passiveness and insecurity which made her heart break, anger swell for all her family had suffered. She had tried every way she knew how to repair the damaged psyche, and now she knew that no one could, that she must resign herself to stacking this, too, upon the pile of shattered dreams haplessly ruptured and outside her control.

On April 28, 1957, Frieda Fromm Reichmann died of an acute coronary thrombosis in her home at Chestnut Lodge, Rockville, Maryland. She was 67 years old. The world of psychiatry had lost an outstanding colleague, Hilde her closest friend.

Common interests bonded the two German refugees, who by the time they met were both American citizens, but who nevertheless were still adapting to life in a new country. Hilde remembered discussing differences in cooking and eating and running a household American style and being amazed how much of one's minor life is related to such intimate things. She remembered in analysis how Frieda hitched her sturdy rocking chair midway to the couch so that you could see her and she could see you. It was an immediate tip-off that this psychiatrist was unconventional and unorthodox. Such insignificant details, symbolically so important....

After the death, Hilde maintained an active correspondence with Frieda's two sisters, Grete and Anna, clinging to keepsakes offered her out of the estate: a robe, a butter dish, a ring, a bracelet, a clock which didn't run, three faded and frazzled oriental runners.... Such memorabilia were comforting, but something important was left unresolved. For Hilde, still intermittently in treatment, Frieda's death had also meant discontinuing therapy before it was completed.

She now turned to Dr. Lawrence Kubie, whom she had previously known only through professional contact, when she approached him for the diagnosis and treatment of certain patients. Often he responded by referring patients to her for treatment in the special areas which interested both. Sometimes she consulted him on difficult technical problems, or asked him to review some of her articles and books.

Now, for the first time, he heard about her personal suffering and was surprised to discover that the traumatic experiences she and her closest relatives were subjected to in Nazi Germany had so sensitized her that any event echoing them was likely to explode into acute panic and paralyzing depression. He concluded that the depressions were directly related to her forcible transplantation from her native land, her separation from her home and loved ones, her anguish over their suffering and deaths. He also considered it imperative that treatment be carried through to completion, so when he retired from practice in New York City to move to Maryland to teach and write at the Sheppard and Enoch Pratt Hospital, he insisted Hilde also visit at frequent intervals.

CHAPTER IX

1960 - 1973

Dorothy

Dorothy Andersen received a diagnosis prescribing surgery sometime in 1961. Fully aware smoking was the cause, she commented that the sweets and chewing gun she substituted for cigarettes were affecting her teeth and gums, and that she was probably the only cancer patient who gained rather than lost weight.

For a while things proceeded normally and the air seemed unusually crisp for September when Hilde joined her at the farm to sup upon stuffed Cornish hens and reminisce about what the simplicity of the place meant to both of them. Dorothy had hired locals to search for water, and when it was discovered a well could be dug rather inexpensively, her reaction, "Imagine, we could have had water in the kitchen all along!" surprised Hilde who considered carrying water from the brook part of the property's allure.

In January of 1963 following the acceptance of a cystic fibrosis award in Philadelphia, Dorothy returned home to discover she was unable to carry her suitcase upstairs. "I felt like such a weakling!" she later told Hilde, checking herself into the hospital for what she insisted was a circulatory disorder, at the same time balking about using a wheelchair and talking about going to the office.

Even after she was settled back into her apartment, Hilde continued visiting Dorothy on lunch time rounds, routinely washing pajamas, hanging them to dry in the little bathroom. The patient's spirits fluctuated. There was serious discussion about what it meant to die early. Dorothy said she wouldn't have minded so much if she were ten years older, since you could still have lots of fun in your sixties, but in the seventies things went downhill, anyway. Conversation of this nature alternated with discourse concerning the future, how to make the farm more livable so that with running water and new appliances she might manage without a housekeeper. Despite an enlarged liver she kept beers cooling outside on the window sill to enjoy beer sessions and poker games with farm friends.

One day she mentioned her liver felt bumpy, what did Hilde think? But Hilde, assuming the role of psychiatrist "who has forgotten how to do these things," refused to examine or express an opinion, advising Dorothy to consult her physician, since he most likely would know what to do.

Apparently the physician felt similarly noncommittal, because a few days later Dorothy explained she had gone for an examination where it was suggested she undergo a biopsy, to which she responded quite matter-of-factly, "It doesn't matter, I don't need to know it that badly." Hilde considered this alternation between knowing acceptance that the end is near and a refusal to deal with it, egregious denial. "If an ordinary person refuses to have a biopsy it is ordinary denial," she declared, "but when a pathologist doesn't want to use the methods of her own trade, we are dealing with severe denial."

Toward the end of February, Dorothy's appetite and weight loss announced the seriousness of her condition. Unlike the shock Hilde experienced when Frieda died, Dorothy's illness was predictable, its outcome inevitable, and still she was shaken, grieved upon returning from her weekend reunion at Hopkins to learn another dear friend had quietly slipped away.

Thirty Year "Itch"

In retrospect, Hilde supposed multiple factors contributed to leaving New York. The City was uncomfortable. Leaving town for a weekend and forgetting to stop newspaper deliveries automatically insured her apartment would be burglarized. She was afraid to walk or drive, yet locating a taxi was like trying to flag and tag a rare endangered bird. The fierce winter of 1960-1961 which produced seven blizzards resulted in mass cancellations of theater and social events. During one of these stymied January weekends she completed and sent a discussant paper to the Psychosomatic Society which was not due to be given until the end of April. It met with cheery surprise. "Who is this miracle woman who sends her paper early like a gift from heaven?" they pronounced flabbergasted, Hilde retorting, "You don't know how right you are because it was due to the heavens that sent us so much snow that I had nothing else to do. I couldn't go out and nobody could come in."

Soon she would be sixty. "This is no place to grow old," she sniffed, continuing to renounce externals, though probably the more flagrant signals for change were happening inside herself. She had come to crossroads similar to those which had coaxed her to Hopkins for a degree in psychiatry. Work was stale, ideas had stagnated, and she was unmotivated to write. She felt tired, saturated with the whole New York-Baltimore experience; she longed to retire into a world of new ideas and adventures.

When she voiced these feelings in a long complaining letter to Lawrence Kubie, he responded sympathetically to her desires, less than sympathetically to her reasons:

> I have to say again that you misunderstand my position with respect to work. To my way of thinking it is never the answer to life for either a man or a woman: but the freedom to work and to take pleasure in it is like a thermometer measuring a temperature. It gives an indication of inner freedom. This is corny common sense. Everyone knows that at times one can escape from external pain or a sense of loss into work, but that this is not always true. In general, one can happily and freely turn one's energies into work only when other areas of life are full. I do not doubt that in your earlier years you put into your work the need for marriage, the possibility of which you had denied to yourself, backed as this was by the attitude of others. This you no longer do. Therefore for the time being, work has lost its full savor: but note, please, that I say "for the time being."
>
> I have no doubt that you will find a more rewarding savor in work when it is being driven with less compulsive urgency. All last year I felt that your work drive and your paper writing were excessive and might be an unwitting effort on your part to thumb your nose at me, to compete with me, to outdo me, and in a sense to burlesque

my position. I did not dare to interfere or even to suggest a slackening of your pace, lest you feel that I was "taking everything away." I cannot help chuckling a little (and hope that you will too) at the fact that so much good work came out of it; but that does not mean that I am happy about the spirit of it, or approved it, or thought that it was the answer for you.

And as for my furthering your inquiries in other directions, you know that I do this primarily in the interests of your finding a setting which would be more rewarding humanly and emotionally, and not of your getting more work done. In this I always felt that if fate should make it possible, marriage would be a happy addition to a full life for you or anyone, but that it is never the *sine qua non* which it seemed to you.

It was Shervert Frazier who actually presented her with the opportunity she was looking for. Like Kolb, Frazier was with the Mayo Clinic when he and Hilde first met. Then, in 1958, they were reacquainted in New York, and now Dr. Frazier was Chairman of the Department of Psychiatry at Baylor School of Medicine in Houston, Texas. "So you don't like living behind triple locks, housebound by snow? I think we've got the place for you...."

Hilde was not altogether sure she could adapt to being a Texan, but she had to try something. By May of 1964 she had written Dr. Kolb for a one year's absence from Columbia in order to "see how I fit into" Dr. Frazier's teaching program at Baylor. The appointment, Professor of Psychiatry, was pleasantly salaried, a great relief to this veteran of grants. "I dislike writing grant proposals and consider it actually training in dishonesty, promising more than you can possibly do," she explained as she insisted that salary be a prerequisite for moving *anywhere*.

By June, word of her leave had circulated. Her old lab boss, Donovan McCune, was in Vallejo, California:

...preoccupied with pediatrics, administration, bookbinding, book collecting, and acquiring a fluent command of Latin—the last a lifelong preoccupation, unfortunately suspended for twenty-five years but now resumed.

It always affects me warmly to hear from you...I owe many things to you. Among these not the least is an interest in the Jewish race which, although I had it before we met, was confirmed and rendered a durable preoccupation by the long association we had during the days of Hitler's dominance and fall.

I hope your decision to give up the highly-taxed drudgery of individual practice will be more than 99 percent and that you will again become a school teacher. You have a great deal to give to the developing minds of the young. I think you have more than the right, even the obligation to do it. Could be that when you get as far west as Texas, we may see each other from time to time.

Former chief of Babies, Rustin McIntosh, from his Berkshire retirement hideaway in Tyringham, Massachusetts:

> Your news constitutes quite a bombshell. I've heard of people "going native," but going Texas is of a different order of magnitude. In my imagination, I can see you now in a ten-gallon Stetson and cowboy boots, both prerequisites for establishing rapport with the *indigeni*. Congratulations on your landing a full time job, complete with professorship. A few years ago I shouldn't have been so surprised as I am now at your undertaking so drastic a change in your *modus vivendi*. But I'm sure it's a good move; and like everybody else who lives there you are sure to go wild over Texas.

Hilde had more in mind for Texans than Stetsons and boots. This most prosperous state of the union could glut itself in oil and ostentatiously exhibit oversized American cars all it wanted, but here was one New Yorker who would not be upstaged. "I will never kowtow to Texans in Cadillacs," she snorted. She had always wanted a Rolls Royce. Only frugality, (who could afford it?) and common sense (where could she park it, how survive the scrapes and fractures of predatory taxis?) had prevented her from investigating the possibility. Now, she discovered a tan beauty waiting for her at a Vintage Car Store in Nyack. A "little old lady story" accompanied the '59 Silver Cloud. It had hardly been driven, and for $7,600 was hers, new battery, seat belts and air conditioner included. Without hesitation she took it.

A couple of months later, she and the Rolls, with Herbert chauffeuring, were headed for Houston. Apart from admiring stares which she pretended not to notice, the trip was uneventful—at least until New Orleans, where they stopped to sample Cajun cooking at one of the

French Quarter's more famous restaurants. Less than an hour later, they returned to mass confusion.

An agitated garage attendant rapidly excused himself: "I turn my back to find space for Rolls. Not easy. Then I hear screeching so I know thieves has got your car. Police come quick. Sorry. Nothing like this ever happen before."

With every pedestrian in the city pointing, "it went that-a-way," much more than nerve is required to execute the successful pilfering of a Rolls Royce. Following a semi-comedic chase, the Rolls wrapped itself around an old-fashioned hitching post while the cops emerged victorious, the culprits were apprehended, the Rolls—with broken headlight—was made driveable by cutting away a torn fender, and less than two hours later, two Easterners were again headed West.

They arrived on schedule, no worse for their experience, and were met at a doctor's conference outside Houston by Dr. Frazier and other members of the department. Charming, jubilant Hilde climbed from her slightly-less-than-perfect-but-still-a-Rolls-Rolls to allow the Texas adventure to begin.

Houston

Until now, Hilde's friendships grafting old world and new were firmly rooted in the Eastern U.S. and had stood the test of thirty years. But also during those years she had antagonized enough personalities and schools of thought to create a host of enemies. "I asked questions, and when you ask questions, that proves something about you—that you are resisting, that you have doubts." She defended the outspokenness, maintaining it was necessary, but the meaner spirited were less generous, labeling her "willful" or "arrogant." Upon this well-worn multi-textured loom, she now was superimposing the newer textiles of the West, discovering in their loose unpatterned weaves, conditions propitious to growth. Such open and natural friendliness greeted her, she was immediately drawn to coworkers, as they to her, since she was something of a curiosity, having as much to do with her person and history, as with her spontaneous Cinderella arrival in an elegant coach.

Reputation preceded her. What sort of person, colleagues wondered, tells humorous anecdotes about Harry Stack Sullivan and consults with Lawrence Kubie and Frieda Fromm Reichmann simultaneously? Books and papers offering clues to theories and ideas did not reveal, could not unpeel her multi-layered, mysterious, and forever fascinating personality. In the end. they admitted she was simply Hilde, sometimes obstinate, sometimes charming, sometimes cranky, sometimes good-natured—but in any case, never apologetic.

Of course, she fully enjoyed being the center of attention, but refusing to let the ambiance interfere with purpose, after a few brief sniffs of Texas air, she headed inside to *work*. On her desk, a letter from Rusty McIntosh inquiring whether fatness in Texas was the problem it was in New York City and describing winter diversions at Mountain Brook Farm: "Milly and I bother New York City just as little as possible; it has enough problems as things stand, and when a hefty snowfall is added, life in Manhattan hardly seems worth living."

Replied Hilde several months later, "You make living on a snowed-in farm sound quite idyllic. It was the nastiness of the winters in New York that made me look for warmer pastures—and I feel satisfied with my choice of Houston. When I first came to this country people kept on asking, 'How do you like America?' When I answered, 'Fine,' I was told invariably "But New York is *not* America.' Funnily enough I feel that way about Houston and Texas. I only know Houston and I like it—I do not know how I feel about the rest of the State.

You asked about the incidence of obesity here in Texas. I have no statistical figures, but apparently there are plenty of fat people around, both adults and children. Something is funny about Houston. One doesn't see many people at a time because everybody drives. As a matter of fact, I no longer saw many fat children in New York when I stopped riding the subways."

If such things as "golden years" exist, certainly these were hers, though Hilde, herself, probably did not notice the ghosts of her past quietly slipping away, dissipating like whiffs of smoke into the broad Texas horizon. But success calculated by productivity, Hilde could and did recognize, and four books stand as tribute to the woman who made her final twenty years the most fruitful.

When McIntosh noted, "You have the thrill of new conquests before you," he did not exaggerate. In leaving New York's Columbia Presbyterian Medical Center, she brought thirty years' experience and recognition with none of its disappointments.

Most of those earlier years were devoted to family, especially mothers and children. She had spent her own childbearing years advising mothers and treating their children, sympathizing and encouraging mothers, while loving their children, through it all, remaining ironically outside the biological experience of motherhood. Often she worked feverishly to achieve in medics what was denied her personally, the dream of raising a large family. Like her own mother, she knew she would have been excellent. Now that the opportunity was gone forever, so, too, was the fantasy, and for its loss came more relief than remorse.

Happier pursuits lay ahead in a plumb role she seemed destined to play, in which even appearance readied her for the part. Youthful eyes, which once squinted suspiciously at matching caps across an ice pond, were softened into specks of grayish blue, alertness peeping out from crinkled corners. Brownish nondescript hair, victim to countless unflattering stylings, was tamed silver and sensible to gently frame her ears. Most convincing was the lap, ample and beckoning, as grandmotherly a perch as could be found anywhere.

Maybe it was all that clicking and clucking that enticed little ones to her nest. "Ooo, ooo, tick, tick, pu, pu," she cooed to bring them flocking. As the fussing grandmother, she was incorrigible, Kurt's children receiving the bulk of her attentions, but soon she had earned a substantial reputation among Houstonians as well.

This was one grandmother who would never be pronounced "dowdy." As if her Rolls had set a precedent for elegance, style became her forte. Clothing was carefully selected to enhance a full figure, creating less an impression of size than of grandness. Baylor ladies clamoring for discards begged advance notice for their benefit clothing sales, perhaps on the sly tucking away a hat or handbag for themselves.

Hilde, undisputed Grande Dame of Baylor, selected a spacious apartment to match her status, where a curious assortment of furnishings collected from many eras and countries created a peculiar but interesting congruity. Antiques purchased from a Chinaman's fire sale in New York balanced teak and Danish modern from Herbert's army visit to Copenhagen. Prints by Chagall and Henry Moore peeped at Paris in the rain. Horses seeking desert watering holes stared upon shawled ladies scuttling across barren Mexican landscapes. Shards collected from "digs" competed for space with Steuben figurines. A bronzed Icarus agonized and writhing, curled wings about him, while "Roman

Spring," displaying a figure curiously like Hilde's, paraded nudity, casting her arms skyward in Bacchanalian celebration. Whether valuable or insignificant, each piece had a story, as within these walls amid a province of book titles equally eclectic, the owner fashioned her lifestyle. Here, colleagues were encouraged to congregate and confer, patients, many of them famous, were coached into cure. Two or three times yearly she threw receptions, presenting fancy gourmet banquets with a debutante's flair for graciousness. Like the larva transformed into a butterfly, Hilde represented that rare being whose appearance improves with age. Time had harmonized her features, mellowed and smoothed them to handsomeness.

That same new harmony, as if time had hewn and worn away roughness, existed in relationships. Perhaps she had finally succeeded in attaining the security and recognition she always unconsciously sought. Still it would be a mistake to underestimate her disposition, to assume contrariness and feistiness were entirely dissolved into a dulled pool of tranquillity. Students and colleagues were quick to testify that her personality remained as peppery and demanding as ever.

As professor of psychiatry, she placed new emphasis on teaching. She had done it in New York, and now in Houston she continued to find working with medical students particularly stimulating. For an unorthodox independent like Hilde, students represented a chance to test ideas without bucking preconceptions or bias. (She realized that any colleague half-way good had already done enough independent thinking to develop his own pet theories.) Her personal bugaboo was with any over-solicitous psychiatric resident who was too busy quoting 'Dr. So and So' to remember how to observe. Instead of becoming one with the therapeutic process, the zealous resident adapted his patients to their symptoms, at the same time exposing one Dr. Bruch to a byproduct of psychiatric dribble: "Is this separation anxiety, does it express an Oedipal Complex, a counterphobic reaction?" On the other hand, the medical students in her eight week seminar, Basic Principles of Psychotherapy, might sometimes be guilty of naive questioning, but never in the expectation of receiving preordained answers. Since she could rely on their simple honesty, it was easy for her to respond, "All right, now let me ask you something. Does such and such an idea make sense to you? Is it valid?"

In many ways the situation paralleled parenting. The very reason she would not prescribe recipes for child care was that if a parent listens carefully to the child, both will respond with secure and appropriate action. The psychotherapist must respond with similar sensitivity, must interact with each situation to appropriately assess what a patient is struggling with. "I have very little of the Pygmalion complex. My approach is to liberate and free what is already there," she declared, believing that a teacher is very much like a sheep dog corralling issues and materials, rounding up ideas. While all the sheep go in a general direction toward a certain goal or implication, the teacher must decide which to follow. Soliciting the unstated, the tacit assumptions underlying patients' complaints was what her own two great teachers, Harry Stack Sullivan and Frieda Fromm Reichmann, had taught by personal example; it was exactly what she, too, wished to convey.

In this endeavor, she emphatically refused to identify with any particular school of thought. All these groups on their own became as orthodox and rigid as the groups they originally protested. Lurking in her own background was the New York Branch of the Washington School of Psychiatry, a painful reminder of Sullivanian discipleship. Well, she would encourage no disciples, take no prisoners. So what if the occasional student asked, "How come you don't have a school of followers?" She would answer briskly that it was incompatible with her style of thinking.

Still, some of her students were outstanding. Stanley Palombo, for one, possessed such an uncanny perception of language, she had agreed to several rare collaborations. Together they explored the use of imagery and its relationship to developmental processes in "Conceptual Problems in Schizophrenia," a paper presented in Atlantic City. At Baylor, she worked with Stuart Yudofsky whose original expectations to become a heart surgeon were quickly superseded by matters of the mind. He and another medical student, Ottis L. Layne, Jr. together wrote a paper, "Postoperative Psychosis in Cardiotomy Patients" which Hilde supervised and felt so proud of, she filed and numbered it among her own papers. Detecting in Yudofsky's excellent grasp of the clinical situation the proper makeup for a psychiatrist, she encouraged him to go to The New York State Psychiatric Institute. What was originally intended as a three month rotation extended nearly indefinitely when Larry Kolb also became impressed by the young man and offered him such a good position in New York, he felt he could not return to Texas.

Teaching duties did not preclude the building of a highly successful private practice which was gradually changing in clientele. As a veteran of treating eating disorders, she had probably seen as many cases as anyone in her field, including the rarer cases of anorexia nervosa. Like everyone who has witnessed this strange phenomenon, she was intrigued by the fanatical pursuit of thinness, starvation in the midst of plenty, but also recognized in it a deep psychological disturbance, not the loss of appetite its name implies. She believed that weight loss and food restriction, like their mirror image, weight gain and over-stuffing, are only symptoms; that similar to obesity, anorexia is characterized by a lack of autonomy, an inability to lead a self-directed life. Rigid dieting is the anorexic's way of exercising control and proving competence, and therefore therapy must be directed to repairing self-esteem and self-expression as well as conceptual distortions.

Hilde's approach was a far cry from behavior modification treatments currently in vogue, where non-eating as learned behavior is modified by rewarding, "positively reinforcing" weight gain, or its reverse, punishing the failure to do so. Because these techniques were conducted under controlled conditions in a hospital under trained supervision, patients often showed temporary weight gains which in the long run turned disastrous. It was against "control" and controlled situations the anorexic rebelled in the first place, and by undermining these last vestiges of self-esteem, the patient felt "tricked" and became even harder to reach through psychotherapy.

Most were referrals, since it was the difficult cases, anorexics whom nobody else seemed able to reach, who increasingly requested her assistance. From every corner of the country they came, arriving with desperate parents to participate in family conferences, later to move to Houston to be near this doctor who genuinely listened to everything they had to say. Mostly they were women, intelligent and often gifted, in temperament not unlike the "difficult" and rebellious doctor, herself. The doctor kept a professional distance from the vicarious experience of parenthood, but as her charges grew in number, so did the family she had always wanted.

"Ghosts"

As her reputation grew, likewise did her demand as featured speaker for conferences all over the world. But even as she enjoyed celebrity, specters out of the past reappeared. In 1965, she attended an international symposium on anorexia in West Germany, organized by Dr. J.E. Meyer, professor at the University of Goettingen. Glowing and sparkling upon meeting the man responsible for producing this successful conference, two years later, most likely with little justification, she was denouncing him for betraying her trust. What Naziism had wrought, psychotherapy could not undo, and the losses and emotional upheavals out of her painful past continued to control her present. Rightfully or wrongfully, she would not make peace with this anger during her lifetime.

> My Dear Dr. Meyer:
>
> You cannot have failed to note my shock when you revealed the truth about your political past. Throughout the time of our acquaintance, you stressed that you had been a "non-Nazi," an honest and courageous German who had refused to join the Party. The simple fact was that as a Quadroon-Jew you were not acceptable. Nevertheless, you cooperated with the regime. Before leaving for Detroit, Dr. Frazier found time to tell me about your letter from Hitler, in which you were promised full German status if you proved yourself a courageous soldier.
>
> I, on my part, was outspoken with you and told you my absolute refusal to have any dealings with former Nazis. Knowing this, you should never have asked me to participate in the Symposium in Goettingen, even less have invited yourself to come as my guest to Houston. If there was the slightest doubt in your mind how I felt about Nazi sympathizers, you could have learned it on the evening of your arrival, when I told you about my intent to publish a paper on how even so-called "good" Germans had been affected by Nazi morality. I notice that you blushed when I mentioned this. It would have been a matter of simple honesty to set the record straight then and there and to terminate your visit. Instead of that, you put me in the embarrassing position of having to apologize to my colleagues for having brought a Nazi manqué to our department.
>
> Needless to say, I feel resentful for having been deceived and made a fool of; and I do not stand alone in feeling this way.

Meyer replied, sending carbons to Dr. S. H. Frazier, Dr. and Mrs. T. Lidz:

Dear Dr. Bruch,

Your letter came unexpectedly and has hurt me to the extreme. These are the facts, which you should know: During the Nazi regime I finished high school, studied medicine and was a doctor in the Air Force. My father died before 1933. My mother, ("arish") consulted, as I remember, many friends at the beginning of the Hitler regime about the future of her children. They were all of the same opinion—that this regime would be either temporary or would relax within time. I was sixteen years of age in 1933.

There are different answers to the question of leaving the country without immediate threat of existence or life, but I feel sure that by not emigrating at that age, without holding any position involved in any cooperation with the party, does not allow any principle condemnation. Today, I still do not know whether my mother, and later on I, did right or wrong (personally and morally as well!) by not leaving the country.

When I told you on our last evening about my ancestors I did this deliberately to make clear that I belong to those German people who, since then, are constantly aware of, even obsessed with the idea that anything like this should never happen again. We feel this as our particular responsibility, having experienced these years within the country. One of our leading psychiatrists, whom Dr. and Mrs. Lidz know very well, functions in such a way that one could call him "das Gewissen" of the German psychiatrists of the present. He is in the same situation with regard to his ancestors, he did not emigrate but joined the army, as I did. Would you consider him and call him a Nazi manqué too?

With regard to the letter from Hitler, which I mentioned as an historical curiosity: I never applied for it—it was added to the official permission to remain as a doctor in the air force in 1944. What has distressed me most is the fact that in our last talk you did not react to my remarks about my situation and did not question. Without giving me any chance to discuss the matter openly you have now hastened to throw your moral condemnation upon me. I do not expect nor wish a reply to this letter.

A more abiding specter was illness. In 1966, she was hospitalized with hepatitis, and since it involved continued bed care at home, doctors insisted she get help. When Else was first called from Aurora, she expected to be in Houston ten days; but then Hilde suffered a severe relapse, and doctors personally asked her to stay so that her sister-in-law would not have to return to the hospital.

Harvey was 23, Mark just turned 17, both sufficiently independent not to be a concern; but two years earlier her husband had suffered a severe heart attack. With constant loving attention she had nursed him back to health, but still she worried. Ernst had left the decision to her, and it would be four weeks before she would go home.

Two years later, Hilde was again confined to her bed.

"You won't believe it when I tell you how I began the New Year," she wrote accountant and long-time friend Nathan Sale of New York City. "I slipped on an over-polished floor and broke my right hip and I am in Methodist Hospital."

"I seem to be doing very well. Today is exactly one week after the operation and I can nearly get out of bed without help, and I can walk quite well with a walker. It makes me look like an old lady (or an infant), but I don't mind. Today I am going to start crutches. It still gets me exhausted even to walk across the room, but I hope it won't be a siege of many months before I can move around."

"Tough luck about your breaking your hip," wrote Rusty McIntosh. "I thought that was reserved for old folks! But I'm glad you're recovering rapidly." Indeed she seemed to be. By mid-February she was hosting the "Psychoanalysts in the Southwest" conference in her own apartment.

But by April, it was apparent something had gone terribly wrong. Her doctors labeled it F.U.O., Fever of Unknown Origin, and like past episodes, it was characterized by moodiness and depression. Four years following her triumphant entry into Houston, it had appeared unheralded and unexplainable, as though her mental and physical energies had built to pressures beyond endurance and now were raging out of control. The patient in her fiery cauldron was unapproachable, but here one must give colleagues some credit. Recognizing the impossibility of dealing rationally with her, they assigned Dr. G. W. Davis from another hospital to take the heat. He was duly unimpressed, shrugged off her tantrums, and refused to capitulate to her whims. It was not a pretty sight.

Immediately she communicated her grievances to Kubie, who, somewhat at a loss, wrote Eppright, the Orthopedic Surgeon, sending carbons to Davis and Bruch. Then he wrote Hilde directly:

> Since talking to you I have thought a lot about this problem. The very next day, Dr. Davis called and we had a long talk about it. I know that you realize that you are going through an intense emotional upset at the moment, probably due in part to the situation in the school, in part to disappointments in your own plans, and in part to your series of physical mishaps. I am confident, as I have always been in the past, that if you will take this upset seriously and give top priority to your physical and emotional safety, allowing your doctor friends to take whatever precautions are necessary, you will make a quick comeback, just as you have in the past.

Two weeks later, strong-willed Hilde was still making waves:

> Dear Dr. Davis,
>
> I hereby state in writing that I wish that you discontinue your professional services. I have requested this repeatedly and also asked you to leave my room. I did so on Monday, April 15, in the presence of my nurse, Mrs. Foley. I consider your entering my room at Methodist Hospital an intrusion on my privacy and urge you to discontinue it.

To Nathan Sale, simultaneous with the disclaimer of Davis:

> How do you do it—find in the wilderness of Texas the most beautiful roses—and they arrive as buds and slowly open up and bloom and bloom. Everybody has been very kind and one visitor called my room "the Garden of Eden." It isn't exactly that to me, but it has been very good to get the many flowery good wishes.
>
> I am still on complete bed rest (with massage and supervised exercise) because a crack had developed in the fracture. I had been encouraged to be active and move around on crutches, etc.—and apparently did more than was good for the fracture. I had increasing pain in the fracture region—and with a special X-ray technique they found the crack.
>
> The whole thing is bad luck anyhow—I feel I have had more than my share since I moved to Texas. Amazingly—I still like living here in Houston but I shall postpone decisions until I am well again.

By May, she was informing Mr. Sale that she was back at her apartment and planning to visit her sister in California; by June, she was walking with a cane and feeling much better.

Often she scheduled conferences to coincide with visits to family and friends. In England, she saw Artur and Lotte and their two boys, both of whom were married with children of their own. Artur had received government money from his five years in the army and had systematically invested it in taxis. By now, he had a fleet of eight or ten, and he and Lotte were enjoying the comforts and pleasures of grandparenthood.

In Chicago, she made a point of visiting Ernst and Else and their sons in Aurora; in Philadelphia, Herbert; in Atlanta, Kurt and family who had recently moved there. Visiting Ester usually meant a conference in San Francisco, but following this episode she headed straight to the companionship and recuperation she needed.

Hilde gave Ester plenty of credit for spunk and enterprise in taking classes to become a nurse, so that by the time her divorce from Viktor became final in 1959 she was entirely self-supporting. It was through her training and work at Marin General Hospital she met Dr. Harold White. When they married in 1962, Hilde was far from convinced. She attended the ceremony expecting to disapprove the new spouse, but when she witnessed her sister's radiance, ended up liking him despite herself.

Richard Alexander

Autumn of 1969 brought unexpected news from another quarter:

"I have a surprise...."

"Yes.... Tell me what it is."

"I'm getting married."

"What? Who?!!!"

Even non-verbal Herbert knew this bombshell warranted special handling and personal delivery. He would fly to Houston to supply details. Quite possibly Herbert's future bride knew even less about Hilde than *vice versa*, but the curiosity was mutual. Consequently, Joanne in Syracuse, Herbert in Philadelphia held telephone exchanges sounding something like this:

"What's she like? Does she enjoy conversation?"

"Oh, yes, she's a great talker. You two will get along."

"Does she know about me, does she know I have *four* kids?"

"She knows we're getting married. I'm going to tell her the rest this weekend. I think it's a good idea to take the snapshots of you and the kids with me."

"Eeeek!"

Days passed in silence, Joanne transfixed by one painful thought: "The wedding's off, he's afraid to call." Yet no one wallows in misery forever, and on Wednesday Joanne hesitantly dialed UNIVAC:

"Were you in Houston last weekend?"

"Oh, yes. Sorry I forgot to call...."

"Your aunt, was she angry with your news?"

"Oh, no. Delighted. She had a little party with a group of friends to celebrate. We toasted with champagne."

Long pause. "Did you show the pictures?"

"Everybody thought the kids were cute. Hilde liked Jimmy's 'Our Gang' hat and said 'He's my favorite.'"

Simple as that. A remarkable person, this Hilde.

A month after the wedding, Herbert met Hilde at the airport, Joanne and children waited at the house. Upon arriving, she leaped from their station wagon, and breezing past Joanne, flounced through the narrow connecting hallways which were the ranch's peculiar construction, looking for children. "Where are the children? Where are the children?" she called. "Come see what Oma has in her suitcase for you!"

Three came running. But the oldest, nine year old William, reserved and overwhelmed, preferred hiding. "Never mind, Wilhelm," she cried to the darkness. "Everybody's shy. I'm shy, too."

No doubt her unorthodox entrance was carefully calculated to win Joanne's favor, since she understood instinctively that a mother's approval is earned by attending her children. In fact, the tactic worked like a charm, for through this overt acceptance of the children a bond of affection between the two women was forged without words.

Certainly she had done her homework. Calling each child by name, she presented an appropriate trinket. "And here, Herbie, See? I've brought you a toy, too," she said, holding out an elaborate crystal-like construction called "Intersecting Parallel Pipeds." Another box of plastic shapes called "Pythagoras," were the beginning of many "games" designed to stimulate or measure the intellect.

Like magicians' tricks, mysterious packets popped from the suitcase. From under a slip came a package of cheese. "Cocktail hour," she declared, cheerfully. Under a dress wrapped in dish towels from her own kitchen, a fancy sausage from Jamail's. "More cocktails! See? Now what do you think about my clever packing? Can you use these?" Joanne caught the towels. The children were fascinated. "Oh, oh, what's this?" she asked pulling another gourmet parcel. "Not for children," she said, wagging a finger warningly, and the children shook their heads in agreement. Now that she had their rapt attention, even "Wilhelm" had the courage and curiosity to emerge from hiding.

"Who's going to take me for a walk?" reaching a hand to five year old Jimmy. Then, petting the head of the little girl eagerly jumping like a puppy dog at her heels, "Who wants to come with us?" To the quiet seven year old, "Dan-i-el, do you come, too?" Off they marched, faces barely above the swish of her skirts, Oma with her diminutive entourage of admirers.

Thus for three up-beat, chatter-filled days, she continued to conquer, at the end of which she declared, "All right, I had a fine vacation. I feel well rested and ready to work again." Wrinkling her nose: "Next time I stay with you. The motel is dirty."

Every Sunday she phoned, "Hi, how is everyone?" not wanting details, merely contact. "It's a beautiful spring morning in Houston." Unstated: "Hi, remember me? I'm here and don't mean to be forgotten." But on one of those Sundays sometime in September or October came what she was waiting to hear all along.

"Hi, how is everyone?"

(Quiet discussion between Joanne and Herbert): "Should we tell her our good news?"

(She had heard.) "What news!! What news!!" already knowing what it was.

Richard Alexander was born April 19, 1971. One week later, Oma was checking him out in his new home in Devon, Pennsylvania. She addressed him "Richard Alexander" or "Richie," never "Rich" or "Richard." He embodied the spirit of Rudolf and of Herbert's lost childhood; he was living proof of the power of the future. In short, he was *das wunderkind,* and nothing was too good for him.

At first she monitored his feeding schedule like a hawk, doing her best not to intervene and "expertize." But it was difficult following her own advice, relying on a mother's confidence and experience in these matters. Fortunately, the mother was aware of Oma's sensitivity on the subject, first making certain her baby was *plenty hungry* before picking him up to nurse. Fortunately for Richard Alexander, both mother and grandmother soon relaxed.

Julie, somewhat sulky, sprawled on the floor drawing pictures. When the much anticipated news of the baby's birth was telephoned from the hospital and greeted with hoots and hollers by her three triumphant brothers, "Yea, yea, another boy!" she had burst into tears. For all the world it seemed as if she would now have to contend with *four* brothers instead of three. Well, at least he didn't *look* like a boy, just a baby, and if she did it very carefully, she could hold him just like a mother.

Oma having heard about the sister disappointment, looked for distractions. "O.K. Julie, see if you can draw a picture of Oma with the baby," and the kindergartner complied with a very detailed sketch. "Hmmmm. I see my hair, my glasses and eyelashes, my nose with its nostrils, my mouth…and hi! here's the baby," she said pointing to a moon face half-way down her dress. "But what is this?" she asked of two round circles further up the dress.

"That's Oma's bottle."

Hilde was so enraptured she told the story at every opportunity. Even years later when everyone assumed the incident forgotten or no longer important, she reminded Herbert and Joanne, "Remember Oma's bottle?"

Sunday phone calls were as habitual as her devotion to her grandson. "Just to show that I am correct about my feelings about the baby, I enclose a recent photograph," she told Nathan Sale, entering a picture far more flattering to herself than to Richard. More often than not, conferences and vacations abroad detoured in Philadelphia, while trips to the Northeast were accordingly increased with always a special one planned in April for the birthday celebration.

Golden Years

"When we try to pick anything out by itself, we usually find it hitched to everything else in the universe," was how she ended the first chapter of her book, *Eating Disorders: Obesity, Anorexia Nervosa, and the Person Within*. The quotation by naturalist, John Muir, is here used to illustrate the complexity of the twin subjects, obesity and anorexia, but it might just as easily represent her life's philosophy. While her papers and books contain relatively few references, they are nevertheless methodically researched for a cross-fertilization of ideas. The mental process is impressionistic, but in extracting wisdoms from abstract sources, she is first and always the astute scholar, assimilating ideas from such diverse sources as Ogden Nash, Joyce Carol Oates, Gregory Bateson, and Jean Piaget as well as A. J. Stunkard, David Garner, Paul Garfinkel and other contemporary experts in her own field. "I never write a paper with 250 or 300 references," she explains, "because when you see something with 350 or 500 references, you know it contains the same errors as all the other papers it was copied from. And when I quote, it's only what I have checked myself." The harmonious written result is pithy, clear and remarkably free of technical language.

An earlier paper, "Transformation of Oral Impulse in Eating Disorders: A Conceptual Approach," which is directed to an audience of psychoanalysts, spoofs her profession through its title, since the title contains the only esoteric reference in the entire piece. Also, when she apologizes for not using "conventional psychoanalytic terminology," she uses this opportunity to make unflattering commentaries about the language of her birth:

> I have the suspicion that my preference for the simplest possible language goes back to some self-observations. When I first began to publish my studies, I made the effort to think and write in English, and on the whole, I succeeded. Yet every so often, I noticed that I had slipped back into German. I came to recognize that the switch to German occurred whenever the data were not quite sufficient to support a statement, or when the thinking behind it was not quite clear. The German language, with its complicated constructions, and its facility in creating new words, lends itself to expressing involved ideas smoothly and gliding over unclear meanings, thus creating the impression of great learnedness through many neologisms. When I

began to study psychoanalysis, my suspicion of the versatility of the German language was reawakened by the psychoanalytic vocabulary, which after all, was invented by a man with unusual linguistic and literary ability in the German language, and with the ambition to be recognized by his nineteenth century fellow-scientists. Freud's style, even when translated into English, reminds me of Victorian "gingerbread" architecture, in contrast to modern functional design and usage.

Not many would brazenly take on Freud and psychoanalysis, but as Hilde's stature grew, it seemed her opposition withdrew in direct proportion, witness the ironic "apologia" on page seven of her book:

> I shall try to present my own views in as simple language as possible, and forego the impulse toward scholarliness with step-by-step documentation of how each point agrees or differs from that of the others, though I shall make some overall comparisons. I shall also forego the temptation of using the conventional psychoanalytic vocabulary, though I regret that this will deprive my presentation of some picturesque and lively imagery.

Eating Disorders: Obesity, Anorexia and the Person Within, published in 1973, was dedicated to "The Memory of Rudolf, Auguste, and Selma, Victims of Nazi Atrocities, and to Richard Alexander and the Future." In it, Hilde examines obesity and anorexia from every angle, biologic and psychiatric, at the same time making clear she is describing only the extreme fringe of eating disorders. The brain is not drive-based and passive, but memory based and capable of learning or relearning past experience. Certain biological clinical studies support this claim, but the emphasis on intelligence or learned behavior also reflects the influence of Piaget in his *The Construction of Reality in the Child,* as well as Gregory Bateson and close friend, Ted Lidz, for various studies in schizophrenia.

To be meaningful, the therapist must ask what went wrong in the learning process, that the body cannot recognize hunger to differentiate it from other signals having nothing to do with the nutritional need to eat. Patients with severe disorders act as if the regulation of food intake were outside their own bodies, as if they had no identity of their own. "Mother always knew how I felt," is a common expression. "How come the brain makes the mistake of experiencing anger or depression or frustration as hunger?" Hilde asks, and the answer is similar to Lidz's description of transmission of irrationality in the schizophrenic, "literally you have got to be taught crazy thinking."

Certainly extreme obesity and anorexia are far too complex—"hitched to everything else"—to be explained simply, and therapy, too, must be individually tailored. Dieting and behavior modification with force feeding bring immediate results but fail to deal with "the person within."

What hope? Again, common sense. Society's preoccupation with slimness and its near emaciation standard for beauty is as harmful as its hostile regard of obesity. There is a happy medium where the health and happiness of "the person within," not just pounds gained or lost, becomes the true measure for regulating weight.

The same year that brought the successful publication of her third book also contained personal loss. Months earlier, she received a telegram informing her of the death of her brother Artur. Never especially close to this English brother, who in recent years she rarely found occasion to communicate with, she was still saddened by his passing, which left Lotte widowed. A greater blow came in September, when out of apparently good health, her brother, Kurt, succumbed to a massive coronary. Dapper, witty and vital at sixty-one, the grownup Kurt was as easy to love as the baby she protected in her youth, yet against all odds, the immediate family was now reduced to three: herself, Ester and Ernst.

Nineteen hundred seventy-four, she would be seventy, March 11. Craftily cognizant of the milestone, she informed Nathan Sale in a letter dated February 20, "I am going to Mexico early in March—I had hoped thereby to escape birthday celebrations. Instead my colleagues have arranged for a whole season of them. The first one was last night, and it turned out very well." In fact her 70th birthday was celebrated by a series of lectures presented by colleagues and close friends and finalized by the most grandiose of affairs, a merry old blast in a cow pasture!

The offbeat setting was a bucolic pecan grove owned by good friend and frequent consultant/confidante, Dr. Dorothy Cato, and to Dorothy also goes credit for its planning and distinctive flavor. Twenty-two fashionably attired guests, sidestepping the occasional dung heap, picked their way through trees and grasses, ladies gowned and glowing, gents tuxedoed or "Texan" in string ties and cowboy hats. From sampling caviar and frozen vodkas, chatter soon matched the strictly cornball setting.

Two long tables crowned with white linen created a "V" where Hilde faced outrageously garish oversized candelabra. For dinner, her favorite, stuffed Cornish game hens accompanied by delectable salads and casseroles, each dish fancier than the next was followed by dessert *magnifico*. Then as dusk faded to darkness a huge Southern moon emerged from behind banks of cloud cover, sending shafts of moonlight perfectly spotlighting the guest of honor, as melodramatic as anything conceived in Hollywood.

Despite constant, sometimes fawning attention, "Hilde's entitlement," as Dorothy aptly phrased it, by July she was back in Methodist Hospital. A note to Nathan Sale, "I am in trouble again—for no reason at all I got a very high temperature. Recovery? Slow, but by mid-August I feel well enough to go away for a few days and I shall visit Herbert and the family—not for any activities, just to sit on the porch. No other visits and side trips."

By September, completely recovered, she was motoring to a departmental conference, fellow Professor of Psychiatry, Dr. Robert Roessler seated beside her in the passenger seat of the Rolls. About fifty-five miles outside Houston, she and Roessler smelled something acrid, but when they stopped to investigate found nothing. Assuming it was the air conditioner, they turned the system off, planning to check again at the next service station. But exactly ten miles later smoke was billowing from the rear, apparently from behind a back seat pillow. When they pulled over to remove the pillow, huge flames shot out, sending them fleeing to escape injury to themselves.

Fortunately, an observant householder was immediately in touch with the Sheriff and Fire Department, so that a fire engine was at the scene in less than ten minutes, in all likelihood preventing an explosion; unfortunately, it was too late for the vehicle, its interior completely burned out.

It all happened so quickly, she did not react, but was later able to put it into perspective, remembering Kurt's death a year earlier and the probable explosion which had been averted. Still, Hilde being Hilde, she would not remain passively in the "wings" watching her trademark being towed off into the sunset. With good reason, she blamed the authorized service dealer in Houston, and when they refused to accept responsibility she wrote the Rolls Royce Company directly:

> It stands to reason that a car that is regularly serviced by only one garage in some way was inadequately handled by this garage. Rolls Royces are famous for many things, but not for suffering from spontaneous combustion or self-immolation. The car had come out of the garage the very day on which it caught fire. However, the garage disclaims any responsibility, and so does the sales manager of your office. I have a series of pictures of the burning car taken by a passing motorist. Since your concern is with public relations and advertising, I feel I should let you know before I show them around.

She ended by making a profit on her original investment of $7,600 by collecting $9,000 in damages and selling the hulk to a dealership which paid $3,500 for the privilege of accepting it "as is." But remuneration was pittance so far as replacing it with another Silver Cloud.

One month later, November 13, 1974, she was writing accountant, Nathan Sale, "Gradually I have recovered from the car tragedy. I have decided to be practical and bought the heavy model Volvo. I have been driving it for a week and I feel rather relaxed about driving 'incognito,' and having a reliable, modern car. We haven't settled things with the insurance company, but it will be near in the ten thousand range. I am asking for more but I doubt that I will get it. After having supported the fancy car for ten years I've decided it should support me with the simple solution of putting the money into a good tax free bond. I shall use the money for some self-indulgence every year." That being said, she surrendered ten years of R.R. memories to her past.

Only one year after her successful book describing psychotherapeutic approaches to eating disorders, she published a slim volume summarizing her experiences as a teacher of psychotherapy, dedicating it to the memory of her own teachers, Frieda Fromm Reichmann (1889-1957), Harry Stack Sullivan (1892-1949), and Lawrence S. Kubie (1896-1973). Entitled *Learning Psychotherapy: Rationale and Ground Rules,* it was designed to initiate medical school graduates into the ways of psychotherapy; and, by its clear descriptions of the psychotherapeutic process, it also becomes an excellent training syllabus for their teachers and supervisors.

It is a text written like a story, and Hilde's lifelong affection for tales and their telling is evident even in the chapter heads: "When Strangers Meet," "The Patient Speaks," "On Talking and Listening," "On Teaching and Learning." These titles are merely shortened versions of what is inside, and her regular readers soon recognized the friendly and familiar strain.

Psychotherapy is defined as "a situation where two people interact and try to come to an understanding of one another with the specific goal of accomplishing something beneficial for the complaining person." Each new patient is a stranger whose anguish and problems are unprecedented and unique, where no single theory is more effective than any other. The patient feels reassured when communication is expressed in his terms rather than lodged in psychiatric jargon. Again, it is, *process,* the interaction between therapist and patient which is all-important. Though it is essential the therapist have a thorough knowledge of psychodynamics, professional expertise is not increased through memorization and repetition. Only by observing what is stated and unstated in each new case can the therapist use past experience and present ignorance in a constructive manner.

One year later, Hilde decided that the concept of ignorance used constructively needed elucidation. Because she had always loved contemplating the past and formulating the workings of the mind, when St. Louis child psychiatrist, James Anthony, called for information on how the research mind functions for use in his book, *Explorations in Child Psychiatry,* Hilde saw the request as tailor-made.

She begins the article, "The Constructive Use of Ignorance," with her favorite Goethe quotation, *"Schadliche Wahrheit, ich Ziehe sie vor dem nutzlichen Irrtum. Wahrheit heilet den Schmerz, den sie vielleicht uns erregt."* "Damaging truth, I prefer it to advantageous error." Out of hundreds, this purely autobiographical article was perhaps her favorite, since it offered complete freedom to talk about herself and her work. Memory returned her to the *Studienanstalt,* where this time her math teacher was on the brink of despair after offering several procedures to an algebra problem.

"Hilde, why won't Mary understand my explanations?"

"Oh," declared the other pupil, "she can't understand you because she's thinking something entirely different." It was true, the teacher had heard only Mary's mis-statements instead of the unstated issues critical to understanding the algebra problem.

She had a fine time composing this professional paper, concluding, "Throughout my life the *leitmotif* of my work has been the effort to diminish areas of ignorance, however small a step any one individual can take, rather than getting involved in debates over the superiority of one or another theory. On danger of being called an unrenegated rebel, I should like to conclude with a quotation from Maimonides, the great physician-philosopher: 'Teach thy tongue to say *I do not know* and thou shalt progress.'"

In 1978, a very popular book found its way to lay shelves, and for many a young high school student faced with the prospect of presenting an interesting and timely book report to her English class, *The Golden Cage: The Enigma of Anorexia Nervosa* by Hilde Bruch was a logical choice. The book was addressed "to physicians, teachers, school counselors, and parents—to all who are in a position of observing these youngsters, before a chronic and often irreversible state develops." Her rare gift for story-telling and the simplified readable descriptions of a complex disease, made this study, dedicated "To the skinny kids who helped me write this book," catch on with skinnies, fatties, and in-betweeners. By now, the previous "rare" disease known to most physicians only through medical books was nearly epidemic.

The writing is based on observations of seventy anorexic patients, ten of them males, in which Hilde presents anecdotal histories including the story of "Ida" who provides the title of her book.

> Even as a child Ida had considered herself not worthy of all the privileges and benefits that her family offered her, because she felt she was not brilliant enough. An image came to her, that she was like a sparrow in a golden cage, too plain and simple for the luxuries of her home, but also deprived of the freedom of doing what she truly wanted to do. Until then she had spoken only about the superior features of her background; now she began to speak about the ordeal, the restrictions, and obligations of growing up in a wealthy home. She enlarged on the image, that cages are made for big colorful birds who show off their plumage and are satisfied just hopping around in the cage. She felt she was quite different, like a sparrow, inconspicu-

Hilde Bruch in 1945

Herbert (left) shortly after his arrival in the United States in 1946; and during college in the early 50's. Hilde kept this 1941 letter from England (below) without knowing that she would later become Herbert's guardian.

DEAR AUNTY
    thank you
for your letter
and chocolate
j was glad
to receive
it, j am very
well and happ
y. Lots of love
    Herbert
↓x↓↓↓x x x x x x x x x x

1954

Hilde on the radio in 1957 discussing her first book
on eating disorders, *The Importance of Overweight.*

Dorothy Andersen's farm in 1941;
Hilde (above) in 1960; and Frieda
Fromm Reichmann (right) in 1948.

Hilde came to Houston in her '59 Rolls Royce Silver Cloud,
which was destroyed by "spontaneous combustion"
two years after this 1972 photograph was taken.

Accompanied by Herbert in 1981 (above), Hilde is given the Founders Award by the American Psychiatric Association. In 1972, with Richard Alexander Bruch (right). Richard's second birthday (below) in 1973: (r. to l.) William, Julie, Richard, Joanne, Jimmy, Hilde, and Danny.

Hilde Bruch addressing the
American Psychiatric Association in 1981.

ous and energetic, who wants to fly around and take off on its own, who is not made for a cage.

As Hilde pointed out, many anorexics express themselves in similar imagery, because their whole life has been one of living up to expectations, the fear that by comparison to others they were disappointing failures. If her first examples seem repetitious, she will not apologize, but explains how perfectly this illustrates the frighteningly similar reactions to hunger. Only during recovery do individual personal features gradually begin to reemerge.

She deplores the "me too" phenomena which has promoted and popularized a serious disease, observing how differently her new patients approach the illness:

> Today, most patients have read or heard about anorexia nervosa before or after they became sick. One had even studied *Eating Disorders* in detail and had compared herself to every case mentioned in the book. The illness used to be the accomplishment of an isolated girl who felt she had found her own way to salvation. Now it is more a group reaction. Recently a new patient said rather casually, "Oh, there are two other girls in my class" (the graduating class of forty girls in a private high school). We might even speculate that if anorexia nervosa becomes common enough, it will lose one of its characteristic features, the representing of a very special achievement. If that happens, we might expect its incidence to decrease again. In the meantime, it is a dangerous illness that not only affects the immediate health of these hapless youngsters, but may cripple them for the rest of their lives.

That anorexia nervosa had become a "fad" and was no longer a statement of isolation or uniqueness but of oneness with other adolescents, Hilde did not debate, but the "whys" of how it happened were open to speculation. No doubt the enormous emphasis placed on slimness by current fashion, "the drumming in day in day out, that one can be loved and respected only when slender," had something to do with it. It might be said that public perception of their "ideal" was reflected in *Playboy* centerfolds, whose curves gradually and mysteriously lost twenty pounds in the same number of years.

Women's lib was another factor. Rules had changed, and with greater freedom came a demand to do something outstanding.

Formerly, a girl had an option: she could be the dependent type, the clinging-vine type of wife. But given so many potential opportunities, the modern teenager was often scared about making incorrect choices. Weight was the only thing she could control.

Pressures generated by greater sexual freedom contributed to feelings of inadequacy. A fourteen or fifteen-year-old could learn everything she wanted from films or sex education lectures, but discrepancies and anorexic episodes followed when she did not feel ready to perform them.

No doubt, media exposure also popularized anorexia nervosa as the "in" disease. *The Golden Cage,* a fascinating array of tales masterfully presented so that anyone can understand…might not Hilde herself be guilty? A review in the National Anorexic Aid Society Newsletter offers a clue:

> Read Dr. Hilde Bruch's new book *The Golden Cage* and you'll gain some fresh understanding about yourself and hear yourself saying, "Hey, that's me too. Why didn't I realize that before."
>
> The advantage point being—you are reading objectively about someone else and easily recognizing similarities through another individual's experiences.
>
> Dr. Bruch's book is easy reading and not just another medical description of anorexia nervosa. The book presents an in-depth look at some specific cases of anorexia and their intricacies."

Hilde herself renounced the oft-made accusation. In a letter to Joanne Greenberg dated March 18, 1983, she wrote:

> I am glad you have sympathy for my problem with the runaway popularity of anorexia nervosa, "bulimia," and all other eating disorders. It looks as if my habit to get interested in unpopular topics nearly produces a boom. When I started to study fat children during the late 30's I got hundreds of comments and letters asking why should I waste my time on such a dull subject. Then suddenly it was big popular news. It looks as if the same is happening with anorexia nervosa, though I do not take responsibility for the boom. At this moment, it looks as if everybody wants to jump on the bandwagon, and meanwhile the illness is gradually changing. In 1960 a book was published on anorexia nervosa and the authors more or less took the stand that no such condition existed, and they proposed that any

psychological weight loss of more than 25 pounds should be considered "anorexia." Now that we have a plethora of authors, the concept is being stretched so that practically everybody who puts some food into her mouth and then worries about it is considered an anorexic. I definitely reject any implication that I "invented" the condition.

Frequent correspondence with Greenberg dated to their mutual friendship with Frieda, when as Fromm Reichmann's patient under the pen name, Hannah Green, she contributed to her psychiatrist's fame in *I Never Promised You a Rose Garden*. Since that first publication, Joanne had published a number of other books under her own name, and Hilde, valuing her critical acuity, enjoyed the novels she recommended, discussing various writing problems as they occurred.

Whether Hilde contributed to the popularity of a disease is moot, but certainly the reverse rings true. Awards piled up: Baylor College of Medicine President's Citation for Meritorious Contributions to the Clinical Sciences, American Society for Adolescent Psychiatry William A. Schonfeld Award for Contribution to Psychiatry, Mount Airy Gold Medal Award for Distinction and Excellence in Psychiatry.

On July 1, 1978, after being appointed Professor Emeritus of Psychiatry, she graciously thanked William T. Butler, Executive Vice President and Dean of Baylor College of Medicine. "It is a position I greatly appreciate, because it keeps me professionally active. I thought it might interest you that several weeks ago I received a Golden Doctor Diploma from the medical school of the Albert Ludwig University of Freiberg, where I graduated fifty years ago." With accountant Nathan Sale, she was more sardonic: "As you know, my position at Baylor reached the state of 'emeritus;' that means all salaries or payments stopped."

By the late '70s, anorexia nervosa was the "hottest illness to have," and the name Hilde Bruch its most prominent connection. Twenty years earlier, she had proven her popular appeal by writing about overweight and dieting for such widely circulated magazines as *Good Housekeeping* and *Colliers*. Now the "skinny disease" appeared even more alluring. Articles about youths trying to starve themselves to death and of the doctor who treated them appeared in newspapers and news magazines all over the country. A write-up in *People* magazine in 1978 showed photos of Hilde enjoying a leisurely lifestyle:

Bruch limits her patient load so that she can read, write, entertain Baylor colleagues and travel—this year to the Andes or China.... Her own appetite intact, Bruch mixes a strawberry daiquiri in her Houston apartment near the Texas Medical Center.

She contributed to *The Ann Landers Encyclopedia, Family Circle* and *TV Guide,* to name a few; even in articles authored by others she was constantly quoted, while bibliographical references directed readers to her publications. She appeared on TV interviews in New York's "The Today Show" and "Feeling Good," given by Children's Television Workshop, as well as "Dialing for Dollars" in Philadelphia.

When she arrived for the annual celebration of Richie's April birthday announcing she would appear on this jackpot show featuring an emcee spinning a roulette wheel, Joanne protested that the program was not dignified enough to be suitable. Hilde immediately phoned her promotion department, "I don't want to be a clown, cancel my appearance," yet somehow was persuaded to keep the appointment.

It was well she did. Emcee was the uninhibited and popular Jim O'Brien, whose wit and charm did not preclude a keen intelligence. To both Herbert and Hilde he offered a firm hand, but to Hilde was extended the special broad warmth one fellow Texan reserves for greeting another. He was well-informed on her subject, painstakingly thorough on background knowledge of the doctor. Watching the program at home, Joanne was particularly impressed with Hilde's poise, deciding that had O'Brien been less than professional, she still would have fared well. Hilde Bruch did not require a dignified setting because she carried dignity with her.

As another successful year drew to a close, the day after Christmas brought sad news. From Aurora came word that brother Ernst, like Artur and Kurt four years earlier, had died of a heart attack. Only the two sisters, Hilde and Ester, remained.

CHAPTER X

1973 - 1984

Valiant Years

If Hilde's first ten years in Houston are "golden," then the last ten are "valiant." She attributed the first painful sensations in her right thigh to a pin inserted in her broken hip two years earlier. X-rays proved negative, but walking difficulties continued. Afterwards came occasional mild tremblings of the right hand. She planned to ask Artur what he knew regarding family tremors, but that very day received a telegram from England that he had died of a cardiovascular incident. The fact that no one in her family had lived past the age of seventy made it unlikely she would ever find out, but two months later it became irrelevant when a definite diagnosis for Parkinson's Disease was made.

She knew little about the illness which London physician James Parkinson in 1817 first described as Shaking Palsy, and most uncharacteristically she cared to know even less. Occasional difficulties experienced turning knobs or faucets or dialing telephones were easily controlled by the medication, levodopa (L-Dopa), and she considered such minor handicaps challenges to ingenuity. Of course, she felt eternally grateful that medical progress had determined L-Dopa could be converted into dopamine, the missing substance in the brain, but her only concession to either the disease or its medication was to carry bread sticks wherever she went to avoid the nauseous side-effect of medicating on an empty stomach.

She was too busy traveling, attending private practice, teaching, and gathering ideas for her latest book, *The Golden Cage* to allow the peculiar, if increasingly familiar, twitch to interfere with her life. Lest anyone accuse her of wasting time by watching the Watergate hearings, she took to knitting with nearly the perseverance of Penelope outlasting suitors. Unlike Penelope, she did not unravel yarn each night, so by the time it was over, four step-grandchildren and one grandson flaunted colorful new "Watergate" sweaters.

Even during these early years, her condition was increasingly obvious and worrisome to others, but because the bearer of the adversity refused to recognize it, whatever troubles she encountered remained her own. Once during a visit to Devon, she experienced a shaking episode at breakfast which was impossible to overlook. "That little tremor worries me," she remarked off-handedly.

On the tip of Joanne's tongue was a two-year worry, "had Hilde seen a doctor, did she know her symptoms resembled those of Parkinson's Disease?" but something held her back, something which said an M.D. already knows these things, or if not, "doesn't need to know it that badly."

Perhaps the greatest irony came from graphologist and good friend Thea Stein Lewinson Hall, who on September 28, 1976 wrote:

> Now, I would like to ask you something which I hate to do and please, feel free to say "no." Could you examine (my husband) Stanley, who developed Parkinson's disease for the last two years with considerable mental symptoms which are not quite obvious in social gatherings?
>
> We have been going on a downhill path, and I wish there would be some help for arresting the process. Also, if I do something wrong in dealing with him, is there a need for a change of tactics?

Whether she chose to acknowledge symptoms or not, they were becoming increasingly difficult to disguise, as a lifetime's independence was eroded by ordinary, nearly petty, everyday occurrences. Domestic chores, sewing buttons, clipping toenails, applying makeup, previously taken for granted, became difficult or impossible. At the office, papers flew helter-skelter while she tried to tame them with a paper clip. "Help!" brought her secretary flying to the rescue. Later, at the

Doctor's Club, she fumbled or dropped a fork while friends and colleagues continued talking to cover the embarrassment.

Nevertheless, changes were gradual and symptoms for a long time were entirely right-sided and completely absent at night. On a trip to Australia and New Zealand in 1975, she discovered something quite by accident when a "Good Samaritan" ordered her a wheel chair, ostensibly because she had sustained a toe infection. A wheelchair was something she had never remotely considered, since it connoted infirmity. Nevertheless, his insistent good deed proved enormously helpful, and thereafter she did accept wheelchairs for traversing airports, but only for that.

Throughout this period she was mentally keen and professionally more productive than ever, a fact she attributed to the magical "upper" effects of the drugs, L-Dopa and Sinemet. While this is unlikely, it was certainly true she remained remarkably free of depression even as her coordination worsened, forcing her to convert creative talent into physical improvisation.

From pantyhose, she switched to stockings. Overhead and back-fastening dresses were discarded for those opening in front. The kitchenette was organized so no movement was wasted and a new microwave oven added to facilitate cooking. Used and unused plates were stored in the dishwasher, washed and re-washed, sparing the exertion of reaching into cabinets. These gradually-acquired habits became so firmly incorporated she set them to rhyme: "One side dirty, one side clean, Heaven help the someone who disrupts my routine!"

By 1977, she foresaw a time when social activities would need curtailment, and in order to spend more time with those she loved, that summer invited six-year-old Richard Alexander to Houston. Then, without explaining motivations, she hosted a grand "farewell-to-my-days-of-entertaining-cocktail party" for colleagues. The following year, she requested Herbert accompany his son to do driving, shopping and other chores. She bought wool, measured Richie, and half-knitted a sweater which both liked, but hand skills had become so unreliable she never completed it. The previous year she had enjoyed swimming at the apartment pool with her grandson (swimming laps was one of the few exercises she liked), but now arms and legs refused to cooperate.

The new secretary beginning work in late November of 1979 was surprised to discover Dr. Bruch thought of herself as a large person.

While pictures confirmed she had been considerably taller and heavier, it was certainly no longer true. Despite obvious effects of Parkinsonism such as posture and tremor, particularly when excited or handling something, Shirley Houston recalls that Hilde took trips every month or so, drove, walked to lunch nearly every day, and never mentioned personal or household problems. She was also planning another book.

Conversations with Anorexics was intended for therapists. By presenting a few very detailed cases, she hoped to unveil the disease in its earliest stages, illustrating the extent to which anorexics camouflage their secret within the human exchange. Behind the present deceptions and dishonesties of the rebellious young women who came to her office, Hilde recognized an earlier period when they actually lived their lie.

As children, they were over-conforming, obedient, and precocious, and this play-acting behavior was rated honest and good by everyone around them. When their bodies changed with puberty, they still craved the security of their so-called "perfect" childhood. As adolescents, they rebelled. They learned to protest by using their eating disorder to remain "little" and ward off the dreadful biological fate of growing up, of entering the world of mature and serious responsibility. Ironically, it was the so-called "good period" of their childhood which was the most dishonest, reflecting the hypocritical aspects of the medical profession and adulthood as a whole: "You *used* to do so well; you *were* such a good student; everybody *was* so admiring of you." All these commentaries represented that inner dishonesty.

As the title implies, her method for uncovering truth was through a relaxed conversational setting whereby the patient makes her own discovery. To justify this approach to a potential publisher she called attention to something she had seen in a recent German publication. "They have invented a new word, *Gesprachpsychotherapie* (conversation psychotherapy), and use in a constructive way things I have used repeatedly in my summarizing writing. For instance, they write, 'In conversation therapy the patient is stimulated to do her own thinking, without interpreting and fitting in theory."

No doubt, the ideas were good, but by 1980 health was betraying her. In November, she fell entering the Library Building, breaking her left hip. After that, Shirley noticed a difference: "It may be hard to separate the hip-related 'neediness' from Parkinson-related disability; but in general the hip caused few problems after a very short period, yet there were more and more things with which Dr. Bruch needed help."

She did resume driving, but discontinued it by early fall 1981. By this time, increasing irritation was evident when the shaking kept her from doing work she wanted to do. (Writing was sometimes impossible, or if she could move the pen she might not later be able to read what she had written). She talked about the bother of shopping for clothes, seemed to have lost interest in such excursions, or at least felt that the effort was so great she would have to forego the fun of shopping, or even browsing through the grocery store.

Still she doggedly reported to her office every day, missing only those days she was confined for the hip. Even during convalescence she continued to work, seeing patients in the hospital and dictating correspondence or manuscript material from her hospital bed.

In 1981 she received several prestigious awards. In May, the American Psychiatric Association honored her twice with the Founders Award and the Agnes Purcell McGavin Award. Colleague Dr. Jane Preston accompanied her by plane to New Orleans and, when she arrived, Herbert was on hand to escort her to various meetings. In June she traveled to Chicago with Dorothy Cato to receive the Joseph B. Goldberger Award from the American Medical Association.

In July, encouraged by good friend and fellow anorexia specialist, Elsa-Brita Nordlund, she decided on an impromptu trip to Stockholm. This time she flew alone, but escort arrangements were made for after her arrival. Barring a few minor mishaps here and there, all three trips went well and were encouraging. She accepted invitations for future conferences in Montreal, Toronto, and Dallas, but the unpredictable Parkinsonism had a final say when she lost her nerve and canceled all three engagements.

Her doctor concurred that medication was losing effectiveness and turned her over to a researcher experimenting with the drug Pergolide. After being hospitalized for ten days without observable side-effects, she was released into a continuing program. During December and January, Sinemet was greatly reduced, Pergolide increased, and another drug, Parsidol, introduced. She understood that her participation in the experiment meant that weekly she would be receiving different pills of unknown strength to take and evaluate. It was a terrible time.

The deeply-concerned patient and scientist in Hilde rebelled at being kept in the dark, treated like a guinea pig. To Joanne Greenberg, she lamented, "Since my Parkinsonism started to make trouble last year, I got myself persuaded to become a candidate for a new drug. I would be very much interested in what happens with other people and how good or indifferent the drug is. But I am being treated like everybody else, and that means I learn nothing. I have had so many ups and downs that I still hope one day it will be effective, but I don't trust my own thinking. Nevertheless, I am better off than I was about three months ago, but not if I compare it to a year ago. At this time my greatest handicap is moving around, or being able to count on doing so three hours or a whole day ahead of time."

Always mixed with these insecurities was a burning hope that the medicine would eventually "kick in," miraculously allow her to resume driving, renew social and traveling plans. But she had not told Greenberg the half of it. One week the little bottle of pills contained placebos and she was shocked to learn the extent of her symptoms, how much the regular use of medication had camouflaged the progress of the illness. Then, after she returned to active medication, the severe physical symptoms were replaced by something worse: fatigue, mental disorientation, even hallucinations.

Shirley recalls she dictated "mystery sentences" while walking and behaving somewhat "drunkenly," often "nodding off" in the middle of the work day. Transcripts of several patient sessions during this time are amazing. Shirley likened the phenomenon to Jerzy Kosinski's book, *Being There*, when such magical powers were attributed Chauncey Gardiner, that the nonsense he spouts is interpreted as unique wisdom.

> Hilde: What was it that was stimulating?
> Patient: I saw a picture in a magazine of some food, a pie, and so I was tempted to go downstairs to the candy machine and buy some candy, but I decided not to.
> Hilde: That is interesting. Have you had other occasions where a luscious picture precipitated the desire? If I understand it correctly, you saw *People* magazine and they have the VIPs who would do what they wanted and the question was what would you do, or what?
> Patient: I've never been that stimulated by a picture.
> Hilde: I know, but in your dream—What do we talk about it?
> Patient: What do you mean, what's my dream?

Hilde: Yes.
Patient: To be able to control myself? And maybe once a week....

Eventually she became adjusted to the new medication, but this period of approximately two months, referred to as the sleepy time when "I lost my mind," was so frightening, at the same time so remarkable, she wanted to talk about it. Friends who had personally witnessed it were embarrassed for her and would not cooperate, but it found its way into many of her letters, most poignantly in a congratulatory response to former student, Stuart Yudofsky, written on her 78th birthday, March 11, 1982:

Dear Stu:
    Congratulations and all good wishes. I can't tell you how proud I am of you, your accomplishments and rapid advancement. I knew from the day you went to P.I. that you had an unusual career ahead. I laughed about Larry Kolb when he kept on asking "When are you sending another Stu?" Anyhow, I am proud you made it, and now I am waiting for the full professorship and wonder where.
    As to myself, I am doing fine, have an emeritus office at the Jesse Jones Library and keep regular hours. You may or may not remember that I have Parkinsonism since about 1973 (that was after your time) and until last summer it (or I) was under control. When I started to cancel meetings, where I had been personally invited, Ben Cooper felt I needed new medication. Since that time I have been an "experimental" subject, and if I were as energetic as I used to be I would have written down all my experiences. I had been on Sinemet which made me hyperkinetic; but I enjoyed its "upper" effect. In October, I was for ten days hospitalized (without paying a penny) but I got plenty of unexpected and undesirable side-effects. The big ones that they worried about, circulatory disturbances, didn't materialize. On the contrary, I came out of it "certified healthy," not even anemic. But it had an effect on my brain. The funny part is, I didn't notice it so much when it was happening, but I canceled all Christmas parties, etc. and at first happily and then not so happily slept my way through December and part of January. A low point was my falling asleep while dictating letters. The worst week was when I was on placebos and faced for the first time how disabled I am without medication.

By that time I was off Sinemet and the new medication was increased. At a certain point I went out of my mind, literally. It was on a day when I had a mother and child in for a consultation and I have the funniest recorded session of a doctor with "loose associations" who at the same time functions as a consultant, to mother and daughter's bewilderment and my amused embarrassment. We are still in the process of adjusting the doses, and I may be two or three days practically symptom-free (I still don't drive) and then comes a day when I can't handle paper and pencil but everything flies on the floor. My talkativeness is also part of the syndrome, though it has been stimulated by my feeling that you might be interested. Anyhow, my traveling days are practically over. I have accepted an invitation to give the *Prager Lecture* in Washington and I finished the manuscript for the lecture in record time. (It is somewhat witty and has, to my surprise, brand-new information. I mention that as example that there is no permanent brain damage; or not yet.) I will take this trip as a test whether traveling is still possible. Jerry Wiener promised me VIP treatment.

That is not all I am doing. I am working seriously on a book, and study now with amazement a few chapters I wrote during the sleepy out-of-my-mind period. They are dull but not incoherent. In addition, I see three patients per day (consultation or therapy), four times a week. I am rather jealous about my three-day weekend, though I can't do much since I don't drive, or often feel too tired to go out in the evening (even though I still accept invitations.)

I think by now your interest will be exhausted if not flattened out. Give my love and best wishes to Beth, and next time tell me about the family. Is it growing? What else is happening?

Affectionately,

Hilde

The letter to Yudofsky is typical of the image Hilde wished and largely succeeded in projecting. Invalidism had no part of it, and only during the last year did correspondence mention Parkinsonism. Herbert and Joanne continued receiving Sunday phone calls, "How is everyone?" glibly describing one social engagement or another, so there was little to indicate the dramatic changes taking place in an illness they already knew about.

April 19, Richie's birthday, and as usual she had scheduled a family visit to coordinate the Prager lecture in Washington. The personal visit almost by definition would be relaxing and enjoyable since the simple act of traveling was not a problem. It was conference procedures after arrival which concerned her and which Dr. Jerry Wiener needed to be made aware of in making the arrangements at George Washington University.

> Dear Jerry:
> I am so glad you found out about the plane connection to Philadelphia. That makes it much easier than chasing the train.
> I like the program and it looks easy, maybe too easy. Open time may be demanding. As to the case discussion, I would rather do it informally, and I hope nobody will mind if I have occasionally to search for a word. This is by the way of indirect information that the new drug seems to be working well and I hope that it maintains its level of performance. I cannot give a paper standing up but need to sit and need a lectern that gives me a comfortable distance for reading the paper. If possible I should like to test that out ahead of time. If I do not see well I stammer and that ruins a lecture.
> A few remarks about myself: even when things are going well, I have difficulties getting dressed. Therefore I will have a minimum of clothes. In particular I cannot manage a long dress, just in case someone considered the dinner afterwards a formal affair. I have to wear a comfortable street-length dress. If the other women don't wear long dresses, it won't be so conspicuous that I do not.
> All I have to do now is to hope and pray for good weather. I prefer to travel without a coat, even raincoat; all such things have become cumbersome and I avoid them. Looking forward to an enjoyable visit.

Many months after the conference Weiner was to write, "People here still mention your visit, how much they learned from you and how much you represented to them a role model for rigorous and lifelong intellectual inquiry unfettered by dogma and ideology. I can assure you your visit here had a real impact."

But by June she was hospitalized for unexpected and expected surgeries which she describes to Elsa-Brita Nordlund:

I did it again: I fell and broke an arm this time. Five days later I had a cataract operation and now I am home, resting and picking up where I left off before this interruption.

It is exactly one year since I came to the Congress, and I remember the weather as quite good. I also remember how much I could do, and now I am worried how to become active again. There is something quite seductive about staying in a hospital room (I had one with a beautiful view) and being taken care of and having an alibi for everything. I am glad to report that the eye operation was a great success, I see better than I ever could see with that eye. And my arm is mending too. I was fortunate that a sister-in-law came to stay with me and we got along fine, and we even rehearsed how I can take care of myself.

It was Else who once again had come to the rescue, and afterwards, it was Joanne. The two family members readily adopted Hilde's routine, at night sleeping on a couch in the library, always listening for the bell she kept by her bedside warning that she needed their assistance. Promptness was important because she was so impatient and anxious to prove autonomy she would often try to maneuver down the long hallway to the bathroom herself. Once, after hearing the bell jingle, Joanne leaped from her narrow couch and was surprised to find herself falling to the floor. A leg had lost circulation during the night and its collapse offered a weird new sensation. Joanne later mentioned it to Hilde. "Now you know how I feel," she commented.

Tyranny ruled the kitchen as the monarch, perched upon a stepstool, barked instructions. "That dish goes over there. No! No! *There!*" she would point as Else or Joanne desperately tried to follow the finger's trajectory. "*Nooo! Nooooo!*" she would scream in anguish as they invariably failed. She was unable to handle or stock in her small refrigerator the heavy gallon-sized wine bottles which saved money and trips to the store, but had nevertheless solved the problem by buying in bulk and storing in small amounts. "Open the refrigerator," she commanded Joanne. Sure enough, hiding in its corners were seven or eight assorted jars and bottles filled with wine, all with tippy lids looking easy to open and easier to spill.

"At home convalescence" began with a small breakfast at 7:00 followed by toilet and dressing. By 8:00 she was seated on her mauve sofa, recording device and small clock by her side, a long teak table spread with papers in front. Her secretary arrived at 9:00 or 9:30 to receive tapes and work assignments, then left for Hilde's office in the library building, returning at designated intervals but always at day's end with mail pickup and completed assignments.

Afternoons she saw patients, while Else and Joanne made themselves scarce by visiting the apartment swimming pool. Later, during social hour, friends dropped by, often with food supplies which Hilde called "care packages," Joanne or Else prepared drinks and hors d'oeuvres while Hilde pondered what the "deep freeze" might contribute for dinner. Devoted friends declared their affection in many ways. By donating time to her family, Joanne and Else were entertained with meals and shopping expeditions even when Hilde could not go.

Unfortunately, family assistance was temporary and recovery slow. She blamed the combination of eye and wrist surgeries for adversely affecting the Parkinsonism, and to Ester on her 75th birthday wrote,

> I am heartbroken that I can't carry out my plan to be with you. But after what I have been through during this past month I don't dare yet to put the improvement to the test of an eight-hour trip. Actually, I had a very good time with TLC from Else and Joanne. I should like to send you a present but haven't come up yet with a bright idea. If everything fails, I hope you don't mind if I use what the Phoenicians invented.

Reluctantly she began avoiding invitations, but one from Stockbridge, the Dr. Otto Allen Will, Jr. Symposium, brought such happy memories she would not turn it down. To Dr. Daniel P. Schwartz, Medical Director of Austen Riggs Center, she wrote:

> I am enthusiastic about the invitation and feel greatly honored to have been asked, and the title of the Symposium, "Illuminations of the Human Condition," might well have been the *leitmotif* for my studies on weight and body size. I also feel very enthusiastic about the format, that of meeting in smaller groups who would freely exchange observations and opinions. It will amuse you that the Red Lion Inn in Stockbridge, Massachusetts, is of historical importance to me personally. That's where I gave my very first American paper, and the first paper on obesity, when I was a young pediatrician, on May 4, 1938. At that time societies were small and would meet in comfortable inns.

Additionally, it would give her a chance to visit with Rusty McIntosh and wife Milly:

> I wanted to tell you that I shall be in your corner of the woods during the last few days of September until October 3. I am scheduled to give a paper on Sunday morning. This invitation stirred up many old memories. In addition, October 3 is the 46th anniversary of my landing in America. The way our circle of friends has shrunk, you and I are probably the only survivors of the great days at Babies.
>
> I do not know whether in previous letters I mentioned that I have Parkinsonism, and it has become more and more disruptive. Since I arrive on Tuesday, I am sure I will have readjusted myself to the time zone and that I can eat properly and do not need spoon-feeding. I am not particularly bothered by the hyperkinetic movements but some of my friends are, so I write about it.

McIntosh answered: "I'll be delighted to drive over to Stockbridge and pick you up on Thursday afternoon, Sept. 30, bring you to Tyringham for a look at our place and a cup of tea." But it was not to be. Instead of attending a joyful reunion, she was forced to cancel first the length of stay and finally the stay itself, while her paper, "The Changing Picture of an Illness: Anorexia Nervosa," was read by Dr. Beulah Parker, Dr. Will's wife.

Following the cancellation, she spent twelve days at the Neurosensory Center being monitored, her doctors discharging her only her on condition she hire full-time help. She argued, blustered, argued some more, then reluctantly accepted the arrangement. Ten days later, however, and to the dismay of everyone, she "fired" the nurse, offering the following "justification":

> I woke up around 9:45 P.M. needing to go to the bathroom. There was a feeling of urgency and I rang the bell for at least two or three minutes as loudly as I could. There was no response. I made it to the bathroom by myself in spite of great difficulty and nearly fell. During that whole time I did not see Mrs. Smith, and I heard nothing of her, but she responded when I closed the door to my bedroom. When she came, she complained that I had not rung for her, that she had been listening to television but had no doubt that she would have heard it if I had rung the bell. I told her to leave, since she was not attentive to my needs. This provoked a long tirade how I had been against her

staying at the apartment, that it was impossible for me to have rung the bell without her hearing. When I told her to leave, since there was no mutually satisfying professional relationship going on, she began to use the telephone, at first in her room. Shortly thereafter the telephone rang and when I lifted the receiver she came into my bedroom, removed the telephone from its bedside stand and kept the receiver and the base so that I had no access to the telephone, and she kept it busy for nearly three-quarters of an hour. I could hear only a few sentences, which sounded to me like recurrent complaining that I had not rung the bell, that she knew I had invented this in order to slight her. By that time I was wide awake, and when she finally left my room and restored the telephone to its place I was too tense and restless to fall asleep for quite some time. She came to my room again, this time without my having rung for her, at about 11:45 P.M. I asked her again to leave and not to disturb me and did not know what she had decided to do. (She had spoken repeatedly of asking another L.V.N. to come.) I was of the opinion that she had left. I woke around seven A.M. and she presented me with a bill, which I refused to pay since she had not rendered any professional services.

Whatever sympathy she aroused was tepid and perfunctory. Hospitalized, she had been the terror of the ward, intimidating nurses and even certain doctors. Confined and cornered, she proved willful and uncooperative, and yet these characteristics, however difficult, were magnified ten-fold when the setting was converted to home ground. Here she became territorial, a trapped bird squawking to preserve her rights, as Else and Joanne soon discovered. It was a striking contrast to her visits in Aurora or Devon, where she was the model of behavior, exuding praise or graciously accepting whatever shortcomings their households might offer.

Her animosity toward round-the-clock nursing might hypothetically be explained several ways. Though comfortably well-off these latter years, she had probably spent too many years scraping for money to be realistic now about her own worth. (Though with family she had always been generous.) More likely, it was exactly as she told Joanne: "I don't like seeing money supposed to be used for the next generation being trifled away on something like this." (Here, no doubt, she was remembering with gratitude her uncles' financial contributions to her own career.)

Certainly, independence and self-image were involved. If she answered Ester's concerned telephone call, "Oh yes, I'm being very well cared for. Joanne treats me just like a baby," she had no difficulty covering feelings of helplessness with irony because Joanne was her guest, Richie's mother, Herbert's wife—in that order. Ester wouldn't be deceived, but knowing Joanne would never treat Hilde like a baby, she would interpret it as playful exaggeration. Paid nursing care offered no variance. Like wheel chairs and chamber pots, it carried one label, "invalid."

Friends and family, trying to convince her otherwise, might as well be addressing a wall. Hilde, perennial axis of controversy, stayed the course. Those familiar with her strife-filled background felt maddened by the stand; it was as if she were clinging to the last remnants of control, savoring the very elements which were her trademark. Did Hilde realize her obstinate existence was made possible only through concerned and loyal friends, "care packages," a secretary who assisted beyond the call of duty, a sister and daughter-in-law who dropped everything to answer SOS calls?

Indeed she did, and graciously responded with thanks, gifts, or other gratuities whenever possible, all of which did nothing to relieve the minds of those concerned, and so the circuitous arguing continued. She retaliated by handing out cards containing an appropriate quote:

> ...avoid undue interferences with life styles of long standing; respect the wisdom and longevity of the elderly....Those who have survived into old age have proven their durability.

She was in charge, always would be. Seated on the far right of her couch as on a throne encircled by colleagues, hyperkinetic movements pushing her head so far sideways it seemed she might soon lose balance altogether, she spoke rapidly in high-pitched staccato tones. All eyes and ears affixed to the slumping figure. Soon her colleagues would know what topics to discuss. No one interrupted, no one changed the subject, no one commented without prefacing, "Do you think, Hilde," or "Could it be, Hilde...." Entitlement. Could royalty have evoked more deference?

"Conversations"

As options rapidly closed, she discovered her manuscript assuming greater importance and dedicated herself mentally and physically to its completion. But the birth of her sixth child would not come easy.

Hilde's unaffected and uncluttered style of writing was deceptive. "If my writing is clear and lucid, then it is the result of very, very hard work," she once told Joanne Greenberg. "You can't imagine how messed up and Germanic my sentences are when I begin. Maybe this sentence is a good example of it. Then there is a constant simplifying and straightening out."

By October of 1983, when she permanently vacated her office, the process of writing had become as physical as it was mental. "My ability to get around on my own two feet varies a great deal," she told Elsa-Brita, "so we have reversed things and brought all the stuff I need for writing to my living room, which you may remember as very airy and empty. The airiness is still there, but the folders and other writing things are piled up on furniture, tables, floors and corners."

Clerical help had always been important, so much so that Hilde had thanked several secretaries by name in her early books. Now that she required their physical assistance, they were even more critical. Word processors, which might have expedited matters, were for the future, and it was only for her final draft of "Conversations" that she used one. Instead, she stayed with the unique system she had developed and refined over time.

Like baking a cake, the most important thing was assembling ingredients, as out of her vast reading repertoire came snips and notes collected from books, magazines, and newspapers over many years. Next, she dictated these details into notebooks using several carbons, saving one carbon for cutting into paragraphs. As a mental outline for chapters began to form, she separated the paragraph pieces into folders, and then from each chapter folder she dictated a first draft to be typed on yellow paper. After that came more reorganizations involving correct sequence of paragraphs on green paper, stylistic corrections on blue, and a final draft on white.

Involved as it sounds, Hilde found the system helpful: Sometimes a particular case in "yellow" might fit in later. She could handle it, at the same time know its stage of correction. A secretary running through yellow could automatically say, "For heaven's sake forget the spelling, I'll leave a space for that word I don't understand." But on blue, it should be ready to be transcribed.

Shirley Houston knew the routine, but in May of 1983, she served notice. Hilde fully understood and accepted it. Secretarial duties had become so intertwined with household and medical ones it was difficult to separate them, and Shirley was too competent to be spending time this way.

In 1983 she dared herself to take two trips, both personal, but was also enticed by an April conference in New York, which coincided with Richie's birthday and her trip to Devon. To Rustin McIntosh, she wrote, "I just received the invitation to the Babies Hospital Alumni meeting on April 22, and I reacted with a strong desire to go there. I don't want to burden you with the decision-making, but how much walking is involved in attending the lectures, the luncheon, etc.? I am still in an unpredictable stage whereby the transition from walking well to being 'frozen' occurs without any identifiable reason. Writing this makes me feel that it is not such a good idea, but maybe I need being talked out of it."

After her Stockbridge cancellation, McIntosh and others, aware of the severity of her handicap, were anxious to discourage and spare her similar disappointments. Her former boss had little difficulty dissuading her. "I feel I ought to warn you that the rate of turnover in personnel in the last two decades has been rapid and the great majority of people who come to these reunions are strangers whose service took place after my time."

Wrote Hilde, "To be honest, I had come on my own to the conclusion that it would be too much for me. As a matter of fact, I shall use that weekend for a visit with Herbert (whom you met when he had just arrived from England) and his family, including a 'grandson' who is going to be twelve years old."

When Herbert picked her up at Philadelphia Airport, he was shocked by her weight loss and the uncontrolled trembling which had been aggravated by the stress of the trip. At night, Joanne, occupying a bed next to hers, watched gradual improvement until the last few days she seemed nearly relaxed. Maybe a change in environment was more beneficial than medicines. Joanne and Herbert wondered if she would consider leaving Houston to make her home with them. Their split level, with its bathrooms inconveniently located was not ideal, but they could work out something. Certainly there was plenty of room now that the three older children were either attending college or living and working elsewhere. Joanne had taught English, done secretarial work, maybe she could help with the book....

Hilde said "thank you," she would consider it. Whether she really did or merely fantasized it through discussion and letters, the thought alone probably brought some pleasure and comfort. Because the trip to Devon was successful, and because she regretted having missed Ester's "75th," she made another courageous decision in August to visit California for her sister's 76th birthday celebration.

Ester recalls the trip: "Hilde wasn't feeling well. She did not want to do much, just sit and read in the easy chair on the deck under the oak trees. Several times going to the bathroom at night, she stumbled, and I helped her and offered her a commode. She said, 'And who is going to empty it?' I answered, 'That's nothing, we don't want you to fall.' But she refused to have anything to do with the commode. When her health worsened, she wanted to cut short the visit and fly home. I suggested our local hospital for a few days, but she wouldn't hear of it. 'My physicians know me and it is better to be in Houston.' Harold and I were terribly worried watching her wheeled to the plane, but late that night she phoned, 'I am in bed and it is O.K.'"

But in fact, things were not "O.K." The replacement secretary had efficiently used her two week hiatus to "offer notice," and a two-sentence handwritten note to that effect topped a pile of letters on Hilde's desk. Almost as calamitous was a powerful hurricane which broke ashore in Galveston just hours after her arrival in Houston. Instead of seeing her doctors as she had promised Ester, she spent the night feeling deserted and sick, shaken by the furious winds and rains beating at her window panes. Perhaps Eastern news reports had down-played the storm, because several weeks later, when Joanne arrived by bus from the airport, she was surprised to see so many lingering signs of violence: uprooted trees and shrubbery lining highways, buildings with plywood or empty spaces for windows.

The trip to Ester's was the last Hilde would attempt. It and the circumstances which followed had shaken her confidence irreparably, but whatever rebound abilities she lost were counterbalanced by a fiery determination to get her manuscript published. With office paraphernalia heaped in her living room, she spent day after day on the corner of her sofa, disciplining herself, building walls with the endless folders and boxes of reprints and case materials. Somehow out of these boxes came eleven chapters, mostly drawn from case histories of the early 1970s, where passage of time allowed for description of long-range changes. But her sense of organization, always so natural, had deteriorated with her health. Constant medical disruptions, hospitalizations, doctor's appointments, and changes in medication, had severely altered concentration. She recognized it, called the efforts "sleepy" and fought to regain her edge, the zip and crispness that had marked her earlier writing.

Obsessed though she was, Hilde had begun to doubt her own motivations. Leo Kanner had once told her that in order to write a book you had to go into a nunnery, and it was so. In the past, she had tucked herself away for large blocks of time, sacrificing favorite activities, the pleasures of social outings, the preparation of gourmet meals.

Once more she found herself isolated for large periods of time. But was it self-imposed exile, or was this "grandiose display of not being involved," merely a cover-up for depression? While her apartment was a pleasing place to be confined, craving isolation was quite different from having it forced upon you.

When she sent Rusty McIntosh a copy of "Parkinsonism: Living with Uncertainty," he had replied, "Please don't stop writing papers." It was heartening and renewed her belief that she still had something to contribute. Sometimes it was difficult to distinguish between what was justifiably productive and what was just "busy work."

"How do I get out of this illness? I get very disappointed when I keep working so hard and it just keeps getting worse. Heavens, when I say I have handled difficult life situations with a certain calm—it's easy. I can pull them out by the dozens. But this is different, this has a destructive element." The "nuisance" disease had become an "insult." Nor could she expect others to understand, least of all her doctor, who, when she complained, replied mechanically, "You need a nurse looking after you. Get off your pride and be realistic."

Nineteen Eighty-Four

On February 2, 1984 she was operated on for metastasized ovarian cancer. Combined surgery, radiation treatments, and regulation of

Parkinson medication, meant lengthy hospitalization, which was further prolonged when she fell and cracked her right hip. No doubt she had been up to her old tricks, impatiently trying to test strength and independence when it happened.

The Department of Psychiatry was planning an 80th birthday celebration. Family and colleagues were invited to attend the gala affair, which would take place in Methodist Hospital. Hilde asked Joanne to come a week early, a strange request since she was already well cared for in the hospital, but apparently she only wanted companionship. Her niece stayed in the apartment, walking the short distance to the hospital each day, where she discovered a sentimental Hilde not wishing to talk about medical problems or professional matters, or even about herself, but about the family she had loved and lost to a long ago past.

It was a soft and gentle and bittersweet time. Poignantly, she spoke of them all, but Auguste, the beautiful promising young woman who had forfeited her own life for Hilde's was a passion. Had Hilde not grabbed all the attention, Auguste surely would have trained for a career and been saved. No argument to the contrary would prevail and she wept without consolation. But there were happy moments, too. Her thirteen-year-old grandson was the identical age his father had been when first she spotted him walking hesitantly beside Frieda, and for Herbert's son the future looked unblemished.

When Herbert and Richie and Else arrived, all gathered in the hospital room, the adults admiring her flowers, the youngster intrigued by a card that played "Happy Birthday" when opened. This particular card, like its recipient, possessed a very definite personality, refusing to turn off merely by being closed, but requiring a proper touch and unique balance to quiet. Richie experimented and found it. Ester had not been able to come, but sent a personal composition, "Analyzing Relationship with Important Figure," all about what it was like to be Hilde's younger sister. So enchanted was Hilde, she asked Else to read it aloud.

While the 80th birthday party could not measure in imagination or scope the wild affair in the cow pasture, its eloquent "thank you" about enriching lives and professions stood as a magnificent tribute from colleagues. With family by her side, an orderly wheeled Hilde to the reception room, where she was greeted by an enthusiastic throng of admirers, toasted with champagne and presented with a delicious gourmet chocolate cake.

Two more awards awaited her in 1984. The one from the Baylor Women's Faculty Club surprised and pleased her greatly:

> First of all, I do not know why and how I deserve it. I had planned to say a few words after you gave me the award. I wanted to tell the younger members how helpful and meaningful the relationship to the group had been when I first came. Even after I was settled here I highly valued the friendship and activities that they developed. The Gourmet Group was particularly generous toward me.
>
> I regretted that my changing health kept me away the last few years. That is why I am particularly moved that you made me an honorary lifetime member. I regret that my physical handicap was more pronounced on Wednesday than I thought it would be, but shuffling or not, I made it into the room and had the great pleasure of receiving your generous gift. I gave it immediately an important place in my home as a constant reminder of your friendship.

Of the recognition she received during her lifetime, the last was probably the most meaningful. The Baylor College of Medicine Department of Psychiatry established the Hilde Bruch Award for Excellence in Psychiatry. Representing the highest medical student award bestowed by the department, it was to be given annually to a graduating medical student chosen by a committee.

She died in her own bed on the morning of December 15, 1984, but not before completing *Conversations with Anorexics* so that with the editing help of Baylor colleagues, Danita Czyzewski and Melanie A. Suhr, the book could be published posthumously. With a lifetime of accomplishments that amazed even herself, Hilde constantly looked to her humble beginnings for answers:

"That beautiful word 'serendipity' comes to mind whenever I think of how I stumbled into discovering that girls can go to the university. I can also imagine that if I hadn't had an authoritarian uncle who said 'go study medicine, that is a good profession for you,' I would probably be doing something entirely different. But since about 1938, eating disorders is the 'red thread' that goes through all my writing, and it so happens it touches on everything. It is biological, with endocrine and growth disturbances and drives. It is psychological, and finally comes the integration with experiential data." In fact, this remarkable ability to assimilate learning wherever she found it was the "red thread" that coded her life.

Legacies were multiple and varied. One can only imagine what pride she would have experienced knowing that her student, Stuart Yudofsky, had finally returned to Houston to become Chairman of the Department of Psychiatry, Baylor School of Medicine. In the February 20, 1987 issue of *Journal of the American Medical Association,* he paid tribute to the teacher who had most influenced his life:

> I mourn and pay tribute to Dr. Hilde Bruch, a consummate teacher. In a field that is worn with words, she taught by involvement and by example. Now that I am also a psychiatrist and a teacher, I must measure myself by her example—vitality, consistency, directness, productivity. Apart from me and a part of me, she is always with me.

APPENDIX

Books by Hilde Bruch, M.D.

Don't Be Afraid of Your Child, Farrar, Straus and Young, New York, 1952. (also translated in Italian, Spanish, and Japanese)

The Importance of Overweight, W.W. Norton, New York, 1957.

Studies in Schizophrenia, Acta Psychiatrica et Neurologica Scandinavica Supplementum 130, Vol. 34, Munksgaard, Copenhagen, 1959.

Eating Disorders: Obesity, Anorexia Nervosa and the Person Within, Basic Books, Inc., New York, 1973. (also translated in French and Italian)

Learning Psychotherapy, Harvard University Press, Cambridge, 1974. (also translated in German, Italian, Japanese, and Swedish)

The Golden Cage: The Enigma of Anorexia Nervosa, Harvard University Press, Cambridge, 1978. (also available in paperback; translated in Dutch, French, German, Italian, and Japanese)

Conversations with Anorexics (posthumous), edited by Danita Czyzewski and Melanie A. Suhr, Basic Books, Inc., New York, 1988.

Awards

President's Citation for Meritorious Contributions to the Clinical Sciences, Baylor College of Medicine, 1978.

William A. Schonfeld Award for Contribution to Psychiatry, American Society for Adolescent Psychiatry, 1978.

Golden Doctor (M.D.) Diploma, Medical Faculty, Albert-Ludwig University, Freiburg, 1978.

Mount Airy Gold Medal Award for Distinction and Excellence in Psychiatry, 1979.

Joseph B. Goldberger Award in Clinical Nutrition, presented by the American Medical Association for contributions to clinical nutrition, 1981.

Agnes Purcell McGavin American Psychiatric Association Founders Award, for numerous achievements, including career-long efforts to prevent mental disorders, 1981.

Hilde Bruch Award for Excellence in Psychiatry, to be given annually to a graduating medical student, Baylor College of Medicine, 1984.

Published Writings

From 1928 to 1984, Hilde Bruch wrote more than 250 articles, which were published in professional journals.

Professional Positions

Instructor in Pediatrics, College of Physicians and Surgeons, Columbia University (Babies Hospital), New York, 1934-1943.

Associate in Psychiatry, College of Physicians and Surgeons, Columbia University, New York, 1943-1953.

Clinical Associate Professor of Psychiatry, College of Physicians and Surgeons, Columbia University, New York, 1954-1959.

Clinical Professor of Psychiatry, College of Physicians and Surgeons, Columbia University, New York, 1959-1964.

Associate Psychoanalyst, Psychoanalytic Clinic, Columbia University, New York, 1947-1964.

Director, Children's Service, New York State Psychiatric Institute, 1956-1964.

Psychotherapeutic supervisor, New York State Psychiatric Institute, 1956-1964.

Professor of Psychiatry, Baylor College of Medicine, Houston, TX 1964-1978.

Professor Emeritus of Psychiatry, Baylor College of Medicine, Houston, TX 1978-1984.

Education

M.D., University of Freiburg, Germany, 1929.

Physiological research and Pediatrics, University Clinic Kiel and Leipzig, Germany, 1929-1933.

East End Child Guidance Clinic, London, 1933-1934.

Psychiatric training, Rockefeller Fellowship, Johns Hopkins Hospital, Baltimore, 1941-1943.

Psychoanalytic training, Washington Baltimore Institute, 1941-1945.

Associations

Diplomat of the Board of Pediatrics, 1937; and the Board of Child Psychiatry, 1962.

Fellow of the American Association for the Advancement of Science.

Life member of the American Psychiatric Association, American Psychoanalytic Association, International Psychoanalytic Association, and the American Psychosomatic Society.

About the Publisher

Since 1980, Gürze Books has specialized in providing quality information on eating disorders recovery, research, education, advocacy, and prevention. They also distribute *The Gürze Eating Disorders Bookshelf Catalogue,* which is used as a resource throughout the world.

Free Catalogue

The Gürze Eating Disorders Bookshelf Catalogue has more than eighty books and tapes on eating disorders and related topics, including body image, size-acceptance, self-esteem, feminist issues, and more. It is a valuable resource that includes listings of non-profit associations and is handed out by therapists, educators, and other health care professionals throughout the world.

Unlocking the Golden Cage is available at bookstores and libraries in the United States. However, copies may also be ordered directly from Gürze Books for $29.95 (plus $3.50 shipping/handling) each.

Gürze Books
P.O. Box 2238
Carlsbad, CA 92018
(800) 756-7533 • FAX (619) 434-5476